969

969

MONUMENTAL BRASSES

by the same author

———

YOUR BOOK OF BRASSES
BRASS RUBBING
(*Studio Vista*)

MONUMENTAL BRASSES

The Craft

MALCOLM NORRIS

FABER AND FABER
London & Boston

First published in 1978
by Faber and Faber Limited
3 Queen Square London WC1N 3AU
Printed in Great Britain by
Ebenezer Baylis and Son Ltd
The Trinity Press, Worcester, and London
All rights reserved

British Library Cataloguing in Publication Data

Norris, Malcolm
   Monumental brasses, the craft.
   1. Brasses—Europe—History
   I. Title
   739'.52'094   NB1846.E/

ISBN 0–571–09891–6

To my father, Ernest de la Mare Norris

Foreword

The subject of monumental brasses, for long the study of a few scholars, has, since 1950, attracted wide public attention and much serious research. In view of this interest Faber and Faber invited the author to write a comprehensive and modern appraisal. Unfortunately, the task took longer than had been anticipated, involving the project in the escalating costs of the last five years. Problems accordingly arose, not only in publishing the work, but in publishing it in a manner which would limit the cost to the private buyer, without prejudice to the material. Fortunately the book, as written, consists of two complementary but independent parts, and it was decided in the interests of publication and economy to divide the work.

Monumental Brasses, covering the subject from *c.* 1180 to *c.* 1800, accordingly consists of two studies. The present volume, *The Craft*, contains the introductory material of the book, and the first nine chapters which relate to aspects of the craft of brass engraving, the engravers and their customers. This is supported by a series of plates which afford an overall view of the products of the craft in Europe, in addition to illustrating points raised in the text.

The companion study, *The Memorials*, published by Phillips and Page Ltd., 50 Kensington Church Street, London, consists of a chronological analysis of brasses by period and region, and is a detailed description. Notwithstanding the independent publication, the relationship of the two studies is retained, and reference is made in *The Memorials* to illustrations published in *The Craft*.

Preface

Anyone who is involved at all seriously in historical, art-historical or archaeological matters is likely to be struck eventually by the remarkable durability of much that was written about them in the nineteenth century. Many terminologies, attributions, theories and basic classifications in these fields have been handed down to us by the great Victorian pioneers, as have also—such is the power of the printed word—many errors. There is no subject to which these remarks are more appropriate than the study of monumental brasses, for until quite recently it was almost entirely supported on a framework that had been set up as long ago as 1861 by the Revd. Herbert Haines in his *Manual of Monumental Brasses* and reinforced by the Revd. H. W. Macklin in his popular textbooks *Monumental Brasses* and *The Brasses of England*, published respectively in 1890 and 1907.

All these books were outstanding in their day, as was another influential work, Herbert Druitt's *Manual of Costume as Illustrated on Monumental Brasses* (1906), but they came to acquire an almost sacred character that was by no means justified. This undoubtedly had a stultifying effect on the wider development of their subject and for nearly sixty years after the publication of Macklin's *Brasses of England* no original textbook of monumental brasses appeared. During this period students, with a few notable exceptions, were disinclined to look beyond Haines, Macklin and Druitt for basic information, even when this related to studies—such as the general development of mediaeval metal work, armour and costume—which, though essential to the proper understanding of brasses, are entirely independent. New developments in these subjects, published in their own specialized literature, were largely ignored by the brass fraternity, many of whom seemed to think that the study of, say, armour and costume on brasses was something quite distinct and separate from the study of real armour and costume. A curious situation thus arose in which, until as recently as the early 1960s, publications on brasses treated some of these ancillary matters in a manner that would have been perfectly intelligible to a nineteenth-century antiquary, but which someone familiar only with modern specialized writings about them might well have found confusing!

If students of brasses were unwilling for so long to extend the boundaries laid down by their illustrious predecessors, they were far from being inactive within those boundaries. Despite the near-disastrous decline of general interest in the subject that followed World War I, a small and devoted band of enthusiasts continued to study and record the monuments themselves in the greatest detail and to publish the results of their work. Immense credit is due to them for keeping the subject alive and, by reviving the Monumental Brass Society in 1934, ensuring that when a general revival of interest in brasses and brass-rubbing began again in the 1950s there was an organization in existence to provide guidance and a measure of control. The quite phenomenal development of this revival has resulted in more people studying and rubbing brasses than ever before, and this has produced its problems for those who are concerned about the conservation of these monuments. It has also, however, had the entirely satisfactory result of revitalizing the whole subject and creating an atmosphere congenial to the growth of new ideas and new methods of research.

The first clear indication that the old order was changing was given by the publication in 1965 of a book by Mr. Malcolm Norris entitled *Brass Rubbing*. Though modest in size, this was a revolutionary piece of work, for it provided what many people had been awaiting for years, a textbook of the subject that was new in every sense of the word. Here at last was a writer with an original and scholarly mind who realized that brasses simply cannot be studied *in vacuo*, but must always be viewed in the context of the general artistic, historical and social conditions of their time, and that where such subjects as costume and armour are concerned they are to be regarded primarily as illustrations that have to be interpreted in the light of information available from many other sources. The result was that he was able to provide a fundamental reappraisal of the whole subject that was limited only by the small amount of space provided by his publisher.

As soon as *Brass Rubbing* appeared hopes were expressed from many quarters that Mr. Norris would turn his attention to writing the major textbook of which he was so clearly capable. This he has now done, and the result, *The Craft* and its companion study *The Memorials* is a work of the same calibre as Haines's *Manual* and will certainly hold the same position in the future as that great book has held in the past. It is both an honour and a pleasure to introduce *The Craft* to the public.

Claude Blair
Keeper of Metalwork
Victoria and Albert Museum
London

Contents

Illustrations

The illustrations consist of photographs of brasses, drawings and rubbings. The rubbings shown are of two types, *negative*—in which the surface is black and the engraved lines white, and *positive*—in which the surface is left white and the lines are black. To avoid misinterpretation, illustrations based on the former are indicated by the letters N.R. and the latter by P.R. In some cases negative rubbings have been turned into positives photographically and P.R. is applied to these also. Acknowledgement is made on the captions of the sources of all rubbings other than those from the author's collection.

Acknowledgement is also made for all photographs of original brasses. Abbreviations have, however, been applied to the names of commercial and private photographers, who have taken subjects at the author's request and whose full names are as follows:
Britain: C. S. Bailey, K. Hubbard, L. W. Hutchins, K. & S. Commercial Photos Ltd., C. Love, D. Newell, Photo Mayo Ltd., E. & A. Wright.
France: M. Chuzeville, Studio Photo-Cine-Bellot-Galloy.
Germany: W. Castelli, A. Münchow.
Most of the photographic reproductions of rubbings were made by C. S. Bailey, K. & S. Commercial Photos Ltd. and E. & A. Wright.

2

Maps

Acknowledgements

I should like to acknowledge a great debt to many friends and scholars for help in the completion of this book, and to clergy and museum authorities throughout Europe, who have given me every facility for studying the treasures in their charge.

I should like to thank the following particularly: H. J. B. Allen, M.A., K. O. Butter-field, M.A., the Revd. J. N. Coe, Dr. H. T. Norris, I. T. W. Shearman, and my late father, E. de la Mare Norris, for companionship and aid over many years in making rubbings of brasses in England and on the Continent. F. A. Greenhill, F.S.A., F.S.A.Scot., for reading and checking the entire manuscript, and making innumerable contributions and suggestions; J. A. Goodall, F.S.A., for valuable advice and notice of unpublished original references, and the late Major H. F. Owen Evans, M.B.E., F.S.A., for guidance, help and support in the conception of this work. A. Baird, J. Bertram, C. Blair, M.A., F.S.A., J. Bromley, F.S.A., J. Coales, F.S.A., A. C. Cole, O.St.J., B.C.L., M.A., F.S.A., R. Emmerson, J. R. Greenwood, Dr. W. N. Hargreaves-Mawdsley, F.S.A., L. James, M.A., N. H. MacMichael, F.S.A., and J. C. Page-Phillips, M.A., for information on various aspects of English brasses. Dr. H. K. Cameron, F.R.I.C., F.S.A., for advice and information over many years on brasses in Belgium and Germany. Dr. H. Nowé and Dr. A. de Schryver, for information on brasses in Belgium. Dr. H. Eichler, Dr. M. Hasse, Dr. J. Mundhenk, Dr. and Mrs. M. Tennenhaus and most especially Dr. H. P. Hilger, for information on brasses in Germany; also the Gesellschaft für Kulturelle Verbindungen mit dem Ausland for generous help in studying examples in the East German Republic. Magister J. Chrôscicki, Magister R. Kaletyn, Dr. H. and Dr. S. Kozakiewicz, Dr. P. Skubiszewski, and Magister K. Wróblewska for information on brasses in Poland. I am especially grateful to these Polish scholars whose unstinted help and kindness during my journey in Poland in 1959, and subsequent answers to queries, have made available a wealth of information on European brasses. The remnant of the Polish series still contains several of the finest examples in existence.

Acknowledgement for the use of rubbings is made on the figure captions, but particular thanks are due to H. W. Jones, F.C.A., whose superb collection has greatly enriched the illustrations, including examples made at my request. I am also most grateful to the Monumental Brass Society for use of Portfolio plates and other illustrations, and to the Society of Antiquaries of London for unrestricted use of their collection, and for the reproduction of plates from their publications.

The sources of photographs taken of the actual monuments are clearly indicated. The interest shown and considerable journeys undertaken by C. S. Bailey of Bromsgrove, K. Hubbard of Croydon, K. & S. Commercial Photographs Ltd. of Leicester, and E. & A. Wright of Stansted Mountfitchet, are greatly appreciated.

In conclusion I should like to record my thanks to J. H. Hopkins and J. Kenyon, Librarian and Assistant Librarian of the Society of Antiquaries, for much assistance in research, to W. E. Rupprecht for translation and correspondence to Germany, and to my wife Laurie for typing the manuscript.

Abbreviations

c.	circa
d.	died
engr.	engraved
Portfolio Mon. Brass Soc.	Portfolio of the Monumental Brass Society
Trans. Mon. Brass Soc.	Transaction of the Monumental Brass Society

Introduction

The term memorial brass has been used to describe any inscription, figure, shield of arms or other device engraved for commemorative purpose in flat sheet 'brass'. Brasses acquired their distinctive title at a period of popularity. Richard Hunt of Shipley in Sussex willed in 1546 that 'A stone be leyed over my grave and also a *brasse* to be nayled on the same stone.'[1] The term in English has the blessing of long usage, and is retained throughout this study, notwithstanding the fact that some brasses consist of bronze or copper, and mediaeval brass or latten plate was of a different composition from the modern alloy. Brasses most commonly take the form of personal memorials. Their situation is usually in churches, set into floor slabs or raised tombs or, more conspicuously, fixed against walls. Their history can be traced continuously from the thirteenth to the present century, and samples of all periods still exist in surprising numbers throughout Western Europe.

Brasses have been subjected to more detailed study than any other class of monument in England. Their remarkable qualities are well known. The figure brass may be regarded as a less expensive alternative to the sculptured effigy, and as such reflects many features of tomb design, while representing a more comprehensive section of society. As a consequence brasses are precious as a source for historical reference. Primarily they, together with monumental effigies and incised slabs, are the only consistently dated works of art of the Middle Ages, and, with necessary reservations, provide a potential key to the chronology of mediaeval art.[2] The inscriptions, in which the date of death is a detail, are valuable in revealing the development of our native tongue, and to the study of palaeography. The usefulness of figure brasses as records of costume and armour is undeniable, although the flat presentation of the figure and the absence of colour both limit the accuracy of the portrayal, and the rendering of armour on late fifteenth and early sixteenth century English brasses is admittedly inaccurate. Nevertheless, the breadth of the record is of the greatest value, especially until the mid-fifteenth century. Brasses are as precious as seals to the student of heraldry and the genealogist. As early as 1408 the brass of Sir Hugh Hastyngs at Elsing, Norfolk, had been called into evidence of title in a major lawsuit. Research into the style of figure representation, ornament and architectural features in brasses is rewarding for the art historian. Designs of Albrecht Dürer and Lukas Cranach, to name but two famous artists, have been identified on German brasses. Furthermore, facility of reproduction through the medium of 'rubbing' with black wax and paper has added immeasurably to the usefulness of brasses for reference. Brass rubbings are sometimes the object of slighting comment, but the collections of rubbings in the Society of Antiquaries, London, and the Museum of Archaeology and Ethnology, Cambridge, afford a comprehensive source of reference for which no other form of monument has yet a counterpart.

Finally, and of greatest importance, brasses are an integral part of monumental art. Their forms and details are indispensable for the interpretation of monumental design. Brasses must be classed as a subordinate type of memorial to the sculptured tomb. The brass engravers adapted the fashions of sculpture to their own purpose. But within the limits of their media they were not troubled with structural problems. They could work out a design in its entirety, subject only to the purchaser's requirements and the scale of the task. There are probably no monuments richer in iconography, allusions and symbolism than the great Flemish rectangular compositions of the fourteenth century.

This last claim may be a statement of the obvious, but the obvious has not been sufficiently recognized. It is these aspects of brasses, the motives and influences which moulded their development, and the course of the development itself which form the main themes of this book. Published studies of brasses have too often emphasized facets such as costume or occupation at the expense of the basic subject-matter. A brass of a fourteenth century priest may be related with advantage to other brasses of the same style, to other brasses of the same period, or to other monuments of the same period. Its relationship to a priest's brass of the sixteenth century is remote, save for the common feature of Mass vestments. Yet classification by dress and profession has persistently prevailed. Intense study has been devoted to brasses for the last hundred years but the subject is far from exhausted. The reasons for this lie not only in the richness of the subject itself, but in the particular lines on which research has been pursued. It is necessary to describe the history of this study to appreciate both the achievement of past scholars and the need for further research and reappraisal.

In the view of the English antiquaries of the seventeenth and eighteenth centuries, brasses were monuments, receiving due, albeit incidental, attention with memorials of all types. Such is their treatment in Gough's great work *Sepulchral Monuments in Great Britain*, published in 1786–96. Specialist treatment of the subject began in the nineteenth century. There can be little doubt that this interest was greatly stimulated against the background of the Gothic Revival both by the number of brasses in the south and east of England and by the process of brass rubbing which began to attract its devotees. The impressions made by Craven Ord, Esq., Sir John Cullum and the Revd. Thomas Cole at the end of the eighteenth century are recognized as the earliest known collection of such facsimiles.[3] Two books by the Revd. Charles Boutell—*Monumental Brasses and Slabs* (1847) and *The Monumental Brasses of England* (1849)—were followed in 1861 by *A Manual of Monumental Brasses* by the Revd. Herbert Haines. Boutell's first book gave some notice to incised slabs and other tombs as well as brasses, though his later book was devoted entirely to brasses, the greater part being illustrations. Haines's two-volume study is a classic, even though the second volume, a list of brasses in England, has since 1926 been completely superseded by the later compilation of Mill Stephenson. His first volume is an introduction of immense scholarship and great breadth of conception. Haines's interpretation of evidence even on a conjectural level has proved astonishingly accurate. The manual has remained an indispensable textbook for a century, and will always so remain. During this period the brothers J. G. and L. A. B. Waller, brass engravers by profession, illustrated a selection of English brasses. Their handsome book *A Series of Monumental Brasses from the Thirteenth to the Sixteenth Century* (1842–64), contains accurate tinted reproductions of brasses combined with a scholarly text, and is still intrinsically the most beautiful book on the subject.

The interest of English antiquaries in brasses was intensified by Haines's book. A considerable number of studies of uneven merit on county series were being published, and in 1886 a society was formed in Cambridge devoted to the completion of the list Haines had compiled. After 1893 the society adopted the name of The Monumental Brass Society. A similar society begun at Oxford gradually lost its specialist interest. The Monumental Brass Society was the meeting place of many serious scholars whose research was published in the Society's Transactions and Portfolio Plates of Rubbings. Its progress was inevitably halted by the First World War. Among the many books on brasses written between 1880 and 1910 three were outstanding. *The Brasses of England* by the Revd. H. W.

Macklin, was a major textbook providing a comprehensive introduction to English brasses. It has become established as a standard work on account of its admirable composition, illustration and description. It is, however, often overlooked that Macklin's book contains few references, and the student must return to Haines for authority. *A Book of Facsimiles of Monumental Brasses on the Continent of Europe* (1884) by the Revd. W. F. Creeny provided an important introduction to brasses outside Britain, illustrated with numerous large plates. It was the first book of its kind and scope and justifiably earned European recognition. *A Manual of Costume as Illustrated by Monumental Brasses* (1906), by H. Druitt, concentrated specifically on problems of costume. These were thoroughly and competently worked out, and fully illustrated with small direct photographic plates as well as reproductions of rubbings.

This great period of research, initiated by Boutell, Haines and the Waller brothers, was completed in 1926 with the publication of *A List of Monumental Brasses in the British Isles* by Mill Stephenson. Mill Stephenson is properly regarded as the supreme authority on English brasses. The list is not merely an exact and laborious compilation, but represents in its accuracy and detail a lifetime's investigation. An appendix to this list drawn up by Stephenson's fellow scholars Ralph Griffin and M. S. Giuseppi was published as a memorial to him in 1938.

These distinguished books represent the most notable achievement of the pioneers of this study. They have become the recognized sources to which most authorities refer, and on which most substantial treatises have been based. Their standing is a tribute to their writers.

Yet the books described above have inevitable limitations. Haines appreciated the need to examine these monuments in the widest geographical context, but his example was not followed. Creeny's volume written as an introduction to Continental brasses has been widely accepted as a final authority. Furthermore the concentrated interest in brasses alone to the exclusion of other allied and broader studies had intrinsic dangers. Classification of brasses is a beginning, not an end in itself. Sources of documentary evidence and comparative studies with allied art forms offer endless and essential lines of research. Much fact in which these early writers appeared to be justified in trusting has now been called into question, especially in connection with costume and armour. Many questions of importance have hardly been asked. There is a need, while taking advantage of the great progress made, to review the subject more broadly, and to some extent return to the perspective of Gough.

Fortunately there are many sources for further reference. The Monumental Brass Society was resurrected in 1934. The researches of R. H. Pearson, R. H. D'Elboux, Ralph Griffin and other experts both past and present have been published in the Transactions of this and other learned societies. It is particularly necessary that the subject of brasses should be reassessed in relation to the research of the last thirty years. Progress in certain directions has been very substantial. Reused brasses, generally known as palimpsests (Figs. 267, 268), have become a major source of fresh evidence. The study of re-engraved fragments effectively begun by Mill Stephenson, was most successfully pursued by R. H. Pearson and has become the subject of a comprehensive analysis (as yet unpublished) by J. C. Page-Phillips. Indents or matrices of lost brasses have attracted increased attention, though their study is still in its early stages. The examination of wills and other documents has proved highly rewarding. Mrs. A. J. K. Esdaile identified for the first time several English engravers of the seventeenth century. Appreciation of Continental brasses has greatly increased, especially as the work of Belgian, German and Polish scholars has become better known. Research into incised slabs by F. A. Greenhill and H. A. Beetlestone has helped to place brasses in a more correct perspective. No recent books dealing with brasses have been conceived on a sufficiently broad scale to deal adequately with these matters. It is accordingly the author's intention to present the subject as it now appears. There is no possibility of offering a completely authoritative study, as so much fresh evidence is continually being brought to light. It is, however, both possible and appropriate to review the subject as a means to yet further discoveries.

It is necessary to define the scope and explain the format of this study. Its primary intention is to give a comprehensive view of English brasses, and a general introduction to the brasses of Europe. *The Craft* is devoted to an analysis of general aspects of the subject, and reference is made to English, Flemish, French, German, Polish and other sources wherever appropriate. *The Memorials* then describes brasses chronologically, separating them according to their place of origin. Brasses in England of Flemish origin are accordingly examined in appropriate sections on Flanders. Certain groups of brasses have been given special consideration but these generally fall conveniently within the chronological order. The author acknowledges some influence of *The Brasses of England* in deciding on this format, in preference to one based on types of brass. The latter is convenient to the reader, but is based on artificial and superficial distinctions. The introduction of so much Continental material may be questioned by some, but it is the author's conviction that the treatment of English brasses as a discrete study should be ended. The inclusion of Continental brasses as miscellaneous items is both inadequate and misleading.

Particular attention is given to the following types of evidence. Existing brasses are the most obvious. Reference is made to outstanding examples, and most lists included are selective. Mention is made of indents where these indicate features of which no example survives. Similarly, the reverses of reused brasses are described in the text where they show unique or valuable details. As far as possible documentary evidence (derived mainly from wills, contracts and letters) is quoted to support opinions. Rubbings and drawings of lost brasses are discussed where necessary. Especially important in this connection are the drawings of Flemish brasses, later published by J. Gaillard in *Inscriptions Funéraires et Monumentales de la Flandre Occidentale* (1866), and the drawings of François-Roger de Gaignières presented to Louis XIV in 1711. The latter, now preserved in the Bibliothèque Nationale, Paris, and the Bodleian Library, Oxford, alone indicate the former magnificence of French brasses. Comparisons with other types of monument or works of art are made where relevant. Monumental plates cast in low relief (Fig. 1) are regarded as another type of monument in spite of their extreme similarity to engraved brasses. These reliefs are especially important in Germany and Poland, where they greatly outnumber engraved plates. Their three-dimensional form does, however, associate them more with raised sculptured or cast monuments than with engraved compositions. Plates on which the relief effect has been achieved by casting and engraving below the overall surface of the metal, described in the text as recessed relief, are included as engraved brasses. Notes at the end of the text provide the sources of quotations and other references.

Photographic illustration of brasses is used liberally, and would by choice have been used more extensively. It is unfortunately very difficult to photograph large-scale horizontal brasses satisfactorily. Rubbings reveal the design of brasses with admirable clarity, though obscuring the texture of the brass, the depth of the engraving and the nature of the stone setting. It is hoped that the photographs included will compensate for their limitations. There has in the past been a tendency to illustrate brasses from Kent, Norfolk and the Home Counties to excess. Many equally interesting examples from the Midlands and northern counties have been ignored, and the selection here has been made to restore the balance.

The dating of brasses described in the text requires explanation. The actual year of the engraving of English brasses is known in hardly more than forty cases. It would accordingly be precise to precede almost all dates given with the letter d., to indicate the date is that of death only. Yet in the circumstances this would serve little purpose, and infer a greater degree of uncertainty than need exist. It may be deduced from evidence already available that the majority of brasses were laid fairly promptly after death, and where uncommonly long periods elapsed the inconsistency is detectable. The author has accordingly preferred to treat the year of death as sufficiently close to that of engraving to require no particular qualification. A margin of error of about two years should in consequence be allowed. Where qualifications are applied, the letter *c.*, placed before the date, denotes an approximation of five years before or after the date stated. In cases of great uncertainty a span of two dates, prefixed with a *c.*, is adopted. The letter d., placed before date, denotes the year of death exclusively, and is not to be interpreted as having any close relationship to the time of engraving.

The dates of English brasses, stated in the authoritative Mill Stephenson List, have been accepted with modifications. There has been detailed research in recent years, especially by such scholars as Dr. J. P. C. Kent, and J. R. Greenwood, into the finer points of brasses that appear to have common or related patterns, and the author, with these writers, has felt obliged on stylistic grounds to differ from some long accepted dates. Arguments to support such views are in controversial cases given in the text or chapter notes. Deductions based on stylistic grounds alone are at this stage of typological research admittedly vulnerable, but recorded dates are by no means entirely reliable. In order to avoid confusion arising from redating, Mill Stephenson List and Cameron List number references are given to the brasses listed in the index. The author hopes that gross misdating has been eliminated, but systematic research in future should permit a more exact dating, especially of brasses belonging to identifiable series.

There have been, and continue to be, extensive changes in the boundaries of English administrative counties. The locations of places given are correct for the period preceding the creation of the Greater London Council, and include in consequence the County of Middlesex. The decision to adhere to these well-established areas has been taken, both to accord with the practice of historical societies and organizations affected, and to facilitate reference to earlier publications.

There have been considerable changes in place-names on the Continent, especially in connection with the German/Polish boundary. In some instances, especially in Silesia, the former German name is still better known in Britain than the Polish and is initially included in brackets. The spelling of names is with few exceptions that used in the country of location. However in Belgium the French forms are so well-established for such important towns as Bruges and Ypres, that they are used in preference to the Flemish Brugge and Ieper. Places in the Eastern and Western Republics of Germany are described as being in East and West Germany respectively.

It is impossible to describe all aspects of this great study, and pointless merely to restate the views of earlier writers. The intention is to reappraise the subject within a European context in the light of recent research. The function is not only to evaluate facts, but to disclose lines of further enquiry.

1 · The origin of monumental brasses

Sepulchral floor slabs, an important class of monument to which memorial brasses belong, have a long history within the Christian Church. In contrast to Roman pagan practice, which denied the association of dead bodies with temples or shrines, Christians sought burial in churches as places of sanctity and spiritual protection. The dead were buried in church, and it was an early Christian practice to mark the spot of this resting place with a sacred symbol and occasionally some form of personal identification. The cross incised on the grave slab was the most common form of decoration, one, moreover, which was carried on throughout the Middle Ages. The Irish monastery of Clonmacnoise still retains a long series of cross slabs dating from the ninth until the sixteenth centuries.[1] Representations of persons on tombs were less usual. Professor E. Panofsky has, however, drawn attention to an early and interesting group of funerary portraits in mosaic, which originated in North Africa and were apparently introduced to Europe via Spain. These depicted the deceased on the slab with an inlay of coloured mosaic and were set horizontally in the floor (Fig. 2). Few examples survive, but they may well be regarded as the precursors of the mediaeval incised figure slab.[2]

Floor slabs acquired a new importance at the close of the twelfth century, especially in northern Europe. Church burial and the fashion for personal sepulchral representation became increasingly widespread.[3] Sculptured effigies, which were hitherto regarded as appropriate for royalty, the episcopate and church founders, were very expensive, while within the church buildings there was limited room for three-dimensional monuments. Decoration of grave slabs economized in both purchase and space. Twelfth and early thirteenth century incised slabs generally followed the shape of the coffin beneath with a marked tapering towards the feet, and exhibited boldly engraved figures.[4] Throughout the thirteenth century incised slabs, especially those made in France and the Low Countries, became more elaborate both in design and execution. The insertion of contrasting materials of figures and canopies, white compositions, resins, alabaster and various metals, added a richer quality to the finished composition. Heads, hands and details of ecclesiastical vestments were most usually chosen for special inlay.[5] The drawings of Gaignières illustrate a few highly elaborate French examples in which the entire inlay was composed of enamelled copper (Fig. 3).[6] A small monumental plaque of this type to Geoffrey Plantaganet (d. 1149), father of King Henry II of England, is still preserved in the museum at Le Mans, France, though this never formed part of a floor monument.[7]

The inlay of brass details, whole figures or complete compositions was one variation of this type of decoration; latten or bronze were effective materials to use for the purpose. Their texture was hard, their colour attractive, and cost moderate. Latten however, as shown by Cameron, had advantages in the overall thinness of plate readily attainable.[8] Low-relief plates in bronze were already an established monumental form in Germany, the tomb at Merseburg to Rudolph von Schwaben (?c. 1080) being a particularly notable and early example. It was a fortunate coincidence in northern Europe that the demand for decorative and representational floor monuments expanded at a time when craft in metal work had already attained an excellent quality and could be applied with skill to enrich the conventional slab. Monumental brasses developed from this association.

Haines suggested that brasses were derived from Limoges enamel inlays, as a cheaper and more durable form of memorial. It would appear that the use of such enamels for this purpose was contemporary with, and did not precede, the earliest brasses. The Le Mans plaque was a small feature on a tomb, and was in no respects equivalent to an effigy. Flat, recumbent figures in enamelled copper date from the second quarter of the thirteenth century, when brasses were already in use in France.

Experiment with different forms of inlay and types of metal continued throughout the Middle Ages. The combination of different coloured stone inlays, mastic and brass remain in the slab of Simon Bocheux (1462), in the church of Notre Dame at St. Omer, France. Hereford Cathedral possesses worn slabs in which the entire figures were inlaid with a white composition. Lead occurs as an inlay for lines on two slabs at Tintern Abbey, Monmouth. The tomb of Elizabeth Corbet (1516), Burford, Shropshire, is an engraved rectangular plate of lead. Flat memorials were cast in iron in Sussex, such as the cross to John Colins at Burwash. Wooden inlays formed part of the brass to Arnold Wlome, and his wife (1329), formerly at the Marienkirche, Lübeck, West Germany.[9] The extent to which inlays were incorporated in incised slabs may be readily appreciated from the numerous slabs in the nave of St. Botolph, Boston, Lincs. Continental examples illustrated by Greenhill are numerous, and these constitute a small proportion of those existing.

There can be little doubt that memorial brasses in their well-known forms originated in the early thirteenth century. The rectangular plate brass and the separate inlay brass, in which the figures, inscription and accessories are set in the slab as individual items, developed together with many other types of inlay exploited by the *tombiers* of France, especially those of Paris and the North. The earliest conventional[10] figure brass of which the design is known was that of Archbishop Pierre de Corbeil (d. 1222) of Sens, formerly at Sens Cathedral.[11] Among its earliest successors was that of Phillipe and Jean, the sons of King Louis VIII of France, apparently engraved between 1230 and 1250 (Fig. 4). The large censing angels, the bold background of fleurs-de-lys, and the posture of Phillipe, holding a hawking glove in his left hand, are all consistent with French incised slab designs. These were moreover in no sense isolated memorials. Gaignières illustrates a considerable selection of thirteenth century French brasses, a particularly good and early series having been at the cathedral of Sens.

This type of monument was quickly adopted in England and the Low Countries, especially in Tournai, a city of western Hainaut in the hinterland between France and Flanders.

Brasses with figure representations were engraved in Germany during the first half of the thirteenth century, and it is now clear that memorials of a similar type were occasionally made at an even earlier date. It is in fact difficult to resolve what should properly be classified as an engraved monumental brass. A particularly interesting case, recently exposed for a short period, is the lightly engraved copper plate over the coffin of St. Ulrich (d. 973), laid in 1187 within a vault in the church of St. Ulrich and St. Afra at Augsburg (Fig. 7).[12] The plate, tapering towards the base, bears the figure of the bearded Saint. Over his head is the simple inscription +San*Ctu*S VDALRI*Cus* EP*iscopu*S. The work is apparently that of a Swabian goldsmith, but should, despite its unusual form and concealed situation, be classified as a memorial brass. This is, indeed, the earliest recorded figure brass, though evidently a work without influence on, or direct association with, the craft of monumental brass engraving.

It is clear that the early German examples developed on lines different from, and having little connection with, their counterparts west of the Rhine. Low-relief bronze effigies, such as those of the eleventh and twelfth centuries in the cathedrals of Magdeburg and Merseburg, antedate the flat brass, and in central Germany throughout the Middle Ages engraved brasses remained a subordinate form of representation to relief. The early German brasses at Verden, Hildesheim, Halberstadt and Paderborn are very different in character from those of France, Flanders and England, and evidently had a separate and unrelated origin. A contrary view has been expressed by Trivick in *The Craft and Design of Monumental Brasses*, who writes 'that there was once a considerable number of brasses with effigies in Western Europe of thirteenth-century date is almost certain, and all indicates that Germany was the originator and was the first country to produce them in quantity.'[13] Yet there seems little to support this interpretation. St. Ulrich's plate is an isolated work. The brass of Bishop Yso (1231) at the Andreaskirche, Verden (Fig. 8), though engraved in a region where evidence of later brass engraving is more substantial, has no companion for half a century. There is furthermore no indication of a prolific German workshop until the fifteenth century. The combined evidence of existing brasses, indents and records of destroyed memorials strongly points to the conclusion that the only notable European workshops of the thirteenth century were in northern France, being complemented towards the close of that century by others in the Low Countries and in England. References to isolated early thirteenth century brasses in Liège, London and elsewhere do not compromise this conclusion, especially when it is considered that the style and origin of the monuments is not known. It would require very powerful arguments, supported by facts as yet uncited, to justify a more easterly source for their origin or inspiration.

The development of brasses from a decorative variety to a monumental form, comparable in importance to the incised slab, may be attributed to a number of factors. Reasonable cost combined with durability were undoubtedly important. The contrast between the condition of the brass and stone portions of composite monuments as in those of Johann von Heringen (1505) and Heinrich Gassman (1481) in Erfurt Cathedral, East Germany, is very striking.[14] Latten was not subject to flaking and did not suffer seriously from the effects of damp. The colour of the metal was pleasing, especially when contrasting colour in the form of resinous inlay was applied to the engraved lines. Furthermore, brasses could be made in a wide range of sizes without incongruity. Diminutive sculptured effigies appear curious unless representing children. Even the designs on incised slabs tend to be related to the scale of the stone itself, the engraved lines being an integral part of the stone base. This is not so with a monumental brass. The stone is essentially a background against which the metal plates may be arranged at will. Differences in both texture and colour set the latten apart. The small inscription and pair of gloves commemorating Peter Denot, glover (c. 1440), at Fletching, Sussex (Fig. 239), are most happily placed in their setting, and would not easily pass unnoticed. This quality of adaptability was perhaps decisive. It enabled the engravers to cater for a wide social range of purchasers and reduced the difference in effective minimal cost between the brass and incised slab.

Once established as an acceptable form of monument, which even royalty occasionally adopted, and all of some means could afford, figure brasses remained in demand. Their decline in popularity coincided with that of all floor monuments bearing effigies. Brass inscriptions on the other hand have survived in uninterrupted use into the present century.

Brasses were the fortunate product of a period of experiment in monumental forms. By fulfilling their function admirably, yet proving adaptable in cost, they emerged as a widely favoured and lasting type of memorial (Fig. 5).

2 · The manufacture of brasses

The casting, engraving, setting and finishing of fine brasses constituted a skilled craft. The completion of a single memorial involved a variety of processes and a surprising range of materials. The precise methods used by mediaeval engravers are not completely known as literary sources are inadequate. Nevertheless, much information can be derived from the examination of brasses. Monumental brass engraving is still practised and most techniques have changed very little over centuries.

A useful summary of the processes involved is recorded in an item from the account book of the noted seventeenth century English sculptor Nicholas Stone. Stone was employed to make a memorial brass to Cecily Puckering, aged thirteen. The brass consists of an inscription and arms, and is preserved in St. Mary's Church, Warwick. The following details are stated for the month of July 1636.[1]

'For the use of Sir Thomas Puckering one grave stone of blake marble five foot nine Inches long and two foot tenne Inches brod and 6 Inches thicke: £6. o. o.
For squaring and smothing of the same stone: £1. o. o.
For three plats of brasse: £1. 12. o.
For cutting the inscriptions in the three plats of brasse and letting them into the marble stone and rivetting of them fast: £1. 16. o.
For gilding those three plats of brasse all over and picking the letters out with blake: £1. 8. o.'

The stone

The first and most important item was the stone itself, and the procuring, cutting and polishing of a suitable slab was the initial task. The stone and the metal work were usually carried out under the supervision of the same master, who was skilled in the use of both materials. The majority of engravers were marblers. The main sources of stone for English brasses were the limestone quarries of the Isle of Purbeck, Dorset, the Sussex Weald near Petworth, and the Kentish Weald at Bethersden. All these limestones polish well, though the fossilized shell deposits of Purbeck marble are more compact than in the others. The Purbeck quarries were the most important in England. The marble was obtained from a relatively thin vein halfway down the northern slope of the southern ridge of the Purbeck hills between Peveril Point and Warbarrow Tout. A considerable quantity of marble was reached easily from the surface. The main disadvantage of this source was the thickness of good material, which varied from twenty centimetres to sixty centimetres only. This imposed limitations on the uses of the marble for the purposes of sculpture, but did not affect the preparation of tomb slabs. Purbeck marble was favoured for making altars, fonts, lecterns, aumbries and piscinae as well as shrines and sepulchres, and was used extensively in the twelfth century for architectural features. The Company of Marblers and Stone Cutters of Purbeck was an influential body under Crown patronage, and outlasted the Company of Marblers of London, but there is no evidence that they were engaged in crafts other than their quarrying, masonry and carving. The marble was dispatched by sea from Poole Harbour and slabs were sent in great quantity to the brass engravers in London.[2]

There is evidence that limestone from other English quarries was used in conjunction with brasses. Indents have been recorded at Haughmond Abbey and St. Julian, Shrewsbury, Shropshire, cut into white coralline limestone from Wenlock in the same county.[3] Similarly it is suspected that a limestone with a distinctly different fossil content was quarried near Peterborough and used by East Anglian engravers. Some indents at St. Mary's, Bury St. Edmunds, Suffolk, are of a compacted sandstone. There is practically no evidence of the use of brasses in direct conjunction with alabaster.

The most famous sources of marble in the Low Countries were the quarries near Tournai especially at Chercq and Antoing. This dark blue or black limestone is most usually found as a setting for Flemish brasses and was very occasionally used in England.[4] Local sand and limestones were widely used in Germany and Poland. A relevant Tournai contract, of 17 April 1314, describes the purchase by a brass engraver Jean Alous of twenty slabs from Pieres de Saint Andriu and Jean li Clers de Morkendiu. The slabs are classified according to length—ten, nine and eight feet, and pairs of seven and seven and a half feet. The largest slabs, quoted at a cost of 'XXI gros Tournois et 1 estelin', were proportionately far more expensive than the smaller stones.[5]

Cutting the stone to a required size, polishing the surface and preparing an exact indent to receive the brass plates to a sufficient depth to allow the brass to be flush with the surface, was work carried out by the engravers. It is interesting to note that in the sixteenth century, when numerous memorials sold from despoiled English religious houses were sent to London for re-use, the engravers did not merely turn over the brass plates for reworking but also reversed or polished down the surface of the stones. The slab of Sir Henry Sacheverell (1558) at Morley, Derbyshire, has on its reverse the indent of a priest. The slab of Sir Richard Catesby (1553), Ashby St. Legers, Northants., has been so reduced in thickness that only the buffed-down rivets of the earlier brass are discernible.[6]

The metal used

The second main item in the Stone account is the manufacture or procurement of brass plates. The term 'brass' as applied to memorial plates has been noted in English wills of the fifteenth century. William Norreys of Ash-next-Sandwich, Kent, described in his will of 1486 a memorial 'with an ymage of the Trinity graven in brasse and pykture of my body and Armes there yn sett in lyke form'.[7] Before this period the term 'latten' spelt latun or laton, is generally applied. Letters of 'laton' are mentioned on the indent of William de St. John (*c*. 1325) at Ramsbury, Wilts. The same metal is described as laiton in Flemish and French records. The origin of this word is difficult to establish. The generally accepted derivation from the Latin *latta* meaning a lath is in effect seriously questioned in an interesting article by Dr. B. Dutton,[8] who draws attention to an Arabic term *lātūn* in use as early as the ninth century. The word is applied to metal ornaments, and may well have been adopted during the crusades. The Latin word *aurichalcum* (golden copper) is also found quite frequently to describe this metal, as is the looser term *aes*. A fuller discussion of the origin of latten is given by Dr. H. K. Cameron in his important article 'Technical Aspects of Medieval Monumental Brasses'.[9] The meaning of the term is fortunately clear, as drillings from the cast figure of Richard Beauchamp, Earl of Warwick, which was required by contract to be 'perfectly made of the finest latten' show the consistency to be copper 84·1 per cent, zinc 8·2 per cent, tin 3·6 per cent, lead 1·2 per cent and iron 2·6 per cent. As Cameron states, 'This then is the composition of latten. It is not a straight bronze or brass but contains the ingredients of both. It comes well within the range of what Collon-Gevaert calls "the best bronzes".'

Dr. Cameron describes the preparation and casting of plate in detail. His researches are based in part on two sixteenth century metallurgical treatises—*Alterfürnemsten Mineralischen Ertz und Berchwerksarten* by L. Ercker, first published in 1574, and *Pirotechnica* by V. Biringuccio, first published in 1540—and on metallurgical analysis of brass samples. Mediaeval brass was calamine brass, formed by the permeation of copper by zinc vapour. Calamine ore (zinc carbonate) was ground and mixed with charcoal and pieces of copper. The mixture was heated in a crucible sufficiently to reduce the zinc in the ore to a metallic state but not to melt the copper. After the zinc vapour had permeated the copper the temperature was raised, and the melted brass was poured from the crucible into moulds. This process is fully described by Biringuccio and in the much earlier writings of an eleventh century monk, Theophilus, and the thirteenth century scholar Albertus Magnus.[10]

Metallurgical analysis of samples drilled from a variety of brasses has shown the content of the metal produced. The samples reveal considerable differences in the proportions of copper and zinc. A sample (1461) from All Souls, Oxford, showed a copper content of 84·7 per cent, while another of 1597 from Penn, Bucks., showed only 64 per cent. The same Penn sample had a zinc content of 32·3 per cent, while zinc from an early fourteenth century sample at the Cambridge Museum of Archaeology and Ethnology formed only 11·8 per cent. From a considerable number of samples now tested it appears clear that the copper content of brasses was very high until *c.* 1550—in the fourteenth century averaging 80 per cent, and about 75 per cent for the remaining period. After 1550 English brasses show a marked reduction in copper, averaging rather less than 70 per cent, with an increased proportion of zinc. A high zinc content hardened the metal but imparted a yellowish colour. Traces of tin and lead discovered in the composition of most samples were probably included deliberately to impart greater fluidity to the metal. The absence of tin in late English manufactured plate has been identified by Dr. Cameron as a cause for their susceptibility to corrosion. The following is a selection of samples analysed.[11] The provenance stated refers to the engraving and not to the source of the plate.

	copper %	zinc %	tin %	lead %	iron %
Fourteenth century Flemish					
1349. Walsokne. King's Lynn, Norfolk.					
Top left corner.	77·31	19·34	1·94	1·41	—
Ditto. Bottom right corner.	77·41	19·35	1·79	1·45	—
1364. Braunche. King's Lynn.					
Top right corner.	79·60	17·53	0·64	2·23	—
Ditto. Bottom left corner.	78·94	18·49	0·61	1·96	—
c. 1390. Reverse Dow. Oxford Cathedral.	77·10	13·20	2·20	5·50	1·60
Fourteenth century English					
? *c.* 1320. Letter T. Cambridge Museum of Archaeology and Anthropology.	79·00	11·80	3·60	2·85	1·24
c. 1320. Bures. Acton, Suffolk.					
Figure, not shield.	79·8	17·8	1·3	1·1	—

	copper %	zinc %	tin %	lead %	iron %
? 1348. Gifford. Bowers Gifford, Essex.	78·3	18·6	1·7	1·4	—
c. 1380. Quintin. Cliffe-Pypard, Wilts.	77·8	18·6	2·7	0·9	—
Fourteenth century Silesian					
c. 1300. Buswoyz, Lubiąż.	77·1	16·3	6·4	0·2	—
c. 1305. Boleslaus, Lubiąz.	75·1	18·9	5·7	0·3	—
c. 1305. Premislaus, Lubiąz.	73·4	20·3	5·4	0·9	—
Fifteenth century Flemish					
c. 1460. Reverse Dow. Oxford Cathedral.	65·00	20·20	trace	13·50	1·20
Fifteenth century English					
c. 1420. Reverse Rufford. Edlesborough, Bucks. Top of figure.	77·80	14·01	3·26	5·03	0·60
Ditto. Bottom of figure.	76·90	14·18	3·35	4·87	0·70
c. 1415. Spetyll. Luton, Beds.	68·45	22·54	2·90	6·11	—
1456. Moor. Tattershall, Lincs.	67·54	24·16	1·16	7·14	—
c. 1470. Reverse Fermoure, Somerton, Oxon.	80·65	12·20	2·21	3·16	1·12
c. 1475. Willoughby. Tattershall, Lincs.	66·81	28·50	2·56	2·13	—
c. 1490. Reverse Fermer. Easton Neston, Northants.	72·9	26·9	—	—	trace
1499. Reverse Rufford, Edlesborough, Bucks.	68·50	21·50	trace	8·70	1·20
Sixteenth century Flemish					
1504. Cortewille. Victoria and Albert Museum.	64·00	29·50	3·00	3·50	
Sixteenth century English					
c. 1500. Reverse Fermer. Easton Neston, Northants.	68·4	23·0	—	8·4	trace
c. 1500. Reverse Fermoure. Somerton, Oxon.	69·93	21·10	trace	9·71	1·12
c. 1510. Knight from Peckleton, Leics.	68·50	21·50	—	8·70	1·20
c. 1520. Reverse Coorthopp. Oxford Cathedral.	75·50	23·20	trace	trace	1·20
c. 1520. Reverse Fermer. Easton Neston, Northants.	79·40	20·20	—	—	trace
c. 1520. Reverse Pen. 1597 Penn, Bucks.	68·00	18·40	0·10	11·70	—
c. 1530. Reverse Fermer. Easton Neston, Northants.	70·80	21·00	trace	7·00	1·30
1540. Rok. Penn, Bucks.	74·20	23·00	0·20	trace	0·60
c. 1540. Reverse Fermer. Easton Neston, Northants.	80·20	19·20	trace	—	trace

	copper %	zinc %	tin %	lead %	iron %
1584. E. Brudenell. Deene, Northants.	70·5	28·4	0·2	0·9	—
1597. Pen. Penn, Bucks.	64·00	32·30	0·20	1·20	1·30
Seventeenth century English					
1610. Ecclesiastic. Cambridge Museum of Archaeology and Anthropology.	68·10	29·30	—	0·93	0·68
1612. Reaynoldes. Hawkhurst, Kent.	68·9	30·2	0·1	0·2	0·6

Not all brasses were made of such alloys. The high temperature required for the firing of enamel necessitated the use of copper plate when enamel decoration was required. The shield of the elder Sir John Dabernoun, Stoke D'Abernon, Surrey, is inlaid with special enamelled copper trays.[12] The red enamelled figure of Margaret Gaynesford (*c.* 1490), Carshalton, Surrey, is of copper. Enamel appears to have been applied to the important brasses at Broxbourne, Herts. (1473), and Little Easton, Essex (1483). No metallurgical analysis has been made of these, but both are composed of multiple plates, probably so constructed to facilitate firing. The will of Bishop Brown of Norwich (1445) specified the preparation of both latten and copper shields, which may well have been made necessary by their colour inlays.[13] Two documents concerning the foundry of the Hilligers (bell- and cannon-founders) of Freiberg, East Germany, record the content of the metal used for various brasses in the years 1593, 1594 and 1624. According to the treasurer of the Elector of Saxony in 1593, old brass left over from the casting of statues in the mortuary chapel of Freiberg was to be used for five brasses of the Elector's family, but refined copper from the refining house at Grüntal and tin from Altenberg was also supplied for them so that the casting was made with an alloy of forty parts copper, thirty parts brass and twenty parts tin.[14] In a memorandum of Hans Hilliger of 15 December 1624 about the cost of a statue and three monumental brasses, it was reported that there was sufficient copper and brass available in the foundry, that no other was required, and that the ten hundredweight of tin lacking could be taken from the tithe of tin due from Altenberg.[15] It would be interesting to establish if brasses made by English bell-founders contained a similarly substantial proportion of tin.

Casting

The process of casting the sheet brass has been described by Ercker who in a diagram illustrates the transfer of the metal from small crucibles to a large one and the moulds made out of two stones (Fig. 6). These are shown as fixed at an angle but not vertical. Ercker was in fact illustrating a mould to produce an ingot fit for battery, rather than a plate for direct use, and moulds for mediaeval latten plate would have required a far closer set. It can hardly be doubted that the majority of latten plates were cast in open earth or sand trays, a simple process confirmed by the appearance of unworked plate surfaces.

It would seem that the plates used in England were cast in a regular size of about 0·76 metres by 0·61 metres (30 in. by 24 in.). The plate joins of most brasses are consistent with these dimensions. The surface of the plate was smoothed by beating the cold metal with a wooden mallet, a process known as planishing, and then polished. Air bubbles trapped in the metal during casting produced defects which were immediately apparent or subsequently revealed themselves when the surface became worn. The insertion of small pieces of brass within regular shaped plates is indicative of repair of such damage. A very noticeable rectangular piece appears on the gown of Amy Lambard (1487), Hinxworth, Herts. The finely 'pocked' surface of many fifteenth century brasses presumably only appeared after centuries of wear and exposure.

The methods of preparation described were subsequently modified by the process of battery, which was introduced into England from Germany in a commercial venture started in 1565, the investors being incorporated by Royal Charter in 1568 with the title of the 'Society of the Mineral and Battery Works'. In the battery process heavy water-driven hammers were used to beat metal ingots, which had first been annealed in a charcoal fire. It was possible by this method to produce a far thinner sheet of metal. Whereas the thickness of fifteenth and early sixteenth century plate was generally about 4 millimetres, that of English battered plate was often 1·5 millimetres or less. Brass plate was, in fact, not the main product of the Mineral and Battery Works, which was primarily established for the making of brass wire for wool combs. Most English brasses of the reigns of Queen Elizabeth I and King James I are engraved on such plates, their undersurfaces bearing the hammer dents. Though such preparation undoubtedly reduced the cost of the metal, the sheet itself was liable to indentation and other forms of distortion. It is significant that some of the finest English brasses of this period are engraved on much heavier cast plates which were probably imported. A very clear illustration of the battery process is reproduced by Cameron ('The Metals used in Monumental Brasses') from *Description de la Manufacture du Cuivre* (1764) by Duhamel du Monceau.

The actual preparation of the plate was not necessarily an activity of the engravers, and was evidently not so in England. Biringuccio states that the preparation of brass 'is carried out in various places, for instance, in Flanders, Cologne, Paris', and both Köln (Cologne) and Paris are named by Albertus Magnus. Great quantities of latten plate were imported from the Continent for English use. Köln was a major distribution centre. Cullen or Köln plate was specified for the making of the latten tomb of Richard Beauchamp, Earl of Warwick.[16] The account of the 'Petty Custom' on general merchandise for the years 1420–1 contains several references to the importation of latten plates. The entry on 29 January 1421: 'De Johanne Dasse pro i bala fusti i fardello latone plates pr. £XV', is an example.[17] This, however, is not conclusive proof of origin. Köln was an emporium for copper mined in the Harz, the Tyrol and even Hungary, much of which was exported to the famous metalwork centres of the Meuse and Sheldt valleys. Great quantities of despoiled plate from the churches of West Flanders were imported into England during the late sixteenth century, and it is probable that latten was brought from these nearer sources from which large numbers of completed monuments were obtained. Founders were established in Tournai by the thirteenth century.

In the author's opinion a misleading conclusion has been drawn from this extensive trade. Various writers have stated that the casting of such plate was not carried out in England at all. Macklin writes 'It [the plate] was manufactured exclusively on the Continent—at least until the middle of the 16th century—in Flanders and Germany, and particularly at Cologne.'[18] This generalization, while on the whole sound, is easy to misinterpret. English craftsmen were capable of such casting, as is proved by a number of latten lecterns of English manufacture.[19] These were made from wooden patterns and cast in sand moulds. The book-rests on several are completely flat, that at Yeovil, Somerset, being engraved with a memorial figure (Fig. 37). Furthermore, the argument of economy, sometimes cited to explain the English preference for separate inlay compositions, loses most of its force if the innumerable fragments saved could not be recast into further plate. The explanation would appear to lie in the failure, through ignorance, to exploit local sources of calamine ore. Copper was a valuable material and in consequence was suitable

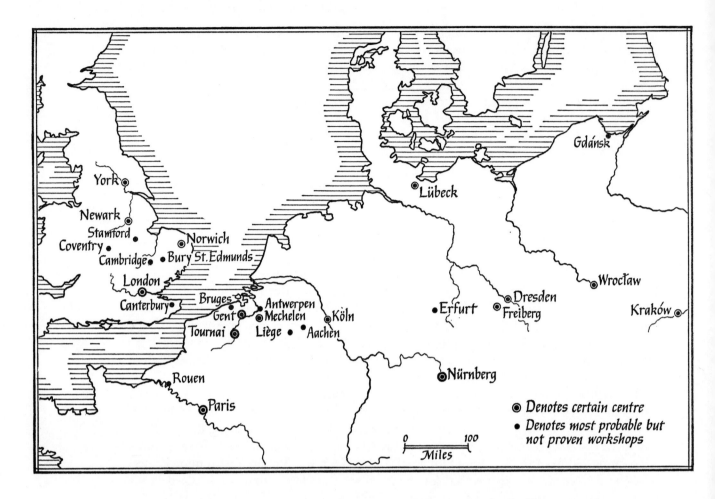

York

Newark
Stamford
Coventry
Cambridge Bury St. Edmunds
Norwich
London
Canterbury
Bruges
Gent Antwerpen
Mechelen
Tournai Liège Köln
Aachen
Rouen
Paris

Lübeck

Gdánsk

Wrocław

Erfurt Dresden
Freiberg

Kraków

Nürnberg

⊙ Denotes certain centre
● Denotes most probable but
  not proven workshops

0   100
├─────────┤
    Miles

1. Certain and probable significant centres of monumental brass engraving in Europe, 1200–1700

for import. Calamine ore, in contrast, was bulky and contained a high proportion of waste. It was more practical to import prepared plate and utensils than to attempt to establish local manufacture with imported raw materials. The mining of calamine ore was a primary function of the 'Mines Royal', incorporated in 1568, and the discovery of the ore in Somerset was a decisive factor in establishing the British brass industry. Yet such an interpretation in no way precludes the occasional casting of plate in England.

Large quantities of scrap latten must have been available, not only from the engravers' workshops, but from other sources where this metal was used. The inscription to William Henshawe, Bell-founder, and his two wives (1519), now in St. Mary de Crypt, Gloucester, is cast in one piece, and is longer than the 'standard' plates used. It is likely that this among others was cast in an English foundry. The casting of latten plates, in contrast to the preparation of latten itself, was hardly an exclusively Continental craft.

Engraving

The plates, whether purchased or cast by the engravers, were cut and engraved to a required design. Some impression of an engraver's workshop can be obtained from relevant mediaeval illustrations. The best known are two fourteenth century illuminations from a manuscript in the British Museum showing the preparation of incised slabs.[20] In these pictures the master is shown talking to the widow of the deceased and others, while craftsmen engrave stones on which the design has already been defined (Figs. 9 and 10). A fourteenth century bench end at Hannover, West Germany, depicts an ecclesiastic working with a fine chisel and mallet, while behind him is a rack containing a range of chisels and a pair of dividers.[21] The workshop is most completely and realistically shown in the engraving by the 'Master of Balaam', of a goldsmith's workshop in which the craftsmen are employed at benches, with their tools at hand or in racks (Fig. 11).

Such illustrations and the evidence of the brasses themselves reveal the type of instruments used. The engraver's most essential instruments were chasing tools and a graver or burin. Chasing tools may be described as fine chisels of hardened metal, the points and edges of which may be shaped to produce a particular required effect. The most numerous are tracers of which the engraver would require a large selection. These are sharp cutting tools, held at a slight angle with the fingers of one hand and struck by a hammer with a specially shaped handle, held in the palm of the other. Broad lines could be engraved by a succession of parallel lines cut flat by the wide front edge of the tool or planed down with a scorer. On a few brasses lines have been left incomplete, only the outer incisions being made. The 'I' in TIMOR on the Acworth inscription (1513), Luton, Beds., is a clear example.

The burin is a hard engraving tool with a triangular or rectangular section. Force is imparted by the hand and forearm and the effectiveness of the tool depends on extreme sharpness. It is difficult to establish from the condition of old brasses whether tracers or a burin had been used on any particular detail. The Hastyngs brass at Elsing shows evidence of the use of both. In addition to these cutting instruments varieties of punches were used for dotted features, especially on sixteenth century German brasses, while a ball tool with a hollowed point was probably used to cut small crescents and circles. For the cruder work of cutting out plates for separate inlay, chisels and files were employed, the marks of which are still discernible.

It is appropriate here to refute the fallacy that separate inlay treatment was an English peculiarity. Separate inlay was economical in the use of metal, and was probably attractive to English engravers for that reason. Furthermore, it was well suited to the graceful canopies and lineal presentation of English designs. The technique was, nevertheless, widely used in Flanders, France, Germany and Silesia. The majority of surviving brasses of Silesian origin are of separate inlay (Figs. 113–17), and Flemish examples of the type are numerous (e.g. Fig. 141). Apart from considerations of taste, separate inlay offered the advantages of economy, but was especially subject to damage and mutilation through the smallness and delicacy of its component parts.

Patterns

Before engraving was undertaken the design of the brass was sketched on the metal. The manner in which this was done can only be suggested as no proof is yet available. It is certain that patterns were prepared from which the brass was copied. Patterns are mentioned in several surviving contracts, as for example on page 97. An original early sixteenth century sketch by Willem Loeman of Köln for a tomb and brasses to Duke Johann II of Kleve, was, until the Second World War, preserved in the Haupstaatsarchiv, Düsseldorf, West Germany. Sketches of brasses by Gerard Johnson of Southwark are among the archives of Viscount Gage, and have been published (Figs. 12, 74). These later designs are described in more detail in Chapter Eight. How far these patterns remained miniature sketches or were painted full scale on parchment or paper can only be surmised. The remarkable similarity of certain figures, of which those of William Cokyn, Esq. (1527), Hatley Cockayne, and John Fysher, Esq. (1528), Clifton, both in Bedfordshire, are examples, indicates the occasional re-use of a full-scale design (Figs. 13, 14).[22] The transfer of the lines of the drawing onto the metal could have been easily achieved by rubbing the under-surface with wax and heavily defining the obverse. This process is still used. Alternatively the lines could have been perforated and coloured. The main outlines would then be clearly painted. The brass engraver W. E. Gawthorp records that on examining the reverse of the figure of Isabel Hay (1455), Luton, Beds., he found the lines of unfinished canopy work of the same period. The continuation of partially engraved lines in black paint was then discernible.[23]

A unique record of painting, presumably carried out in the workshop, is on the brass of Johann and Lambert Munten (1559) at Aachen Cathedral, West Germany. The obverse consists of an engraved inscription, below which is a cadaver and the words 'O Minsch Dirch Am Mych Op Erden dat Ich Byn Moys Du Werden' (Fig. 15). On the reverse is the painting, consisting of a different inscription to the same persons and the cadaver, which lies on a mat and a table inscribed with the 'O Minsch . . .' text (Fig. 16). The painting may have been done to show the purchaser the proposed design. Had it been approved it might have been engraved, though the cadaver is both too small and detailed to be executed without modification. Alternatively it may have been a means of allowing both sides to be exposed. The author is indebted to J. C. Page-Phillips for notification of the existence of this curiosity.

Another approach to transferring the main lines of a pattern was by using dividers and making superficial scratches on the metal. Evidence of this process can be seen on the brass of Archbishop Jakub (1480) at Gnieźno, Poland, where thin guidelines cut across the intended design (Fig. 93). It is clear from the faults in some brasses of good quality that the parts were engraved separately and then assembled, probably as a consequence of an urgent order. Serious inconsistencies arise at the junction of the plates, and are especially noticeable round the hanging mufflers of the figure of Sir Robert or Sir William de Setvans, Chartham, Kent (Fig. 121). Overall detailed definition of the lines would have prevented such errors. It is very likely that many small designs were freely drawn upon the metal from patterns well known to the craftsmen. No process was used exclusively.

Whether after having set out the design the entire monument was engraved by one craftsman or team, or whether certain parts were allocated to specialist workers, is an interesting question for investigation. Separate inlay compositions facilitate such division of work. As explained in Chapter Two of *The Memorials* it is now clear that the separately inlaid letters of fourteenth century inscriptions in England were cast in quantity and independently, and frequently in later brasses the quality of inscriptions and arms is superior to that of the figures. Thorough analysis of English brasses of the early sixteenth century may well expose conclusive evidence.

Setting

After costing the engraving, the Stone account refers to the setting of the brasses and 'rivetting of them fast'. The method of fixing brasses to their setting changed considerably during the fourteenth and fifteenth centuries. The earliest brasses were set into their indent, secured with pitch only. The pitch was run hot into the indent and the brass pressed down upon it until it had cooled. Both Sir John Dabernoun 'the Elder', Stoke D'Abernon, Surrey, and Sir William Fitzralph (*c.* 1330), Pebmarsh, Essex, were found to be so fixed when they were repaired. Indents of similar brasses give no indication of former rivets. Four large brasses (*c.* 1300–05) at the Silesian monastery of Lubiąż were also found to have no other form of fixing. The great weight of the brass plates themselves was a favourable factor. In many instances reinforcing bars, at the junction of the plates comprising the brass, were set into deeper indents, and must have helped to secure the whole. These bars are a feature of Flemish brasses, and were discovered on the reverse of the two large rectangular brasses at King's Lynn, Norfolk, when these were repaired by D. H. Wippell. Their recesses are discernible on many indents, especially in St. Alban's Cathedral. It is interesting to note that bitumen as well as latten was imported. In 1293 eleven ships of Germany and Frisia put into Scarborough with copper from Lübeck and ninety-nine barrels of pitch and tar.[24]

The use of rivets (dowel pins) in addition to the bitumen fixative became universal practice in the fourteenth century. A Tournai contract of 1301 or 1311, recorded in Chapter Eight, Appendix I, refers to their insertion specifically. Rivets were generally made of latten, though also quite commonly of copper. Their ends were made bulbous (Fig. 17) or flanged so as to set securely in lead, which was poured into specially prepared recesses in the indent. Two methods seem to have been adopted to secure the plates.

In the first method the brass was probably laid upon the stone with elongated rivets protruding through the plate. When it had been ascertained that the position of the rivets matched the recesses, the pitch was spread and the brass lowered into position. Before the plate was pressed down, lead was poured into the recesses through prepared channels. These channels may be observed in many indents, and at Blatherwyck, Northants., much of the lead had set within them, having been poured in from the back of the slab.[25] The brass was then pressed to the required level, a task which must have been completed rapidly as lead sets quickly. The rivets were then cut down nearly flush with the surface of the plate and flattened.

In the second method the elongated rivets were set into position in advance of the brass. Lead was poured directly into the recesses, and was often punched with a tool to give greater security. The pitch was then spread and the brass pressed into place. This process appears simpler than the other and more economical of lead, though both were concurrently used in the sixteenth century.

Late fifteenth and sixteenth century brasses set against tomb backs or on the top of high tombs were often fixed with pointed headed rivets driven into wooden plugs. Clear examples of such plugs are found in indents at Blythburgh and Bures, Suffolk, and Dedham, Essex. Bitumen was frequently omitted in these vertical positions. Paper has been discovered at Holy Trinity, Coventry, and even under the floor brass at Lambourne, Essex, as substitute backing. Until the sixteenth century, rivet heads were generally skilfully polished and it is often extremely difficult to locate fifteenth century rivets on the surface. This work was probably effected by abrasion either with a metal tool or a water stone. No such trouble was taken to finish many late sixteenth century brasses which are clumsily marred by obtrusive rivet heads, the rivets themselves occasionally being of iron. Plate joins were reinforced with solder and carefully polished on the obverse.[26]

Colouring and inlays

The colouring and gilding of brasses, and the blackening of their lines (as in the Stone account) could be an elaborate process. It is reasonable to assume that the lines of all engraved brasses were originally inlaid to contrast with the surface of the plate. Black inlay was most common, using the same bitumen or pitch which was used as the fixative. Traces of this inlay will generally appear if heat is applied to brasses under repair. This was a simple treatment. Many brasses were highly coloured with a variety of pigments. Particles of malachite (green), vermilion (red) and azurite (blue) have been identified. The binding component consisted of rosin or a mixture of rosin and beeswax.[27] The Tournai contract I mentioned above required that 'all the colour thereon must be fine, hard, and made of good oil and resin'. Few brasses remain highly coloured, though fragments of pigment can usually be traced in armorial tabards and shields. Coloured inlays remain substantially intact on brasses at Ávila, Spain (engr. *c.* 1505), and the Victoria and Albert Museum, London (1535).

An easier form of colouring, but only appropriate to mural brasses, was to apply paint to the metal surfaces. The small French brass to François Senocq and wife (1552) at the Musée de la Princerie, Verdun, is so treated (Fig. 19). The votive composition of Canon Johann Pollart (1534), at Aachen, is richly painted. Two English examples are Ralph Flexney and wife (d. 1578, engr. *c.* 1590), St. Michael, Oxford, and John Prideaux and family (1639), Harford, Devon. The application of gold paint was quite common in the seventeenth century.

The use of enamel for colour was complicated, and as a consequence, rare. Four examples have been cited on page 36.

The surfaces of mediaeval brasses were often gilt, as appears not only from the Stone record but in a contract of 1515 (Chapter Eight, Appendix IV). The Hastyngs brass at Elsing was described as being gilt, and traces of the gilding remain at Ketteringham, Norfolk (1499) (Fig. 227). Occasionally a selected surface would be silver gilt. A face has been so treated at Westerham, Kent. preserved on the reverse of a group of children (1529).[28] Lead was used extensively as an inlay for shields and tabards of arms (Fig. 18), and to represent white material such as the woollen pallium of archbishops or the fur almuce worn by priests. Ladies' kirtles were sometimes heavily inlaid. The greater part of the figure of Dame Elizabeth Fynderne (1444), Childrey, Berks., is engraved on lead inlay, including the lion at her feet.

Mention has already been made on page 29 of the decorative inlay of brass details into incised slabs, and the equivalent inlay of alabaster, wood and other materials into brasses. The alabaster face of Queen Ingeborg (d. 1319), Ringsted, Denmark, is original (Fig. 135),[29] while indents at Dundrennan Abbey, Stewartry of Kirkcudbright, Scotland, reveal the insertion of faces and other details within the brass. A deacon (*c.* 1325) at Noyon Cathedral, France, has his tonsure and hands of marble. The Tournai contract cited specified that the head, hands and the white of the alb on an archdeacon's brass should be of 'good alabaster'. This type of treatment was probably confined to Flemish and French brasses. The head of Bishop Yo(u)ng (engr. *c.* 1523), New College, Oxford, was for a while of alabaster or white composition, though this has now been shown to have been an early nineteenth century restoration.[30] The use of enamel inlays has been described (p. 36). The adoption of coloured glass as an inlay, at Elsing, Norfolk (1347), and of mosaic, at Westminster Abbey (1276) (Fig. 68), was highly exceptional.

Transport of brasses

The maker's final responsibility, having completed the stone, the brass and all required decoration, was to ensure the safe transport of the monument to its destination. Delivery to a specified destination is a requirement of most surviving contracts. Water transport was preferred for such bulky articles. The clumsy two- or four-wheeled carts used for transporting heavy loads over land were uncertain means of conveyance on roads of poor quality. In 1612, for instance, the brasses of Thomas Windham, Esq., and his sister Jane Pope were brought by sea from London to Yarmouth, by river from Yarmouth to Coltishall Bridge, and from there in two carts to Felbrigg, Norfolk.[31] According to the records of Belvoir Castle, Gerard Johnson, the Southwark sculptor, brought the tombs of the Dukes of Rutland to Boston by sea from London and carted them in fifteen carts across country to Bottesford, Leicestershire.[32] This, however, did not save him from a broken axle and the necessity of placing a night watch on his crippled cart. Water transport was also cheaper than land carriage, a point well illustrated by J. E. Thorold-Rogers in analysing the cost to the bailiff of Elham, Kent, of transporting lead to repair the church roof in 1330.[33] All the main centres of brass engraving were appropriately situated on navigable waterways.

It may be presumed that brasses in their slabs were conveyed by ship or barge to the nearest convenient point, and then transferred where necessary to horse-drawn carts. Occasionally the plate alone was dispatched. In September 1661, the lozenge-shaped brass of Sir Owen Wynne was sent from London to Llanrwst, Denbigh, Wales, by Will Harrison, carrier.[34] It is only rarely that the engraver's last duty can have been so simply resolved.

3 · The geographical distribution of brasses

Memorial brasses were a monumental type of northern European origin and development. They were apparently very rarely made south of the Alps,[1] unlike incised slabs which are common in Italy. Their distribution is concentrated in the northern states of Europe west of Russia, and there are no grounds to doubt that this was always the case.

The establishment of monumental brass engraving in any particular city or region was influenced by a variety of local factors. The existence of a large population, the flourishing of allied crafts, facilities for trade, especially access to river and sea communications, the absence of alternative types of memorial, and the availability of raw materials all had importance. An examination of the main centres of engraving discloses their significance.

Distribution in the British Isles

ENGLAND

Brasses are far more numerous in England than in any other country. The following table giving a breakdown by period and county accounts for 7,616 examples. These figures have been obtained from a revision of the revised Mill Stephenson List and include brasses found in the last twenty years and exclude those lost. They do not, however, include museum collections and a large number of insignificant fragments, shields, children groups and other details; a complete list of every fragment would exceed eight thousand. Furthermore many early eighteenth century inscriptions have yet to be recorded. This total is only a small proportion of those originally laid. Thirty thousand would be a conservative estimate, and proposals of one hundred thousand are not impossible.

The most striking feature of these figures is the great preponderance of brasses in the Home Counties and on the east side of the country. This imbalance is especially marked for brasses earlier than 1500. The uneven size of counties gives some misleading impressions, without invalidating the general pattern. Essex has more brasses than Cornwall, Devon, Somerset and Dorset together. There is no reason to suspect that this was brought about by exceptional destruction. Indents indicate that the East was richer than even now appears. Certain great churches in the West in places of particular prestige and wealth had, and some still retain, large collections of brasses. The cathedrals of Hereford, Salisbury and Wells were outstanding. There is nevertheless in the parish churches no counterpart to the series of indents at St. Mary, Beverley, Yorks.; Boston, Lincs.; Fotheringay, Northants.; Lavenham and Letheringham, Suffolk; St. Andrew, Norwich, Norfolk; and Saffron Walden, Essex. These are but choice examples of a great selection. The cathedrals of the East and South-East, especially Canterbury, Chichester, Ely and Lincoln, possessed splendid series, and still retain superb indents. The City of London was undoubtedly the richest centre for these monuments, many of which perished in the great fire of 1666.

	Total brasses	Inscriptions & inscriptions with arms only	Total brasses by period				
			13th & 14th C.	15th C.	1500 to 1559	1560 to 1599	1600 to 1710
Norfolk	946	681	19	260	434	86	147
Kent	742	349	34	192	159	135	222
Essex	473	201	15	76	105	122	155
Suffolk	436	236	5	65	91	96	179
Oxfordshire	402	175	21	101	94	52	134
Yorkshire	351	278	9	58	31	28	225
Buckinghamshire	340	138	10	87	105	42	96
Surrey	284	141	10	65	63	41	105
Hertfordshire	281	90	13	101	67	44	56
Sussex	266	152	8	58	40	32	128
Berkshire	251	102	11	60	57	43	80
Gloucestershire	215	133	3	37	33	16	126
Northamptonshire	212	101	5	53	48	27	79
Lincolnshire	210	112	13	56	32	24	85
Hampshire	199	136	5	35	40	41	78
Wiltshire	168	118	4	15	19	19	111
Bedfordshire	167	56	4	45	56	12	50
Somerset	158	102	–	25	18	25	90
Cambridgeshire	152	66	6	45	46	12	43
Middlesex	148	57	5	23	42	33	45
Derbyshire	109	69	2	18	21	12	56
Dorset	108	78	2	19	30	19	38
Devon	104	52	2	12	16	20	54
Warwickshire	91	37	–	13	25	16	37
Lancashire	87	60	–	3	11	4	69
Shropshire	75	54	3	4	9	7	52
Cornwall	73	15	1	18	14	18	22
Nottinghamshire	68	52	2	11	10	4	41
Cheshire	62	56	1	2	4	7	48
City of London and Westminster	61	25	7	13	14	13	14
Herefordshire	61	35	3	15	7	13	23
Leicestershire	58	30	1	19	7	5	26
Worcestershire	55	30	1	8	8	5	33
Staffordshire	51	33	3	4	5	10	29
Durham	41	30	1	17	6	7	10
Cumberland	29	19	1	4	9	3	12
Huntingdonshire	29	17	–	5	5	2	17
Westmorland	24	22	1	–	1	1	21
Isle of Wight	17	11	2	1	2	–	12
Rutland	9	5	1	2	3	2	1
Northumberland	3	2	–	2	–	–	1
Total	7,616	4,156	234	1,647	1,787	1,098	2,850

The concentration of brasses of recognizable types and indisputable documentary proof show that London was the greatest centre for the engravers' workshops. Norwich, York, probably Bury St. Edmunds, almost certainly Cambridge and probably Coventry were at times important centres of the craft. Engravers are known or may be suspected to have worked at Canterbury, Lincoln, Newark and Stamford. The very high figures for Norfolk are accounted for by the industry of the Norwich engravers whose easily recognized inscription plates exceed six hundred in number. Many of the Suffolk and some West Norfolk brasses were probably made in the Bury workshops, and many of the northern brasses may be confidently ascribed to York.

These centres of engraving had much in common. London, Norwich and York were, by the standards of the Middle Ages, cities of great importance. All were famous for tomb-makers, glass painters, goldsmiths and workers in textiles. All had good water communications both inland and to the sea. The other centres had similar advantages to a lesser degree. The East, South-East and Home Counties were, in mediaeval England, the most populous regions of the country, while Coventry enjoyed outstanding prosperity on account of the cloth trade. The importation of latten plate from Köln and Flanders favoured the ports of the eastern shores. The only serious rivals to brasses were incised slabs, engraved in especially great numbers by the craftsmen in alabaster at Burton-on-Trent. Incised slabs are more numerous than brasses in the North and Midlands, especially in Derbyshire, Leicestershire, Lincolnshire and Staffordshire. Yet it is more likely that the makers of these slabs supplied a region distant from the brass engravers than that they limited the sale of brasses. All circumstances favoured the situation of the brass engravers in the East. The distribution of brasses is, accordingly, not surprising. Coastal trade from London was exploited to the full, and brasses of undoubted London origin predominate in coastal towns even in areas possessing their own workshops. Most of the brasses at Cley, Norfolk, Aldeburgh and Lowestoft, Suffolk, and many at Ipswich, were evidently brought from London.

WALES AND IRELAND

The dearth of brasses noted in the western counties extends predictably to Monmouthshire, Wales and Ireland. Wales and Monmouthshire possess only two brasses of the fifteenth century, five for the period 1500 to 1560, eight for the period 1560 to 1600 and sixty recorded examples from the seventeenth century, the majority being inscriptions only. The revival in the seventeenth century, stimulated by a spreading population and the rise of local engravers when English-made plate was manufactured, follows the overall pattern of western England. Eire has four recorded brasses with figures, all in Dublin. Three of 1528, 1537 and 1579 in St. Patrick's Cathedral are all London work. Another of *c.* 1580 at Christchurch Cathedral may be local. Two indents in Dublin are apparently of London-made brasses, while a large indent at Youghal is undoubtedly Flemish. Most interesting is an indent of a figure at Old Leighlin, Co. Carlow, ascribed to Bishop Matthew Saunders (d. 1549) which forms part of a composite monument including an elaborate incised cross and inscriptions, all cut in Kilkenny marble. The figure in pontificals was small and may possibly though improbably have been a local engraving.[2] Large numbers of brasses are recorded as having been stripped from Waterford Cathedral in the seventeenth century.

SCOTLAND

The distribution of brasses in Scotland may be better appreciated from indents and documentary records than from existing monuments. An inscription at St. Giles's, Edinburgh (1570), is known to have been engraved by an Edinburgh goldsmith and

Miles

⊚ Nousisainen

Oslo

Roskilde
Skanör *(now in Lund)*
Ribe
Ringsted
Iona
Lübeck
Stralsund
Wensley
Schwerin
Topcliffe
Toruń
Newark
Shrewsbury
King's Lynn
St. Albans
?Little Shelford
Tolleshunt Darcy
Altenberg
North Mimms
Aveley
Bruges
Gent
Köln
Tournai
Noyon

Rocca Melone
⊚ *(now in Susa)*

Castro Urdiales
(now in Madrid)
Solzona
(now in Paris)
Leça do Balio

Sevilla

⊚ Denotes existing examples

• Denotes places having fragments,
or where rubbings and drawings
of lost examples afford conclusive
proof of the former existance of
such brasses

2. Distribution of Flemish brass, *c.* 1301–*c.* 1400, based on existing or illustrated examples

another from Ormiston (1563), is probably also by his hand. Two brasses at Aberdeen were made (*c.* 1450) and (*c.* 1619) and another at Glasgow is of 1605. The later Aberdeen brass to Dr. Liddel is a fine plate made in Antwerpen and the earlier is probably French or Flemish. Poor relations with her southern neighbours favoured the import of brasses from the Continent. All of the recorded Scottish indents as at Perth, Withorn Priory and Dundrennan, are undoubtedly Franco/Flemish, most probably made in Tournai. Brasses were rare in Scotland, and restricted to far wealthier classes than in England. Less than forty indents have been noted.

Distribution on the Continent of Europe

It becomes increasingly speculative to generalize about the number and distribution of brasses in the rest of Europe. How far the remaining monuments are a minute proportion of those laid is difficult to assess. A fair number of indents in the Low Countries indicate splendid brasses that once existed. Documentary records prove that very large numbers of brasses have been lost from Antwerpen, Bruges, Gent and Tournai. Bruges still retains an impressive collection of thirteen figure brasses and a considerable collection of inscriptions, arms and other devices. France has been practically stripped of these memorials, though the drawings of Gaignières show considerable numbers of elaborate plates from Paris, Normandy and several of the more southerly cathedrals. The existing collections in the cathedrals of Freiberg and Meissen in East Germany and in the city of Lübeck, West Germany, are exceptional but are suggestive of a greater production of brasses than now appears.

FRANCE

The most outstanding centres of Continental engraving may be identified with some certainty (see Map 1). Judged on the basis of Gaignières's drawings, Paris and probably Rouen were important. Both were large and prosperous cities, celebrated for their wealth and arts, and situated advantageously on the river Seine. The brass at Beauvais Cathedral to Louis de Villiers de L'Isle-Adam (1520) was signed by Mathieu Le Moine: 'Tumbier à P[ar]is'. The cathedral of Laon possesses an interesting series of indents which may have contained brasses from another workshop in north-east France.[3]

THE LOW COUNTRIES

Engraving in the Low Countries first centred on the three cities of Bruges, Gent and Tournai and extended to Antwerpen in the latter part of the fifteenth century. Substantial documentary proof has been preserved of the activity of the Tournai and Gent marblers. The importance of Bruges in this craft other than as the chief emporium is more controversial. There seems, however, reason to expect the participation of Bruges craftsmen. Brasses were very numerous in the city. A Scottish document, the Halyburton Ledger, reveals the export of brasses from Bruges at the end of the fifteenth century,[4] while a Polish reference of 1426 names Bruges specifically as the place where a brass had been 'made ready'.[5] All three cities enjoyed a most favourable trading situation, though Bruges gave place to Antwerpen at the close of the fifteenth century. The river Sheldt served both Gent and Tournai. Tournai and Gent were famous for metal work and Tournai had a particular advantage in its proximity to excellent sources of marble. Whereas it seems probable that brasses in France were limited in numbers by the immense production of incised slabs, such slabs and brasses developed together in Tournai and in west Flanders, enjoying a common fame. Antwerpen came to the fore in this craft through the deterioration of port facilities outside Bruges and the influx of metal workers from the Meuse towns, following the ravages of Charles the Bold, Duke of Burgundy. The engraving of brasses at Antwerpen and Mechelen is confirmed by the evidence of a document and a signed brass.

The views of scholars conflict over the extent to which the craftsmen of the celebrated Mosan centres of metal work were involved in this speciality. The fame of Liège and Dinant is beyond question, and incised slabs were made in large numbers in and around Liège. There is nevertheless neither documentary evidence, nor significant quantity of brasses in the Meuse country to indicate that monumental brass engraving was carried out there. The author is nevertheless convinced that brasses were engraved in Liège, though not in large numbers.

GERMAN CENTRES

The cities of Köln on the Rhine, Lübeck by the Baltic Sea, and Nürnberg near both the Maine and the Danube, were the greatest centres of German brasses. Engravers from these cities are known, and considerable numbers of brasses still exist in the surrounding regions. All three comply with the criteria of population, allied crafts, commercial facilities and water transport. There are ample indications that brass engraving was practised in a number of centres in Thüringia and Saxony, areas especially rich in copper and calamine ore—notably at Goslar and Annaberg. The ducal foundry at Dresden was used for such work in the latter part of the sixteenth and first half of the seventeenth centuries. Nevertheless, the casting of relief plates provided an alternative to the engraved brass and was more usually adopted.

CENTRES IN POLAND

Further to the east lie the Silesian capital of Wrocław (Breslau), and the old Polish capital of Kraków. Wrocław was an important centre of engravers, and one of particular interest. The city is situated on the river Oder, and was celebrated for the manufacture of textiles and stained glass. Copper and marble were both available in the locality. Kraków was, apparently, a minor centre but favoured by the importance of the city and the variety and high quality of its skills.

It is reasonable to conclude that the numerous and wealthy customers of urban society, the stimulating influence of craftsmen upon each other, and the accessibility of water transport to bring materials and convey completed monuments, were prerequisites for the preparation of memorial brasses on a substantial scale. The relative unimportance of local materials is surprising. The prolific engravers of London imported a great proportion of their plate. The Flemish brass workers obtained much of their copper via Köln from German sources. Lübeck craftsmen imported copper from Stockholm in Sweden.

Trade in brasses

Trade was not confined to materials alone, but involved a great commerce in brasses comparable to that in altar-pieces and other church furnishings. The complexity of their geographical distribution is attributable to this business. A concentration of brasses is indicative of a favourable market and not necessarily of local workshops.

The greatest exporters of brasses were the engravers of western Flanders and Hainaut, whose most celebrated work is described in Chapters Four and Five of *The Memorials*. From evidence at present available it would appear that the engravers working in the Franco/Flemish hinterland, above all in Tournai and its environs, were the first to establish a widespread reputation in this craft, but their special interest in incised slabs and

4

brasses was rapidly assumed in other Flemish centres. Furthermore the designs and conventions first used at Tournai seem to have been adopted at Gent and elsewhere, and it is not possible to differentiate the products of the various workshops with any conviction. The term 'Flemish', though not strictly accurate, is convenient to describe the brasses from these centres collectively, and should be interpreted as having this significance.

Flemish plates have a surprisingly wide distribution,[6] explained by the intrinsic excellence of the monuments and facilitated by sea and river communications and carriage provided by the German Hansa. Within the regions with access to the Baltic Flemish brasses and indents are numerous. Brasses or their fragments still exist at Bremen, Emden, Köln and Lübeck, West Germany; Schwerin and Stralsund, East Germany; Nousisainen, Finland; Oslo, Norway; Ringsted, Denmark; and Toruń, Poland. Others have been lost from Bonn and Altenberg, West Germany; Ribe and Roskilde, Denmark; and Poznań, Poland (see Map 2).

England, Scotland, Ireland and France all possess Flemish brasses or proof of their import. The four great rectangular brasses at King's Lynn, Norfolk, Newark, Notts., and St. Alban's Cathedral, Herts., are the largest of a group of fourteen still existing in the English series, while indents and records of others remain. As has been stated, the majority of brasses in Scotland appear to have been of Flemish import, and the indent at Youghal near Cork, Eire, extends the distribution to Ireland. One of two Flemish brasses in France at the Louvre, Paris, was brought from Solzona, Spain, but a few of the brasses drawn by Gaignières were most probably Flemish and the composite brass at Noyon may well have been made at Tournai. Further south, Flemish brasses were laid in the churches of Spain and Portugal. Examples are preserved in the museums of Madrid and Sevilla and the cathedral of Avila, Spain, and in the churches of Evora and Penafiel, Portugal. Other Flemish plates exist at Funchal, Madeira, Basel, Switzerland and Susa, Italy.

No other workshops enjoyed such fame or the means of exporting their products. Brasses made by the Vischers of Nürnberg were in great demand in Germany and Poland, being found as far east as Kraków. Little has been finally established about French brasses but the figures at Minster in Sheppey, England, are most probably French work. A brass of English origin is preserved in the Musée Lapidaire at Bordeaux, and an indent in the old church of Jamestown, Virginia, U.S.A., is the remnant of a monument attributed to the first English governor.[7] The export of English brasses did not reach beyond English possessions with one known exception. The death of the English Bishop Hallum at the council of Konstanz (1416), evidently led to the transport of his brass to the cathedral of that city.

All available evidence supports the following generalizations. Brass engraving was primarily the activity of craftsmen in large cities and populous areas where the market for their products was favourable. The extent of the market was limited by communications and the competition of other workshops and alternative forms of monument. Local access to raw materials was of secondary importance. The most active centres of the craft lay within west Flanders and Hainaut and the east of England. In France the marblers, while making superb brasses, concentrated on incising slabs; similarly incised slabs and relief plates predominated in Germany and Poland. Around the Baltic seaboard there are few brasses in comparison to the large collections of incised slabs at Visby. Moreover, those which exist are primarily imports from afar and not the products of any local workshop. Likewise, with few exceptions, it is Flemish brasses that are found in Spain, Portugal and south of Germany. In Tournai and Flanders incised slabs were similarly the most prominent form of floor monument. Yet the incised stone and the engraved brass flourished together, produced together in the same workshops, and enjoyed a Europe-wide reputation. In England the marblers made brasses their speciality, though incised slabs remained an equally important type of monument.

The outstanding popularity of brasses in England and the Low Countries may not be ascribed only to the excellence of the makers. Distances between cities were relatively short, workshops were numerous, and the engravers readily made brasses of small dimensions. Numerical concentration of brasses was accordingly matched by a remarkably wide social distribution. Brasses became a common form of monumental representation and from this demand the craft continued to expand.

4 · The social distribution of brasses

Brasses were an adaptable form of memorial in their scale, richness of treatment and decoration. While the finest compositions were costly and only obtainable by the very wealthy, a pleasing monument could be purchased at a moderate price. The classes of people represented are accordingly varied, depicting most strata of mediaeval society, from royalty, ecclesiastical dignitaries and the wealthiest merchants, to craftsmen, parish priests and yeomen. This generalization applies especially to England where small brasses were fashionable.

Cost of brasses

The cost of brasses is difficult to analyse on account of great disparities in the value of money from one generation to another. Comparison between English and foreign currencies is a further complication. Most of the recorded prices of English brasses are derived from wills which only afford a guide to the actual price paid. Jacob Verzelini gave directions in 1604 concerning his brass to be laid at Downe, Kent: '£20 to be expended thereon, or as much as shall be thought meet by my executors and overseers'.

The following selection of English examples includes several large and expensive monuments. The cost of all, though in some cases cited in terms of the mark, having the approximate value of two-thirds of a pound, is recorded here in sterling.

Sir John de St. Quintin (1397), Brandsburton, Yorks. £13 6s 8d. Very large brass with two effigies. Still existing.

Sir Thomas Uhtred (1398), Catton, Yorks. £10. Two effigies etc. Lost.

Sir Philip Darcy (1399), location not known. £10. Two effigies etc. Lost.

Thomas Graa (1405), York. 100 shillings. Two effigies etc. Lost.

Sir Arnold Savage (by son's will 1420), Bobbing, Kent. £13 6s 8d. Two effigies, canopy, still existing.

Richard Bamme (for wife) (1422), Gillingham, Kent. £14 13s 4d. Lost.

Sir Thomas Stathum (1470), Morley, Derbyshire. £4. Three effigies etc. Still existing. (Fig. 72).

Sir John Cursun (1471), Bylaugh, Norfolk. £5 6s 8d. Two effigies etc. Still existing.

John Fastolff, Esq. (1478), Oulton, Suffolk. About £5. Two effigies etc. Lost.

George Catesby, Esq. (1506), Ashby St. Legers, Northants. £6 13s 4d each, for two brasses, one large with two effigies, double canopies etc. and (?) a small kneeling figure, both of which still exist.

Robert Fabyan (1512), St. Michael, Cornhill, London. £2 13s 4d. Two effigies etc. Lost.

Christopher Rawson (1518), All Hallows-by-the-Tower, London. £2. Three effigies etc. Still existing.

Robert Gosebourne (1523), St. Alphege, Canterbury, Kent. £4 10s. Effigy etc. Still existing.

Ralph Hayman (1598), Milton, Kent. £4. Four effigies etc. Lost.

Jacob Verzelini Esq. (will 1604, d. 1607), Downe, Kent. £20. Two fine effigies etc. Still existing.,

Among several Continental examples the following are of particular interest:

Tournai: Unknown (1330). 60 livres. Very large rectangular brass now lost.
Tournai: Huart Platecorne (1335). 26 livres. Two separate inlay figures now lost.
Bruges: Archbishop Wojciech Jastrzambiec (*c.* 1420) for Gnieznó Cathedral, Poland. 400 Flemish guilders. Now destroyed.
Aire, Artois: Sir William and Margery Sandys (1536). 30 Flemish pounds. Two high tombs with brass crosses for Basingstoke, Hants. Parts of these tombs still exist, though the brasses are lost.[1]
Antwerpen: Dr. Duncan Liddel (engr. *c.* 1619). 121 pounds 15s 6d Flemish currency. The brass is in St. Nicholas the west church Aberdeen, Scotland, and the full account has been preserved—31 pounds 0s 6d for the brass plates, 50 pounds for the engraving, 3 pounds for a bounty of salmon. The balance was made up with transport and exchange expenses, and the cost of three visits by John Liddel to arrange for the preparation of the memorial.[2]

Particularly noteworthy features of these records from the Low Countries are the great disparity in price between the fourteenth century rectangular and separate inlay compositions, and the very substantial costs incurred for Dr. Liddel's brass, arising from transport and administration. The recorded charges for this brass excluding the personal costs of John Liddel and exchange expenses, and these cover only part of the transport, totalled 87 pounds 10s 6d Flemish, which was equal to £49 8s 9d sterling. This brass accordingly cost over twice that of Jacob Verzelini, which is an English separate inlay brass consisting of two large figures, inscription, children groups and shields, all of which are very well engraved. The importation of brasses was undoubtedly a very expensive undertaking.

These examples are on the whole unusually large. R. H. D'Elboux, studying a considerable number of relevant English wills, showed that the cost of an average-size figure brass between 1465 and 1538 rarely exceeded £2. Twenty-seven examples quoted by him ranged in price between £1 and £2 13s 4d. Sixteen examples varied between £1 and £1 13s 4d.[3]

A particularly valuable survival is the ledger of Andrew Halyburton, Scottish Consul at the port of Veere, near Middleburg, mentioned in the preceding chapter (p. 48). This ledger records the export of articles, including tombs, between 1493 and 1503. The monuments, which appear to have been brasses, ranged in price from £2 10s to £3 12s (sterling). An exceptional brass was apparently on a high tomb and cost £9. The relative economy of brasses to the tomb effigy and chantries preferred by the great is emphasized by the expense of £40 agreed for the alabaster tomb of Ralph Greene in 1419, and the immense sum of £2,481 spent on the tomb and chapel of Richard Beauchamp, Earl of Warwick, in the mid-fifteenth century.[4]

Status of the commemorated

A brass presented a cheap or fairly expensive form of memorial according to its size and source. Grandness of commemoration depended upon an ability to pay and requirements of status. Brasses were far more adaptable in scale than sculptured tombs and accordingly made acceptable monuments for undistinguished members of society as well as the great.

The majority of English figure brasses represent civilians and wives or females alone comprising, in all, about 1,820 examples. Figures in armour,[5] many with wives, total about 850, and ecclesiastics number about 540. Most figureless inscriptions commemorate unimportant civilians.

ROYALTY

With the possible exception of Queen Anne Neville (d. 1485), wife of King Richard III,[6] no English king or queen is known to have used a figure brass as a memorial, though a small half-figure at Wimborne Minster, Dorset, was laid during the fifteenth century in memory of King Ethelred of the West Saxons (Fig. 39). A larger brass of early fourteenth century date at Wells, Somerset, once commemorated King Ine of Wessex.[7] A near approach to a royal representation was the brass of Thomas of Woodstock, Duke of Gloucester, son of Edward III, at Westminster Abbey (Fig. 20) and it is just possible that a large representation of the Holy Trinity, now in the Victoria and Albert Museum, London, belonged to this composition.[8] A few very small fragments survive of the Flemish brass doubtfully attributed to King James III of Scotland, formerly at Cambuskenneth Abbey. The magnificent Flemish brass at Ringsted of King Eric Menved of Denmark and his Queen Ingeborg (1319) is truly a royal monument in conception and execution (Fig. 135) and King Christopher I (d. 1259) was similarly commemorated at Ribe. In contrast, the figure of Queen (?) Agnes of Sweden (1432) at Gadebusch, East Germany, is surprisingly poor in design and crude in finish.

Several excellent thirteenth century brasses to French royalty are recorded in the drawings of Gaignières, though all were destroyed in the Revolution (Fig. 21).

NOBILITY, CARDINALS AND ARCHBISHOPS

Similarly, brasses to the highest ranks of secular or ecclesiastical society are rare. English brasses commemorate Elizabeth, Countess of Athol (1375), Ashford, Kent; Eleanor de Bohun, Duchess of Gloucester (1399), Westminster Abbey (Fig. 173); Thomas de Beauchamp, Earl of Warwick and wife (1406), St. Mary, Warwick (Fig. 163); Henry Bourchier, Earl of Essex and wife (1483), Little Easton, Essex; William, Lord Beaumont (1507), Wivenhoe, Essex; John, Lord Strange of Knockyn (d. 1479, engr. 1509), Hillingdon, Middx.; Elizabeth de Vere, Countess of Oxford (1537), Wivenhoe, Essex; and Sir Thomas Bullen, Earl of Wiltshire (1538), Hever, Kent (Fig. 212). Brasses to the Earls of Cumberland at Skipton in Craven, Yorks., have been restored, while an indent remains at Pleshey, Essex, to Humphrey Stafford, K.G., Duke of Buckingham and his Duchess (1480).[9] Both the earls at Little Easton and Hever were Knights of the Garter, the first shown wearing the garter and the mantle of the Order, the second in full insignia. Other members of that Order are at Spilsby, Lincs. (d. 1410, engr. *c.* 1405); Exeter Cathedral (1409); Felbrigg, Norfolk (d. 1443, engr. 1416) (Fig. 24); and Trotton, Sussex (1421) (Fig. 178). Ralph Lord Cromwell (d. 1455, engr. *c.* 1475) was High Treasurer of England, and the magnificence of his mutilated brass at Tattershall, Lincs., was appropriate to his rank.

Four English figure brasses represent archbishops, at York Minster (1315), Westminster Abbey (1397); New College, Oxford (1417) (Fig. 22); and Chigwell, Essex (1631). Only the inscription and scrolls now remain at Kirk Sandal, Yorks., to Archbishop Rokeby of Dublin (1521), while fine archiepiscopal indents exist at Canterbury and Maidstone, Kent. Cardinal Morton was represented at Canterbury with his cardinal's hat placed above him. There are two Continental brasses of cardinals—Cardinal Nicholas de Cusa (d. 1464, engr. 1488) at Kues, Germany (Fig. 94), and Cardinal Fryderyk, son of Kasimir IV of Poland (1510) at the cathedral of Kraków, Poland, Archbishop Jakub

Szienienski (1480), at Gniezno Cathedral, Poland, is the sole survivor of a series of brasses to Polish archbishops (Fig. 93).

The ducal and electoral houses of Saxony are well represented over a period of two hundred years in the East German cathedrals of Meissen (Fig. 23) and Freiberg, and in the churches of Stolberg and Torgau. These are exceptional series illustrating particular family preference for this type of memorial. Isabella, Duchess of Burgundy, with her husband and son appear on a brass at Basel, Switzerland (*c.* 1450) commemorating one of her grants (Fig. 149). Four brasses at Wroclaw and Lubiąż, Poland, (e.g. Fig. 113–15) represent dukes of Silesian principalities. In West Germany at Kleve there are two brasses to dukes of Kleve and their families (Fig. 202), a duchess of Geldern is at Geldern, and another at Hamm to Count Gerhard von Mark was destroyed in the Second World War. Yet there is no doubt that as a general rule persons of eminence preferred sculptured representation.

BISHOPS, KNIGHTS, ESQUIRES AND MERCHANTS

Brasses are more prominent as memorials of bishops, abbots, knights, esquires, lower church dignitaries and wealthy merchants. These classes were represented in considerable numbers in England, though the monastic and episcopal brasses have suffered exceptional losses on account of the dissolution of the religious houses and pillage of the cathedrals. Figure brasses to thirteen bishops, three abbots, two priors and two abbesses survive though indents of others are numerous. About one hundred and thirty brasses commemorate deans, archdeacons and canons in processional vestments. Several of these brasses are among the most splendid extant, surpassing those of the episcopate. Many military brasses commemorate persons of standing and achievement. Sir Symon Felbrygge, K.G. (d. 1443, engr. 1416), Felbrigg, Norfolk, was banner bearer to King Richard II and is appropriately shown with his banner (Fig. 24). John Peryent, Esq. (1415), Digswell, Herts., was pennon bearer and esquire to the body to King Richard II and esquire to both King Henry IV and Henry V. Thomas, Baron Camoys, K.G. (1421), Trotton, Sussex (Fig. 178), commanded the left wing of the English at Agincourt. Sir William Bagot (1407), Baginton, Warwicks., achieved great influence and unpopularity in the reign of Richard II, while William Catesby, Esq. (d. 1485) Ashby St. Legers, Northants., was 'the cat' associated with King Richard III.[10] William was one of nine Speakers of the House of Commons represented on brasses, among whom was the much maligned Sir John Say (1473), Broxbourne, Herts. Among the merchant classes the woolmen (Fig. 180) and the Baltic traders are most outstanding. William Grevel (1401) is described on his great brass at Chipping Campden, Glos., as 'flos mercatorum lanar' tocius Anglie'. Notable families of woolmen—Pagge, Taylour and Fortey—are handsomely represented at Northleach and Cirencester, Glos. The leading Lincolnshire woolmen similarly laid brasses, while other merchants such as Alan Fleming of Newark, Notts., Adam de Walsokne, and Robert Braunche of Lynn (Fig. 139), purchased grandiose Flemish brasses for their monuments. Two barons of the Cinque Ports have brasses at Faversham, Kent. Among several brasses to lawyers Sir John Cassy (1400), Deerhurst, Glos., was chief Baron of the Exchequer. Two chancellors of Cambridge University are commemorated on brasses. Among a few brasses to Lord Mayors of London Sir George Monox (1543), Walthamstow, Essex, wears his chain of office (Fig. 25).

Equivalent classes on the Continent have substantial representation. It is nevertheless noteworthy that with few exceptions figure brasses are confined to the upper strata of these groups. In 1939 churches now within Poland had twenty-seven known figure brasses. Of these, one at Toruń represented a merchant, noted for great wealth and influence. Ecclesiastical brasses consisted of one archbishop, eight bishops and two canons. Four brasses commemorated Silesian dukes, while among the nine lesser military figures, most were notable castellans, and one honoured a distinguished knight of the Teutonic Order. Engraved figure brasses in Germany have a comparable social distribution. Forty brasses commemorate the families of Saxon dukes and electors. There are altogether twenty-one brasses to bishops, abbots and an abbess and at least twenty to canons and deans. All the military brasses are to persons of high rank. Brasses commemorating civilians are found at Lübeck, though the majority of these commemorate rich burghers and are large memorials. The life-size figure of Bruno von Warendorp (1369), at the Marienkirche, is one of the least imposing. A similar pattern of distribution in France may be inferred from the drawings of Gaignières. The majority of the brasses drawn represented nobility or important ecclesiastics. There is no evidence that small figure brasses were common in France.[11] Only in Flanders is it apparent that the engravers scaled down their compositions to benefit the less ostentatious buyer. The delightful but miniature brass of the béguine Griele van Ruwescuere (1410), at the Bruges Béguinage (Fig. 27), is an excellent example. In spite of this, almost half of the Flemish brasses surviving are on a grand scale. Civilians are well represented as might be expected from such a highly developed commercial society.

MINOR GENTRY, TRADERS, PARISH PRIESTS AND OTHERS

The widespread use of brasses by the minor gentry, craftsmen, small traders, parish priests and yeomanry is an English peculiarity. The English series has an exceptional value as a social record. The majority of military brasses represent gentry of very local importance or minor officials of the Crown. Early sixteenth century brasses record an interesting variety of royal officers. Among the more important, John Borrell (1531), Sergeant-at-Arms, is shown at Broxbourne, Herts., holding his ceremonial mace (Fig. 28). No brasses of heralds remain, though Thomas Benolt, Esq. (1534), Clarenceux King of Arms, in official robes with sceptre, existed in St. Helen's, Bishopsgate, London, until the eighteenth century (Fig. 26).[12] Inscriptions record the offices of a variety of officials of the royal household whose figures reveal no peculiarities. Among the more unusual are Chief Mason to the King's Works, Chief Cook to the King, Sergeant of the Woodyard, Master of the Jewel House to King Henry VIII, Governor of the Pages of Honour, Master of the Buckhounds to King Henry VIII, Keeper of the Goshawks to Queen Elizabeth, and Officer of 'removing wardroppe of bedds' and Groom of the Privy Chamber.[13] Crown keepers or Yeomen of the Crown bore a crown on their left shoulder, and are depicted on the brasses at the Society of Antiquaries, London (*c.* 1475), and at Slapton, Bucks. (1519). Yeomen of the Guard are also represented, as at East Wickham, Kent (1568), with the crown and rose embroidered on their doublets.

Several military and civil brasses commemorated servants of the nobility or gentry. Outstanding among these are the two marshals to the Earl of Arundel, both holding staffs of office, at Stopham (1462) and Arundel (1465), both in Sussex. Thomas Forest, park keeper of Dunclent Park (1511), Chaddesley Corbett, Worcs., is shown with shields appropriately bearing a hunting horn and crossed arrows. John Selwyn, gent. (1587), 'keeper of her Ma'tis parke of Otelands under ye right honorable Charles Howard', Walton-upon-Thames, Surrey, is not only shown with his hunting horn, but is also depicted riding a stag, a feat he performed in the presence of Queen Elizabeth (Fig. 29). William Morys (1509) 'Sumtyme fermer of Cokyswell'—a gatherer of rents and dues—is commemorated with his children on a simple brass at Great Coxwell, Berks. Of lower status, Thomas Cotes, Porter at Ascot Hall (1648), is represented at Wing, Bucks., with his hat and porter's key.

Brasses to tradesmen and craftsmen are common. Members of the trading companies of

London are prominent. An early example is that to a rich London fishmonger, Nichole de Aumberdene (*c.* 1350), Taplow, Bucks. Mercers, haberdashers, grocers, brewers, skinners, poulterers, butchers, bakers, smiths, masons, bell-founders, weavers, tailors, a printer, a carpenter and an organist are commemorated along with many others. James Rodge, Honiton, Devon (1617), was a 'bone lace-siller'. John Waliston, Chenies, Bucks. (1469), was a blacksmith. Peter Denot (*c.* 1440), Fletching, Sussex, was a glover and his brass depicts a pair of gloves (Fig. 239). John Deynes (1527), Beeston Regis, Norfolk, was presumably a ship's captain, and wears a seaman's whistle round his neck.[14] Among the lowly, who had evidently improved their lot, was the milkmaid, Alice Ryder (1517), said by Weever to have been represented at Hackney, Middx., with her pail on her head.[15]

Representations of parish priests in mass vestments are numerous. About two hundred and twenty-five examples exist, of which sixty are half-effigies and many others are small in size (Fig. 30). Few of this status could afford fine brasses, though there are notable exceptions. The remaining brasses to the regular clergy below the ranks of abbot and prior, and the great majority of brasses to university doctors, masters and bachelors are unpretentious. A few students and several children were given individual commemoration (Fig. 31).

It may be concluded that brasses in England were a basically inexpensive type of monument, well within the means of a purchaser of quite limited wealth. Splendour and scale could, nevertheless, be adapted to satisfy the most egotistical patron, as the vast indent of Bishop Beaumont at Durham still bears witness.[16] In contrast, brasses on the Continent were sought by a far narrower and richer class of buyer. It is on account of this difference in demand that English brasses have so clear a numerical superiority, while falling behind Flemish or German standards in scale. The English series is unrivalled in value both for historical reference and its comprehensive record of costume. Continental brasses are more promising subjects for the research of an archivist or art historian.

Having described the widespread use of brasses from the fourteenth to the eighteenth centuries in England and Europe, it is appropriate to consider the motives which prompted the purchase of these memorials.

5 · The importance of motive in commemoration

The desire for commemoration and a belief in the value of prayers and masses for the dead promoted in the Middle Ages the extensive use of memorial brasses and incised slabs. The preparation of a tomb was not primarily an act of personal or family vanity. While monuments were an important record of a family's pedigree and lineal integrity, they were also a unique means of attracting the prayers of the living to succour the departed souls in purgatory.

Many brasses were laid to commemorate an individual. All remaining brasses prior to 1315 are of this form. Nevertheless it became increasingly fashionable, when the deceased was married, to prepare a brass as a family monument showing husband, wife and children together. In England the children were usually grouped below the parents on separate plates, or arranged behind them in kneeling compositions. In Flanders they were often engraved in front of the main figures. The will of John Bowyer of Basingstoke, Hants., dated 1536, gives specific directions for a family brass. Bowyer required his executors to 'ordeyne a ston of ij yardes long and a yarde of bredyth wt a pycture of a man and ij women and under the same stone a man childe and iij maydyns and scrypture consarnyng the same'.[1] It was the usual English practice for all to be depicted on the death of one parent (Fig. 32), though a space was often left in the inscription for including the date of death of the other. These blank spaces were not surprisingly rarely completed as intended, even though members of the same family were often interred nearby later, and represented on other brasses. The brasses of Thomas Peckham, Esq. (1512) and Reynold Peckham, Esq. (1525) at Wrotham, Kent, are examples. Even the date of death of such a notable as Sir Symon Felbrygge, K.G., at Felbrigg, Norfolk, was left unrecorded.[2] Quite frequently several adults are represented in families where the deceased married several times. Many women died young in childbirth. William Sharp (1499), at Great Chart, Kent, is accompanied by his five wives. Four wives together occur at Cirencester, Glos. (1442) (Fig. 33); Hackney, Middlesex (1562); Ingrave, Essex (1528); and Writtle, Essex (c. 1510). Occasionally a deceased person would be twice represented, both on a personal and on a family memorial. This understandably took place when the husband and wife were buried in different churches. Susan Fetyplace, wife of John Kyngeston, is shown in fashionable dress on her husband's brass of 1514 at Childrey, Berks., but is dressed in the habit of a vowess on her brass of 1540 at Shalston, Bucks. Anne Duke is twice represented, on a family memorial of 1551 at Frenze, Norfolk, and on her own of 1577 at St. Margaret, Norwich.[3] More unexpectedly duplication is found in the same church. Joan Urban is twice depicted at Southfleet, Kent, on her brass of 1414 and on her husband's of 1420. At Sherborne St. John, Hants., John Brocas, Esq. (1492), is depicted alone, and again together with his two wives and family. Dame Anne Danvers is twice depicted at Dauntsey, Wilts., on her husband's brass of 1514 and her own of 1539. These repetitions are explained by the preference for a family representation, especially on the husband's death.[4] The brass of Anne Drewry (1572), at Depden, Suffolk, is a curiosity in that she is shown twice on the same brass with her two husbands (Fig. 34), and at Filleigh, Devon, Richard

Fortescue (1570) has two separate brasses to his memory, one having been set up by his brother-in-law.

Very rarely a brass would become composite, additional members of the family being added at a later date. An early example is that of Tomesin Tendryng (1485), Yoxford, Suffolk. This unusual brass, depicting an adult and separately inlaid children, all but two of whom are in shrouds, poses a sharp stylistic contrast. The shrouded figures and inscription are of London workmanship, though of an uncommon design. The living daughters are clearly good quality Norwich work of *c.* 1495, presumably added later because they died in their youth or wished to be represented on their mother's memorial. The brass of Elizabeth and Robert Cheyne at Chesham Bois, Bucks., is a well-known case with a figure, shields and inscription added in *c.* 1565 to a brass of 1516. The memorial of Richard Covert, Esq. (d. 1547) and his wives at Slaugham, Sussex, is another. The figures of Richard and his first two wives were apparently prepared *c.* 1525 and show the group kneeling. Jane, the third wife, is shown standing, and was probably added in 1527. The main inscription, mentioning a fourth wife, was engraved in 1547 (Fig. 35). The composite brass of Valontyne Edvarod and wives (1574), together with Thomas Parramore at St. Nicholas-at-Wade, Kent, is a peculiar example of rearrangement. An inscription to John Sedley and wife of 1594 has been added to the brass of John Sedley and wife (*c.* 1520) at Southfleet, Kent. Such additions were rather less exceptional in Flanders. The brass of the Willebaert family at St. Jacques, Bruges, consisting of plates of 1522 and 1601, may be cited as an example.

The message of inscriptions

The inscriptions relating to the figures generally contain factual information necessary for a monument, such as the names and rank of the dead and the date of death. Identity is further clarified where appropriate by shields of arms, merchants' marks and occasionally a rebus. But it is primarily in the content of the inscription that the special function of a brass becomes clear, and a difference in motive becomes apparent between brasses laid in the Catholic tradition or in another. All brasses have a commemorative purpose, and a lasting significance to the families involved. Their chief importance to Catholic belief lay in their service to the dead.

The value of the prayers of the living for the relief of the dead is a tenet of Catholic faith. The dead may no longer help themselves, but for those in a state of grace the period of purification may be eased by the prayers and pious acts of others. It was of the greatest concern to a Catholic that prayers for his or her soul should be said and masses sung. Preparations to this end were often elaborate. The endowment of chantries and chantry priests was possible for the rich, and several Flemish brass inscriptions record such grants at length. The inscription to Isabella, Duchess of Burgundy, at Basel, states that she founded 'In the Conventual Church of the Carthusian Order . . . two Anniversaries and two Religious of the same order, to be perpetual intercessors with God, to celebrate two Masses on any day for the health of the Souls of the most excellent Prince Lord Philip, Duke of Burgundy, her husband, and also the Lord Charles . . . their son, and for the prosperity of themselves while they live and when they shall have left this life' (Fig. 149). The inscription further lists the donations made to the church in money, vestments and sacred vessels.[5] Most persons of means arranged for the preparation of a memorial for a similar purpose. Duke Wenczeslaus of Sagan in Silesia spent much of his adult life in the concerns of a society formed to ensure the adequate commemoration of its members. His own tomb at the Church of St. Barbara at Wrocław, Poland, consisted of a brass covered with a tester, and a large painting set above, all intended to remind the viewer of the Duke's virtues and his own pious duty.[6]

The mediaeval brass was laid with a very practical and devout purpose, which seems to have dominated all others. Joan Cobham willed in 1369 to be buried in St. Mary Overy, London, and required of her memorial 'quod sculpantur una crux de metallo in medio lapidis et in circuitu lapidis ista verba in Gallico –

> Vous qi par ici Passietz
> pur lalme Johanne de Cobham prietz.'[7]

A similar message is stated with great clarity in four verses to a civilian (*c.* 1400), formerly at the Temple Church, Bristol, and now in St. Mary Redcliffe Church, Bristol. This has been translated as follows:

> 'Thou art witness O Christ, that this stone is not
> here laid to adorn the body, but that the soul may
> be remembered. You who pass by, whether old, middle-
> aged or youth, make supplication for me that I may
> attain hope of pardon.'[8]

The plea for prayers almost invariably begins or closes all inscriptions laid before the religious revolution of the sixteenth century. The appeal was directed to the piety of the reader, and as a consequence long inscriptions described the generosity of the dead in preference to the detail of his personal achievements in secular affairs. The early inscription in English to Herry Notingham and wife (*c.* 1405), at Holme-next-the-Sea, Norfolk, is an excellent example. It reads:

> Herry Notingham & hys wyffe lyne here
> that maden' this Chirche stepull & quere
> two vestmentz & belles they made also
> crist hem save therfore ffro wo
> and to bringe her saules to blis of heuen'
> sayth pater & ave with mylde steuen'

The request in the last two lines is justified by the endowments made by the deceased. An equally interesting and less well-known inscription is that to Thomas Amys (1495) at Barton Turf, Norfolk, which reads:

> I beseche all' peple fer and ner'
> To prey for me Thomas Amys hertely
> which' gaf a mesbook and made this chapel' her'
> And a sewte of blewe damask also gaf I
> Of god .M°. CCCC°. xc°. and .v°. yer
> I the seid Thomas decesid verily
> And the iiij. day of Auguste was beried her
> On hoos sowle god haue mercy.

Also in Barton Turf are the inscriptions of Thomas Amys and wife (*c.* 1495) and of John Idewyn Vicar (1497). Of the first it is written 'Of such godes as God had the seid Thomas lent, dede make thys Chapel of Seint Thomas to a good intent', and of the second 'Qui Dedit usui eiusdem unum integrum vestimentum de rubeo velvet'. The examples are numerous. William Hyklott (1508), Athorne, Essex, 'paide for the werkemanship of the walls of this churche'. William Complyn (1498), Weeke, Hants., is recorded as having given to 'frest dedycacion of ye Church XLs + to make nawe bellis to ye sam Church X£ also gave to ye halloyeng of ye grettest bell Vis. VIIId + for ye testimonyall of the dedicacion of ye sam Church Vis. VIIId.' John Frankeleyn (1462), Chearsley, Bucks., purchased land for a graveyard 'leystowe'; Thomas Prude (1468) at St. Alphege, Canterbury, has a shield set into a pillar of the church with the inscription 'Gaude Prude Thom Per que*m* fit ista colum*p*na'; while at Withersfield, Suffolk, an inscription (*c.* 1480) reminds the reader of Robert Wyburgh and all benefactors 'Qui istam ylam fieri fecerunt'.

Rather than the citation of benefactions, some inscriptions offer a moral discourse. The earliest surviving inscription in English to John the Smith (*c.* 1370), at Brightwell Baldwin, Oxon., is an instance. The reader's attention is drawn to the transitory nature of human life, and the lasting value of good works. The message is well expressed in the marginal inscription to William Chichele and wife (1425) at Higham Ferrers, Northants., part of which reads:

'Lerneth to deye . that is the lawe.
That this lif . yow to wol drawe .
Sorwe or gladnesse nought letten age .
But on he cometh to lord & page .
Wherfor for us that ben goo
Preyeth as other shall for you doo .'

In certain cases the message of human frailty is reinforced by a representation of the deceased in a shroud, or as an emaciated corpse or skeleton.

In contrast to such religious expressions the content of late sixteenth century and later inscriptions is mainly concerned with the character and achievements of the commemorated. Many record the virtues of the dead in a manner that can only be regarded as gross flattery. The verses of Alice Cobham (1580) at Newington, Kent conclude:

'Who in her lyfe did well deserve to have a future fame,
For that she was unto the poore a good and gratius dame
With Charitie and modesty and all the gyft of grace
Accquainted so she was to good to tarry in thys place.'

On some other inscriptions achievements almost obscure identity. At Clewer, Berks., it is written of Martine Expence (1600), a talented local archer:

'He that liethe under this stone
Shott with a hundred men him selfe alone
This is trew that I doe saye
The matche was shott in ovld felde at Bray
I will tell you before you go hence
That his name was Martine Expence.'

The official rejection in England of the Papal authority and much traditional Catholic belief and observance, limited the function of brasses. The efficacy of prayer for the departed was denied, and any reference to it was regarded as 'Popish' and superstitious. A brass could only serve as a memorial. In place of the services rendered to the church good works found expression in grants to the poor or to schools. The brass of John Lyon

(1592), at Harrow, Middx., states that he left lands to a corporation for a free grammar school for the poor, for poor scholars at the universities and for the repair of highways. In many inscriptions the allocating of sums of money is listed in detail. Other men were honoured for more local and limited achievements. John Gladwin the Elder (1615), Harlow, Essex, 'with longe and tedious sutes in lawe with ye lord of ye mannor of Harlowe did prove the custome for the copieholds to ye great benifitt of posteritie for ever'. It would, however, be wrong to ascribe the change in emphasis entirely to changes in religious thought. Concentration on the secular and individual is evident throughout the monuments of western Europe. The brass of Don Parafan, Duke of Alcalá (1571), in the University Chapel of Sevilla, Spain, is a highly egotistic memorial, expressing pagan rather than Christian sentiments.

Indulgences on brasses

The influence of the religious motive in mediaeval brasses is not confined to the inscriptions. This motive profoundly affected the importance and content, the form and situation of brasses. The appeal for prayers had to be attractive to be effective. Attention was secured in a number of ways. In certain cases the piety of the spectator was rewarded by a grant of indulgence to anyone saying select prayers on behalf of the dead. The inscription of Dame Jone de Kobeham (*c.* 1320) at Cobham, is the earliest surviving example. The brass of Roger Legh and family (1506), at Macclesfield, Cheshire, is particularly striking. Above the figures is a representation of the Mass of St. Gregory and the words:

> 'The pardon for say
> ing of v pater noster
> & v aues and a cred
> is xxvj thousand
> yeres and xxvj
> dayes of pardon.'

The original inscription to John Marsham and wife (1525), St. John Maddermarket, Norwich, concluded 'Ye shall not lose your charitable devotion; XII Cardinals have granted you XII dayes of Pardon.'

While the fictitious character of these extravagant indulgences current in the later Middle Ages is now recognized, they were accepted at the time, and panels depicting the Mass of St. Gregory or the Christ of Pity (the subject of his vision) were accordingly a feature of brasses in the late fifteenth and early sixteenth centuries. The history of the Mass of St. Gregory, which has been studied closely in the last hundred years, still remains obscure and no traces of it can be found in the mediaeval legends of his life.[9]

Duplication of brasses

Duplication of monuments was another effective means of attracting notice, and should be distinguished from the circumstantial double representations of individuals discussed on p. 58. John Cottusmore and wife (1439), appear twice at Brightwell Baldwin, Oxon., and Sir Edmund Tame and his two wives (1534) at Fairford, Glos. Important features of these two sets are that in each, the adult figures, depicted recumbent on the floor, are shown kneeling on mural monuments nearby, and that the kneeling composition is rather

later than the recumbent. Both mural brasses bore representations of the Trinity.[10]
Another example is the group of five brasses of Ralph Hamsterley, Master of University
College, Oxford. This Master arranged for five independent brasses to be laid, at Oddington Church, Oxon., where he was rector (Fig. 61), and in the Oxford colleges of Durham,
Merton, The Queen's and University. At Merton College the brass was a combined
memorial to Hamsterley and Thomas Harper. The inscriptions remaining at Oddington
and The Queen's College both ask for prayers. Later instances of repeated commemoration are found but these only serve to record past service or bequests. Bishop Robinson of
Carlisle (1616) is depicted on almost identical brasses at Carlisle Cathedral and The
Queen's College, Oxford. Robert Rampston, gent. (1585), was represented in a figure
brass at Chingford, Essex. His numerous benefactions are recorded by no less than seven
inscriptions in various churches nearby.[11] Thomas Beri (1586) is depicted, and his bene-
faction of 'XII penie loaves to XII poor foulkes . . . everie Sabothe Day for aye' recorded,
at Walton-on-the-Hill, Lancs., and St. Martin, Ludgate Hill, London.

Situation of brasses

The importance of a conspicuous situation on the wall has been noted, a situation made
increasingly necessary with the pewing of churches in the fifteenth century, and favourable
positions for brasses were much sought after. A place near to the altar, to the blessed
Sacrament reserved and the holy relics, was regarded as beneficial. In addition to the
sacredness of the spot, the monument could constantly attract the notice of the clergy.
Many brasses were accordingly placed in a central position near the altar. High tombs
became particularly popular in the fifteenth and early sixteenth centuries, as their
prominence and richness attracted attention, as well as protecting the brasses from wear
(Figs. 36 and 209). During the mid-sixteenth century such tombs were often appropriated
and inlaid with new brasses to other people. A place connected with the Easter Sepulchre
was highly valued. The will of Robert Morley of Glynde, Sussex (1514), reads: 'On the
north syde, where as the Sepulcre is accustomed to stand, in the wiche place I wyll a
Tombe of marble to be made, wt my picture and myn armes garnisshid thereon, with a
vawte rysing up by the wall, comyng over the same stone of marble, so that at Easter tyme
the Sepulcre maye be there sett to thonour of allmighty God'.[12] Many early Tudor
recessed tombs served this dual purpose. The brasses, usually situated at the back, bright
and coloured, commanded attention. Lecterns, cast of latten, offered an occasional context for integrating a brass. The half-effigy of a friar, Martin Forrester, is engraved twice
on the faces of the book-rest of the lectern at Yeovil, Somerset. The whole was made
c. 1460 (Fig. 37). The lectern at Merton College, Oxford, which was bought out of a legacy
of John Martock, is inscribed 'Orate pro an*ima* M*agist*ri Joh*ann*is Martock'. The effigy of
John Martock (1503), in processional vestments, is at Banwell, Somerset. Even the rim of
a font has been inlaid with a brass inscription of *c.* 1510 at Cockington, Devon.[13]

Haines refers to some indents which are marked with crosses, indicative of use as altar
stones. It is highly unlikely that these grave slabs were designed for such a purpose. A
sepulchre, unless it contained the body of a saint, would not have been acceptable for use
as an altar. It is probable that the slabs noted by Haines were either decorated with
crosses, or were turned into altar stones at a later date, most probably in the reign of
Queen Mary. The indent of Abbot John de Sutton (1349), at Dorchester, Oxon., only
bears four crosses, not the five necessary for an altar slab. The indent of David de Tillebury
(*c.* 1330) at Stifford, Essex, was almost certainly adapted at a later date.[14] A chantry altar
at St. Albans Cathedral bearing indents on the side, is probably composed of unconnected

pieces. The presumption is against the use of high tombs as side or chantry altars, though some were constructed in very close association.[15] After the spoliation of chantries in sixteenth century England, and the sale of their contents, old altar slabs were widely used for the inlay of brasses.

The porch was a particularly conspicuous place and suitable for a modest brass. An inscription to Henry Boyton and son (*c.* 1500) is still nailed to the north door at Thaxted, Essex. John Aleff, parson of Hollingbourne, Kent, willed in 1537 to be 'buried in the way beside the Porch door on the right hand going in, a plate to be set in the wall nigh his grave'.[16] At Edenham, Lincs., the brass to a donor (*c.* 1520), kneeling before (?) St. Thomas of Canterbury (Fig. 47), was raised high on the outer wall of the tower.

A number of brasses were laid, not only to stimulate the thought of the passer-by, but to aid the contemplation and discipline of the commemorated. The inscription to Ralph Eyer (1527), Rector at Sulhampstead-Abbots, Berks., states that it was laid in Eyer's lifetime 'Jugitur de morte cogitans, sibi vivens hoc monumentum posuit'. A documentary reference to a brass of Bishop Andrzej Bninski, formerly at Poznań Cathedral, Poland, discloses that it was prepared on the Bishop's order twenty years before his death. The acts of the Chapter of Poznań for 9 January 1479, record of Bishop Andrzej, 'Fertur finus ad sepulcrum, quod sibi ante annos XX vel circa. Cogitans se semper moritorium, de marmore auricalco superducto elaborari jusserat'.[17] It is probable that many shroud brasses were laid with this purpose in view.

The time of preparation

It is clear that the preparation of a brass, and its appropriate setting were matters of great importance to the person commemorated as well as to the family as a whole. Concern for proper representation influenced the time as well as the nature of the preparations. It is generally assumed that brasses date from within two years of the death of the person commemorated, unless there are strong reasons to suspect otherwise. Surviving contracts show that completion was expected within a year, even for large compositions. An inscription at St. Osyth, Essex, to John Darcy states the date of death and of engraving. Darcy's death is recorded as 1638, but the plate is also inscribed 'Fr Grigs fecit Anno 1640'. The executors had apparently acted with reasonable promptness. However, it is evident that the time margin was occasionally much greater, either on account of the indifference or incapacity of relatives, especially minors, or, as the inscription of Richard Adane (1435) at Kelshall, Herts., complains, 'Executors bith coveytous & kepe all that they fynde.' A man could guard against such negligence. The action of Bishop Andrzej has several counterparts. The inscription at Kelshall reads 'The which Rychard Adane as ye now say, leid here thys ston be hys lyff day.' The will of Dr. Hewke of Trinity Hall, Cambridge, directed his 'body to be buried wher it shall please God I may assigne it. And my gravestone that is ready bought and paid for to be laide over my body shortly after my decease.'[18] Where documentary evidence is available the number of brasses prepared in advance is shown to be quite considerable, especially in the case of important ecclesiastics. Inconsistencies of style and costume on the brasses themselves betray many early preparations. John Hampton and family (d. 1556) at Minchinhampton, Glos., are commemorated by brasses engraved *c.* 1510, the date of death having been clearly added by a later and less expert hand. Changes of fashion in the waiting period could necessitate alterations. The shoes of William Maynwarying (d. 1497), at Ightfield, Shropshire, have been subtly rounded with shade lines. The figure, apparently prepared ten years earlier, had been engraved with pointed shoes. The most common sign of engraving in the lifetime of the commemorated, is the complete absence of a date of decease. The appropriate section was not engraved, leaving blank spaces in the inscription. Striking examples of this feature are the brasses of Abbot Delamare (d. 1396, engr. *c.* 1360), St. Albans Cathedral, Herts., Abbess Herwy (d. 1527, engr. *c.* 1520), Elstow, Beds., and Bishop Yo(u)ng (d. 1526, engr. *c.* 1523), New College, Oxford.

Recognition of a founder or benefactor could influence early commemoration. Sir John de Cobham (d. 1407) at Cobham, Kent, holds a depiction of his foundation there (Fig. 38). The style of the design indicates a date of engraving little later than 1362, the year of the refounding of Cobham as a collegiate church.

In contrast to the above, late commemoration was more frequent, prompted by the concern of the descendants, especially when the heir was a minor on his father's decease, or an unfulfilled obligation to benefactors. The difference in time between burial and commemoration is sometimes extreme. At Wells Cathedral, Somerset, there used to be the brass to Ine, King of Wessex, who resigned his power in A.D. 726. Neither brass nor indent survives, but a rough drawing remains to indicate that the brass was made *c.* 1320. The half-figure to St. Ethelred, King of the West Saxons (d. 871), still lies at Wimborne Minster, Dorset. The brass figure can hardly be earlier than 1440 (Fig. 39). Robert Fitz Haimon was buried in Tewkesbury Chapter House, Glos., in 1107, reinterred in the presbytery in 1241 and moved again in 1328 to the north side of the choir. His brass, which is completely destroyed, was laid on the second transfer.[19] The brass of Duke Boleslaus of Silesia (d. 1201) at Lubiąż, Poland, is an important existing example (Fig. 114). It is tempting to regard this as the second earliest figure brass in Europe, but comparison with others in the same church will not support this view. The Duke is described in his inscriptions as 'FUNDATOR LUBENSIS' and it is clear that his brass was engraved a century later, when the monastery church was rebuilt.

Descendants belatedly laid brasses to parents and ancestors from a sense of family duty or pride. The inscription of Mikołaj Tomicki at Tomice, Poland, states that the memorial was set up in 1524 by Bishop Piotr of Kraków, son of the deceased. Mikołaj died *c.* 1495, and a poor stone-relief monument had already been erected to his memory. His successful son was apparently not satisfied with it. The will of Richard Brasyer of Norwich (made 1505 and proved 1513), directed that brasses should be laid to the memory of his grandfather Robert and his father Robert, as well as to his own. These brasses still exist in St. Stephen's Church, Norwich. At Stopham, Sussex, the brasses of John Bartelot (d. 1428) and John Bartelot (d. 1453) were both engraved *c.* 1470 presumably to bolster the family pedigree. There are several individual brasses of a patently posthumous category. Thomas Quatremayn and wife both died in 1342, but their figures lie with those of their son Thomas (d. 1396) and his wife on a brass (*c.* 1420), Thame, Oxon. William Whappelode died in 1398. His brass was engraved at the time of his son's commemoration in 1446, and included on the same slab at Chalfont St. Peter, Bucks. Sir Robert Swynborne (d. 1391) and Sir Thomas Swynborne (d. 1412) are represented on a magnificent combined memorial at Little Horkesley, Essex (Fig. 177). Sir John Lysle at Thruxton, Hants., died in 1407, but his brass was clearly engraved *c.* 1430. Stylistic inconsistencies reveal many other examples. The brass of Richard and Elizabeth Wakehurst, who died respectively in 1454 and 1464, at Ardingly, Sussex, was engraved *c.* 1500. John Sacheverell was slain at Bosworth in 1485. His brass at Morley, Derbyshire, was engraved *c.* 1525. A more notable victim of Bosworth, William Catisby, was executed after the battle. His brass, laid in accordance with his son's will after 1505, records William's date of death as 20 August 1485, five days before his actual tragedy. George Verney, of Compton Verney, Warwicks., died in 1574. His brass is a typical engraving of fifty years later. Certain brasses, though consistent in appearance, are shown by the information of the inscription to have been laid some years after death. At Cranford St. Andrew, Northants., the wife of John Fossebrok, Esq., is described as a dry-nurse ('sicca nutrix') to King Henry VI. The inscription is dated 1418 but could not, by reason of this reference be earlier than 1422.[20]

Commemoration of ancestors long dead or even fictional was undertaken in the late sixteenth century and more particularly in the seventeenth century. Tombs were accepted as evidence of ancestry and arms, and certain gentry attempted to display their 'credentials' in complete series of family monuments. The small sculptured tombs of the Poyntz family at North Ockendon, Essex; the curious series of spurious tombs to the de-Montforts and Wellesbournes at Hughenden, Bucks., and the even larger collection of adopted Lumley tombs at Chester-le-Street, Durham, are products of this activity. Brasses were used for the same purpose. The most carefully fabricated series, to the Dering family, are at Pluckley, Kent.[21] An elaborate brass with the same intention is that of Thomas Beale (1593), at Maidstone, Kent. Kneeling in six tiers are Thomas Beale, William of 1534, Robert of 1490, John of 1461, William of 1429 and John of 1399, all with their families. Smaller series are found at Newton Flotman, Norfolk, and Norton Disney, Lincs. The figures of Richard Blondevyle (d. 1490), Ralph Blondevyle (d. 1514) and Edward Blondevyle (d. 1568), kneel in a row at the former, the brass being dated 1571. At Norton Disney half-effigies in tiers represent William Disney (d. 1540) and family and Richard Disney (d. 1578) and family. The inscription of Edward Turpin, gent. (d. 1683), at Bassingbourn, Cambs., also commemorates John Turpin of 1494 and other ancestors. An effective but curious representation is the brass at Otley, Yorks., placed by Frances Palmes in 1593. This depicts a recumbent civilian from whose body springs a genealogical tree of the Lyndley and Palmes family, rather in the manner of a Jesse tree. The most surprising of all is a Polish brass of 1602, signed by Walery Kunink of Poznań. The brass was ordered by Stanisław Czarnkówski for his family chapel at Czarnków, and commemorates Mikołaj Czarnkówski of the twelfth century, Sędziwój of the thirteenth century and Sedziwój of the fourteenth century. All three were castellans. They are presented as rising above an inscription, which contains much questionable information about their achievements and those of Stanisław himself. The conception of the monument is grandiose, the treatment is naïve, but the result is imposing as well as humorous. The three figures are richly armed, two hold banners and one a mace. The designer hardly attempted an antique effect, the style of the armour, the great moustaches and the hair-net of the central figure being highly fashionable (Fig. 40).

External brasses

Concern for complete family commemoration brought further consequences in England. The private ownership of chapels, and the virtual acquisition of portions of churches by private families, forced the minor gentry to place high tombs in the churchyards. This led to a substantial increase in the number of churchyard brasses, which had occasionally been laid in the fifteenth and early sixteenth centuries. The earliest indent noted in a churchyard, probably in its original place, is of *c.* 1450 at Bridge, Kent. Another of 1531 is at Houghton Conquest, Beds., and three sixteenth century Kent wills express a desire to be buried in the churchyard, a brass also to be set there.[22] External brasses—usually in the form of inscriptions—are common in the West Country and found also in the South and East. Brasses with figures are at Staverton, Devon (1592), High Halden, Kent (1601) (Fig. 45), Burford, Oxon. (1609), Mudford, Somerset (1617), Ringsfield, Suffolk (engr. *c.* 1630) (Fig. 99), and Birstall, Yorks. (1632) the last now being inside the church. Inscription plates are far more numerous. Some of these are found associated with buildings and were laid to commemorate the construction. These brasses form a group of their own, though they serve as memorials to an achievement. Early examples are on the alms-houses, at Saffron Walden, Essex (*c.* 1475) and Lambourne, Berks. (1481), at Browne's Bedehouse, Stamford, Lincs. (*c.* 1490) and on the Market Cross at Shepton Mallet, Somerset (1500). An inscription of engraved copper (*c.* 1382) is set upon the gate tower of Cooling Castle, Kent.[23]

Apology brasses

Most extraordinary of such plates, recording acts as much as persons, are the inscriptions set up in several of the civic halls in the Low Countries to commemorate offences. These were made at the expense of the accused and constituted part of the punishment. The inscriptions were accompanied by cast heads or fists in brass, indicating abuse or assault on officials in the course of their duty. The most important collection is preserved in the Town Hall at Veurne, Belgium, consisting of seven inscriptions dating from 1499 to 1623, two heads and two fists.[24]

From the facts summarized it will be apparent that the motives behind commemoration influenced not only the form of brasses but also their presentation and situation. Certain aspects of brasses which seem peculiar are fully and reasonably explained in terms of their intention. This conclusion has a special application to design. Catholic theology and practice greatly influenced the preparation of brasses in the Middle Ages, and are reflected not only in the place, form, age and message of the memorials but in every aspect of representation. Similarly, the desire for artistic realism, the influences of humanism and the Renaissance, and the rejection in most of northern Europe of Catholic belief brought important if subtle changes to the appearance and content of brasses.

6 · The interpretation of monumental brass design

The meaning underlying brass design has been a neglected subject. Brasses have been judged on their face value, and the detail of representation has attracted most investigation. Why a figure brass should have a particular arrangement or pose, or be within a setting of a particular type, has not been seriously examined. This chapter is, accordingly, an innovation, and the author is particularly indebted to J. A. Goodall, F.S.A., for help in this summary.

It is fortunate that much guidance on monumental brass design can be derived from comparisons with tomb sculpture. It will be shown that many of the engravers were marblers and the crafts of stone carving and brass engraving were closely allied. Furthermore it was the most sumptuous sculptured tombs which set fashions that were adopted in modified form in cheaper monuments, brasses and incised slabs. Brass design was accordingly involved in the incongruities of tomb sculpture, and added to them by interpreting in the horizontal plane what was originally conceived in the vertical plane, and rendering in two dimensions what was essentially three-dimensional.

Inconsistencies in design

Professor E. Panofsky has shown that an unavoidable inconsistency arises in recumbent tomb sculpture, unless the figure represented is unequivocally depicted as in death.[1] Once the figure acquires the attributes of life—vigour in pose and alertness in expression—the recumbent posture is not explained. The confusion is further emphasized when drapery folds and other details are arranged in a manner consistent with a vertical representation. These problems arose in pre-Christian memorials and remained unresolved. The only solutions to achieve consistency lay in replacing the recumbent with a kneeling or vital posture, portraying the deceased as a corpse, or reducing the inconsistency by setting the tomb against a pillar or wall. The third solution was widely adopted in Germany.

Most brasses of the fourteenth and fifteenth centuries embody such contradictions. The figures appear alive and standing, though animals at their feet and helmets or cushions behind their heads suggest repose. Semi-profile representation became fashionable and the incongruity was thereby exaggerated. The logic of design was further confused when vertical canopies, weepers and other secondary figures were introduced into it. The horizontal head canopy, or gablet, is a feature of several of the finest English tombs, such as those at Westminster Abbey to Queen Eleanor, King Edward III and King Richard II. These tombs are also enriched with vertical canopies of loftier design rising above the recumbent figures. It was the latter type of canopy which generally attracted the brass designer, greatly increasing the size and impact of the composition. The transposition created peculiar difficulties. Pendant shields with supporting accoutrements, appropriate to a vertical structure, are inappropriate in the horizontal, though decorative and effective in appearance. The brass of Eleanor de Bohun (1399), Westminster Abbey, is a particularly fine example of these conflicting concepts (Fig. 173). Subsidiary figures arranged along the sides of the tomb chest required different accommodation on a brass. The use of wide canopy shafts for this purpose was a satisfactory compromise. The best example for study is the brass of Sir Hugh Hastyngs, Elsing, Norfolk (Fig. 129), which was without doubt designed in the manner of the Westminster tombs to the Earls of Lancaster and Pembroke. The vertical canopy of the Earl of Pembroke with its flying brackets and equestrian figure in the pediment is faithfully reproduced.[2] The weepers of the tomb chest fill the side shafts in compartments. Through this rearrangement Sir Hugh appears as lying within and not under his elaborate canopy. Inconsistencies were further accentuated by late fifteenth and early sixteenth century concessions to realism. The introduction in many Flemish and German brasses of curtains and pavements drawn in exaggerated perspective makes the various parts of the composition totally irreconcilable. It may be concluded that the normal representation of a figure brass was of a recumbent effigy, though the attributes of the figure were not strictly in accordance with this conception. This conflict was not a peculiarity of brasses but of all recumbent effigies.

The character of the figure representation and the issue of portraiture

The importance of a brass in drawing attention to the needs of the departed soul has been described. The individual commemorated is dead, his spirit transferred to another world, and his earthly remains have no value, other than as a symbol of human frailty. The monument is accordingly forward looking in its spiritual interest. Nevertheless the place the deceased filled in his own family succession, and the offices he held which did not perish with him on earth, have a continuing significance. The differentiation of a human being as a physical man, a spirit and a holder of particular status or office was an important theme in mediaeval thought, epitomized in the persons of royalty. These concepts have been examined in detail by Professor Kantorowicz in *The King's Two Bodies*.[3] A concern of the memorial in addition to its pious motive was to record status. For this reason, in addition to a plea for prayers, and the date of death, the inscription almost invariably describes the status of the deceased, whether knight, priest or member of a merchant company. The figure represented on the monument displays this important feature. Armour and vestments are carefully defined. Livery collars, badges and staffs of office and implements of profession are frequently included. Status in the family line is described in heraldic terms, with shields of arms, heraldic dress and even banners. The human peculiarities of the deceased, his facial appearance, stature and age were less important, even irrelevant to the function of the monument. A figure brass may be said generally to represent a type of man, shown as living but recumbent as in effigy.

Contrary views have been and are maintained. Attention is drawn to the use of representational mortuary effigies at important funerals, and the apparent individuality of face on certain brasses. Yet the arguments in favour of mediaeval portraiture, in the sense of a recognizable personal likeness, have little evidence to support them. It is not significant that a face may indicate character, unless it can also be shown that the peculiarity belonged to the deceased. For instance the face of Roger Campedene (1398), Stanford-in-the-Vale, Berks., is peculiar, but is probably no more than curiously engraved. Contracts and will specifications for the making of brasses so far recorded make little reference to the physical appearance of the deceased, though details of arms, marks, vestments and other decorations are carefully specified. No advocate of portraiture could seriously maintain the view that Flemish figure brasses of the fourteenth century were other than stylized representations, their features presented according to the established conventions. Yet these were the most sought-after brasses in Europe. Dr. J. P. C. Kent has shown in a study of military effigies that the peculiarities of nose, mouth and other features in English brasses may be traced to whole series of patterns. Furthermore, the uniformity of feature and expression is usually far more striking than any significant difference. A selection of examples can create a most misleading impression, which is dispelled when all the examples of a period are examined. The majority of English brasses were clearly shop-work, and were not based on special designs.

These considerations do not preclude the existence of mediaeval portrait brasses. They do, however, give cause for profound scepticism, which is reinforced by a further consideration. Painted portraits of the commemorated do not exist with which to make comparison, and an early Tudor exception, that of the Norwich mayor John Marsham (1525), whose portrait is in Blackfriars Hall, shows little connection between the painting and brass in St. John Maddermarket, Norwich. There are nevertheless several instances, to which reference has been made, where brasses are duplicated or a person is by chance depicted twice. If these brasses were indeed portraits it must be expected that a marked resemblance would be discernible on the two representations. This is not the case. There is no significant facial resemblance between the figures on the Cottusmore brasses (1439 and *c.* 1445) at Brightwell Baldwin, Oxon., nor on those of the Tame family (*c.* 1528 and 1534) at Fairford, Glos. Even more diverse are the later representations at Halton, Bucks., and Noke, Oxon., of Henry Bradschawe, Esq., chief Baron of the Exchequer, who died in 1553. On the first he is shown clean-shaven in the fashion of 1553, whereas on the second brass of 1598 he has a beard and moustache, and appears as a typical Elizabethan. This gross discrepancy occurs on brasses to the memory of a distinguished lawyer, and at a period when portraits might be anticipated.

There are mediaeval brasses which show features presumably appropriate to the deceased and which were probably included by specific request. The bearded knight at Stoke-by-Nayland, Suffolk; and squires at Mendlesham, Suffolk (Fig. 41), and Newland, Glos., are notable examples. The civilian figure of Nicholas Canteys (1431), Margate, Kent, is another. Such beards are a distinctive mark of age and may well have a personal significance equivalent to the crutch shown beside William Palmer 'with ye stylt' at Ingoldmells, Lincs. (Fig. 46). It is in fact difficult to achieve a likeness with a few strokes, especially when the face is shown full view and is in part concealed by a helmet or head-dress. It would be incorrect to deny the possibility of a fourteenth or fifteenth century portrait brass, but it is a fact that no satisfactory evidence has been produced to substantiate a single case. Demand for realism in the sixteenth century opened the way for true portraiture, but there are few established examples even in the seventeenth century. The conflict between fashionable and accurate representation is revealed at Llanrwst (see p. 94). Personal likeness was not a necessary attribute of the mediaeval memorial.[4]

Recumbent figures

The figure usually lies as if in prayer, with the hands placed stiffly together. Occasionally the alternative Christian representation is adopted, the hands being shown held wide apart, palms outward. This feature is most common among brasses in East Anglia. Rarely, as at Little Shelford, Cambs., Southacre, Norfolk, and Trotton, Sussex (Figs. 162, 161, 178), the figures of man and wife are shown hand in hand, as if joined in the hand clasp of matrimony. There are many examples of this arrangement in sculptured effigies. The arm-in-arm pose of an unknown man and wife (*c.* 1510), Brown Candover, Hants., is unique and pleasing. Certain poses were apparently adopted to give a vigorous impression. The drawn swords of two military figures (*c.* 1300 and *c.* 1305), Lubią˙, Poland (Figs. 113, 116), and of another (1325), Gent, Belgium (Fig. 142), are effective. The cross-legged pose of six English brasses (e.g. Fig. 120), and many effigies is now only interpreted as a vigorous arrangement. Long-held associations between the crusaders and crossed legs are indefensible, but notable as typical of romantic theorizing when interest in the Middle Ages revived. Episcopal figures are usually shown with their right hand raised in benediction. An extraordinary English design is the figure of the Countess of Athol (1375), Ashford, Kent, who was depicted holding two banners which formed the canopy shafts. This brass is now unfortunately mutilated.[5]

Half-effigies are common in England. These are usually small and were presumably chosen for reasons of economy. Some early examples are, however, large, and it is possible that the type originated from the association of half-figures with or within crosses, which are described on pp. 77–8. Busts are very rare until the seventeenth century, when interest increased in the visage of the deceased. Mediaeval examples are at Blickling, Norfolk (?1378) (Fig. 43) and Halvergate, Norfolk (palimpsest reverse *c.* 1440).

Foot supports

A few early brasses and many incised slabs represent the figure with no form of 'support' or 'rest' for the feet. All four of the early fourteenth century brasses at Lubiąż, and Willem Wenemaer (1325), Gent (Fig. 142), are of this type. An English indent (1507), for Sir James Hobart and wife, Norwich Cathedral, shows such a feature. It was, however, far more usual to introduce some beast or device below the feet, especially on male effigies. The significance of the lions and dogs most often depicted has caused speculation. The lion has been associated with strength and the dog with loyalty. Wilder theorists have attributed death in battle to the lion, an interpretation which would involve some ladies in affray. Whatever the importance eventually ascribed to them, many beasts were originally so placed to represent evil. The deceased is shown stamping down iniquity beneath his feet. An important Old Testament reference is found in Psalm 90:13 (Douay version) 'Thou shalt walk upon the asp and the basilisk: and thou shalt trample under foot the lion and the dragon'. That a real connection exists between this verse and monumental foot-rests is shown by the brass of Bishop Novak (1456), at Wrocław, Poland (Fig. 42). In this brass all the creatures named are depicted, the lions under the bishop's feet, dragons, an asp and, presumably, basilisks to the sides. It is significant that in fourteenth century Flemish episcopal brasses the deceased are shown as thrusting their croziers into the dragons and wyverns under their feet. The fifteenth century Flemish brass of St. Henry of Finland, Nousisainen, Finland, shows the saint trampling his murderer Lalli underfoot. The two Bishops Rupprecht and Heinrich Spiegel von Dessenberg, at Paderborn, West Germany, trample armed figures under their feet. Both prelates were distinguished for their defence of the diocese. The lion beneath the feet of Sir John Dabernoun gnaws at the knight's lance (Fig. 118), while the hound beneath Sir Roger de Trumpington, Trumpington, Cambs., bites at the sword.

Once the precedent for such creatures was established, it may be presumed that many were introduced in the thirteenth century for reasons other than religious symbolism. The heraldic importance of lions and the companionship of dogs made them obvious choices. Though even with these it is necessary to be cautious in interpretation. The lions at the feet of early ecclesiastical brasses as at Horsmonden, Kent; and formerly at Oulton, Suffolk; Peterborough Cathedral, Northants; and Durham Cathedral, most probably were intended to hold an evil significance for the viewer. Dogs had a low reputation in Christian tradition. Psalm 21:21 (Douay version) reads: 'Deliver, O God, my soul from the sword; my only one from the hand of the dog.' Proverbs 26:11 (Douay version) associates dogs with folly, and by inference with apostacy: 'As a dog that returneth to his vomit, so is the fool that repeateth his folly.' The dogs fighting over a bone beneath the feet of Laurence de St. Maur (1337), Higham Ferrers, Northants., are neither companionable nor edifying (Fig. 132).

The symbolic origins of these representations were undoubtedly forgotten in the course of the fourteenth century. Lions take on a benign aspect. Dogs, especially those associated with women, have the appearance of pets. A named dog, 'Terri', lies below the feet of Lady Cassy (1400), Deerhurst, Glos., while another, 'Jakke', resembling a poodle, was below the feet of Sir Brian de Stapilton (1432), Ingham, Norfolk (Fig. 44). Different types of dog can be distinguished, especially the collared leash hounds beneath the knights' feet and the belled lap-dogs at the ladies' feet.

As well as the traditional animals foot-rests also afforded a medium for heraldic display, emblems of trade and witty allusions. In the first category are the whelkshell for Wylloughby (1467), Wollaton, Notts.; the elephant and castle for Beaumont (1507), Wivenhoe, Essex; and the Calopus for Foljambe (1529), Chesterfield, Derbyshire. In the second category are the sheep, woolpacks and shears under the feet of wool merchants at Northleach (Fig. 180) and Cirencester, Glos., and the vintner's tun below Simon Seman (1433), St. Mary's, Barton-on-Humber, Lincs. (Fig. 179). In the third category are the dragon (for St. Margaret's overpowering of one or the Devil) beneath the feet of Margaret Wyllughby (1483), Raveningham, Norfolk (Fig. 50); and the 'mareys' or marsh below William Mareys, Esq., (1459), Preston-by-Faversham, Kent. An unusual example of the canting beast is the hedgehog (*hérisson*) running at the feet of Joan Peryent (née Risain) (1415), Digswell, Herts. A tun appears beneath the feet of John Stockton (1480), Hereford Cathedral. In contrast to this display of subtlety the two bedesmen at the feet of a lady (*c.* 1410) at St. Stephen's, Norwich, return to the theme of prayer (Fig. 48).

Animals, devices and emblems below the feet occur in declining numbers until the late sixteenth century. Sir Richard Catesby (1553), Ashby St. Legers, Northants., has a cat at his feet. The dog at the feet of Anne Bartelot (1601), Stopham, Sussex, is a very late instance. Foot-rests were gradually replaced by simulated pavements or low pedestals, though the heads of many figures in armour were still shown pillowed on their helmets.

The influence of wit on design

Reference to wit in the choice of foot-rests introduces the subject of wit generally, and its influence on design. Allusions to the name of the commemorated were expressed in a variety of ways and were cleverly devised. Foot-rests were one medium, heraldry was another. The allusions of canting heraldry owe nothing to brass designers, but were incorporated into their compositions. The arms of Thomas Salle (1422), Stevington, Beds., *Azure two salamanders salient in saltire or* are a notable example (Fig. 51). The monk with a scourge forming the crest on the helm of Sir (?) William Moyne (1404), Sawtry All Saints, Hunts., is another. The crest on the helm of John Cely, Esq. (1426), Sheldwich, Kent, in which the fingers of a human hand point upwards in the direction of a shield *semeé* of eyes (now lost), was possibly a bilingual pun, 'ciel eye' being a reference to the all-seeing eye of heaven which the shield portrayed.

The rebus was, in origin, a pictographic means of identifying a person by a punning device for the guidance of illiterates. On brasses it may have served this purpose, but many are examples of a simple ingenuity—some, it may be suspected, devised specially for the occasion, having had no other existence than their own mortuary occurrence, to compensate for the lack of arms of the individual commemorated. For example John Shipwash (1457), Hambleden, Bucks., shows the device of a sheep standing in water (Fig. 49). Four tuns are engraved on the arms of a cross at St. Mary-the-Virgin, Oxford for Croston (1507) (Fig. 59). 'Col' and a well are repeated on the brass of Richard Colwell (1533), Faversham, Kent. At Hitchin, Herts., James Hert (1498) is accompanied by hearts of which one remains, and a brass to Dr. John Sperehawke (1474), is lost, on which a sparrow-hawk on a hawking pole was placed at the feet of the deceased.[6] The elaborate tree branch bracket supporting John Terry and family (1524), St. John Maddermarket, Norwich, almost certainly alludes to the name (Fig. 228).

Ornament of garments or equipment could be turned to the same end. The tunic of Walter Pescod (1398), Boston, Lincs., is embroidered with peascods in the form of a W (Fig. 52). The scabbard of Sir William Pecche (d. 1487), Lullingstone, Kent, is decorated with branches which might be those of a peach tree.

The most surprising brass of this type is that of Abel Porcket (1509), now in the Gruut-huse Museum, Bruges, in which the entire design is composed around the name. In the centre Cain is shown in the act of slaying Abel with a jawbone. The quadrilobe medallions at the corners of the border inscription are filled with bristly pigs (Fig. 53).

The wording of the inscription was occasionally arranged to play upon the name of the deceased, such as the phrase 'micuit more mitis bene morigeratus' for William Moor, B.D. (1456), Tattershall, Lincs., and the references to 'mons' on the inscription of Thomas Hylle (1468), New College, Oxford.

A concluding example of rather distorted wit would appear to be the foot-rest of Edward Cowrtney, Esq. (1509), at Landrake, Cornwall (Fig. 54). A dog is depicted between Edward's feet, apparently tugging at a plant-like object to which he is tethered. This is probably an allusion to the legend of the mandrake, suggested by the name of the squire's resting place. The mandrake root was said to scream on being pulled from the ground, a scream lethal to human beings. Hence the need to delegate the task.

Angels on brasses

Significant attendants to the figures are angels. These are placed near the head, most usually supporting the cushion set behind it. Few English examples now exist, though those at Elsing, Norfolk (Fig. 130); Rothwell, Northants.; Hever, Kent (Fig. 55) and Little Easton, Essex are particularly noteworthy. They occur frequently on Flemish brasses. There are many Biblical references to angels having charge of the righteous and bearing them up, notably Psalm 90:11 and 12 (Douay version). Especially relevant to these monumental representations is a reference in the Collect in the Absolution of the Mass for the Dead, 'sed jubeas eam a sanctis angelis suscipe et ad patriam paradisi perduci'. This concept of transport from earth to paradise is fully explained in representations at Balsham, Cambs. (1401) (Fig. 56), and Checkendon, Oxon. (c. 1430), in which the soul is depicted borne up in a sheet by angels. Such groups are found on most fourteenth century Flemish rectangular compositions.

The inscription

The inscription is the most essential part of the brass inlay. The most common place for it if associated with a figure is on a rectangular plate below the feet. On large compositions it often surrounds the whole on a fillet. Clarity of wording is the most necessary feature and few texts are confused with much decorative detail. On a few brasses a mischievous face has been drawn into a capital letter,[7] while on some of the largest Flemish brasses the inscription weaves between a mass of ornament, as the Jesse Tree at Schwerin, Germany (Fig. 146), and the stages in the life of man at the Hôpital Notre Dame, Ypres, Belgium. Great care has usually been taken to ensure that the text is easily read, though verbal contractions are sometimes confusing. Border inscriptions on floor brasses normally read inwards towards the centre. The same type of inscriptions on a raised tomb are usually set in chamfer round the sides, reading outwards. The inscription is accordingly legible though the design on the tomb top is not seen. Concern for legibility explains the reversal of certain inscriptions which appear to be placed upside down in error. The brass of John Symondes and family (1512), Cley, Norfolk, is an excellent example of where the main and subsidiary inscriptions are reversed. This feature occurs when the brass as originally laid could not be viewed from its base without inconvenience or disrespect, for instance if the brass was laid close by an altar. Later repair, poorly carried out, has occasionally produced a similar result. J. Franklyn has associated this feature with the reversal of arms in heraldic usage on the death of persons concerned.[8] This view is unsupported by evidence. Had such a convention been current among the engravers, instances of reversed inscriptions would be common, which they are not. Reversed shields are found at Haccombe, Devon, but these are only two from identical sets of four, and probably served the same purpose of making inspection easier.

Canopies

The canopy work on English brasses surrounding the figures is of recognizable architectural origin, and either directly derived from the canopies of tomb sculpture or their representations in stained glass or illuminated manuscripts. The tall pediment follows the form of vertical tomb canopies, while embattled super canopies indicate a parapet supported above. Flemish canopies, encrusted with tabernacles, pseudo brickwork and other ornament, have a different origin, derived from the miniature architecture of the goldsmiths and latten workers. The models may be found in rich caskets and shrines. The connection is confirmed by the tiled roofs common to both the caskets and the canopy tops.

A particularly interesting feature of the richest canopies lies in the subsidiary figures. These include representations of the Deity, apostles, saints, mourners and weepers who may be relations or attendants of the dead.

The figures most commonly found on large English canopies are those of the apostles St. Peter and St. Paul taking the topmost place within the shafts, and representations of the Holy Trinity, the Virgin Mary with the Christchild, St. George or St. John the Baptist within the pediment or a central tabernacle (Fig. 57). Mary and St. John the Baptist were the intercessors most commonly shown in representations of the Last Judgement, which doubtless ensured their importance in tomb sculpture. St. Peter held the keys to heaven and his natural companion in mediaeval art was St. Paul. The Holy Trinity was the subject of devotion especially marked in England, and St. George held particular local significance.

In the most elaborate Flemish compositions the chief position within the canopy is held either by Abraham or God the Father, accompanied by adoring angels and receiving the soul of the deceased. The angels bearing the soul upwards are shown below. Apostles paired with prophets occupy the niches of the side shafts. This arrangement was derived from the belief that each of the apostles was responsible for a clause in the creed, which was predicted in a particular prophecy. A palimpsest fragment, formerly at Costessy, Norfolk, showed a detail from an English fourteenth century canopy with the figure of St. James the Great holding the scroll—'Qui Co*n*cepit [sic] e*st* de Sp*iritu* sanc[to . . .] Maria virgine', his reserved section.[9] Each apostle is shown with a particular emblem usually associated with martyrdom. An angelic choir fills the shafts round Bishop Rupprecht, Paderborn, Germany, while seraphim are represented in the canopy of Bishop Hallum at Konstanz, Germany.

The fashion for representing mourners or weepers on tomb chests was initiated on the French royal tombs at St. Denis, and was quickly imitated in England. The latten statuettes on the tomb of King Edward III at Westminster are particularly fine. Similar representations are found on a few very elaborate brasses. Comrades are depicted at Elsing (Fig. 129) and ancestors at Hunstanton in Norfolk. Both weepers and apostles surrounded the figure of Bishop Beaumont of Durham, and are still discernible on the indent. Mourning monks are shown in niches at Evora, Portugal, around the figure of Branca de Vilhana (*c.* 1490). The inclusion of members of the episcopal household, differentiated by emblems of their office, is a peculiarity of the brasses of Bishop Novak at Wrocław, Poland (Fig. 42), and Bishop Deher at Fürstenwalde, Germany.

Several of the largest fourteenth century Flemish brasses are decorated at the base of the canopy with pictorial panels. The subjects of these panels are rarely religious, but concentrate on the frivolous and gay. Wodehowses are particularly well represented, feasting, hunting or marauding (Fig. 146). These panels were not entirely decorative but helped to impart a secular or contrasting quality to an otherwise devout composition. They shared the function of the foot-rests, drawing attention to the world over which the deceased had triumphed.

Heraldic devices

Heraldic devices and background ornament were arranged around or within the structure of the canopy work as best suited the composition. Such details include shields of arms, merchants' marks and trade emblems, or a powdering of small scrolls with prayers or mottoes.

Evangelists' symbols

An important feature of large and many modest designs are the symbols of Evangelists occupying corner positions on the slab. These symbols are usually joined by the bands of the marginal inscription, and appear as incidental details. There are several examples of which Stanford-in-the-Vale, Berks. (1398), and St. Michael Coslany, Norwich (1515), are two, in which no marginal inscription is present. The position at the angles of the slab is significant. The biblical origin of these symbols is found in the vision of St. John (Apocalypse 4:6–9, Douay version), in which the four winged creatures, a man, an ox, a lion and an eagle, are described.[10]

The Evangelists' symbols had a varied significance according to their associations. One of the most important in association with the Deity represented the Divine Kingdom, the lion being symbolic of wild animals, the ox of domestic animals, the eagle of birds, and the man of mankind. Such a group is illustrated by the cross of Thomas Chichele (1400),

Higham Ferrers, Northants. A more common interpretation of the symbols, and that relevant to most brasses, is disclosed, along with the first, in the fifteenth century catechetical dialogue between Dives and Pauper. Pauper explains to Dives how the symbols are regarded as having a protective quality, and are, in consequence, painted on the walls of houses 'agenst tempestas and wycked spiritys that fle the evangelistes set i maner of a crosse'. The corner positions of the Evangelists' symbols are accordingly important, inferring their blessing and protection upon the deceased and all represented within the composition. A third and equally appropriate interpretation of these symbols, was to regard them as standing for the faith in which the deceased died.[11]

It would appear that most mediaeval figure brasses presented two main themes in whole or part. The first is the embodiment of status in the recumbent figure. The second is the safe passage of the departed soul to its eternal reward. The more elaborate the brass the greater is the religious meaning. The arrangement of the composition leads the spectator from emblems of earth or evil, through the faith of apostles and prophets to the mediation and guidance of patron saints, the Blessed Virgin, and finally to the Deity or Abraham receiving the ascending soul. The attendant angels and evangelists' symbols have their appropriate place in this scheme. The text of the inscription is directed towards these themes in its piety and identification, while the canopy provides an appropriate framework for the whole (Fig. 58).[12]

Kneeling figures

The recumbent effigy in brass or stone involved the designer in many inconsistencies. An alternative treatment, representing the deceased as kneeling in prayer, avoided such difficulties. Kneeling figures made effective and beautiful memorials (Figs. 149, 151) admirably suited to a vertical position. An excellent brass of this type is the Flemish latten altar-piece of 1368 at Susa, Italy. A small kneeling figure of a lady at Sedgefield, Durham, may be dated as early as *c.* 1320. This type of composition became very common in England and Flanders during the fifteenth and sixteenth centuries, inspired by the donors shown in manuscripts and stained glass, and from Flemish panel paintings.[13] The most usual arrangement shows the adults kneeling opposite each other praying at faldstools, their children kneeling behind. The centre of the group is concentrated on the person or persons to whom supplication is directed—the crucified Christ, the Madonna, the Pietà or the Holy Trinity. The kneeling figures are often assisted by patron saints, who are depicted as guiding and encouraging. Such designs have a pictorial quality and were often (even in England) engraved on quadrangular plates in preference to separate inlay. The prayers offered by the groups in their devotions are recorded on scrolls rising from the hands or mouths of the figures. The plate of the Duke and Duchess of Burgundy (*c.* 1450), at Basel, Switzerland, is among the finest of this type (Fig. 149). The small separate inlay composition of Edmund Croston (1507), St. Mary the Virgin, Oxford, is particularly interesting as the kneeling figure addresses St. Catherine, who in turn addresses a higher placed representation of the Holy Trinity (now lost) on Croston's behalf (Fig. 59).

Votive compositions could be enriched with other and sometimes dominating features. Notable examples are the brasses of John Strete (1405), Upper Hardres, Kent (Fig. 175), and John Spycer and wife (1437), Burford, Oxon. On both these brasses the commemorated kneel at the foot of tall brackets, their scrolls rising up in the first case to Saints Peter and Paul, and in the second to the Madonna. While the bracket is a notable part of the design, its purpose is of secondary importance, serving primarily to integrate the group. The same interpretation may be given to arrangements where the praying figures kneel at the foot of a floriated cross in the head of which a representation is placed. The brasses of John Mulsho, Esq. and wife (1400), Geddington, (formerly at Newton-by-Geddington), Northants. (Fig. 60), and Robert Parys and wife (1408), Hildersham, Cambs., are of this type.

A votive element is introduced into many compositions incorporating recumbent effigies. Scrolls with prayers are inset, rising to representations higher on the slab. The family group of Sir Thomas Stathum (1470), Morley, Derbyshire, is an excellent example of the arrangement, showing St. Anne, St. Christopher and the blessed Virgin Mary with the Christchild addressed by the knight and his two wives (Fig. 72). Such brasses do not appear incongruous as the figures have the superficial appearance of standing. In fact they combine two very different concepts in which that of the recumbent effigy predominates.

Shrouds and skeletons

The presentation of the deceased in death, as a bare skeleton or wrapped in a winding sheet, avoids many inconsistencies. The figure is stripped of all status and serves as a symbol of human decay (Fig. 61). Shrouds, cadaver and skeleton brasses form an important and independent group, different from other types of figure representation in concept and message. They were nevertheless greatly influenced by prevailing conventions. Many English shrouds and skeletons have grass-plot foot-rests, while several embody most of the inconsistencies of their less austere contemporaries. The majority of these figures are recumbent, though there are examples kneeling in prayer. In a few cases the living is contrasted with the dead (Fig. 240).

Emblem representations

Representation by an emblem or device only was common. These brasses, though often small in size, emphasize the importance of status in commemoration. The chalice emblem for the priest (Fig. 236), the mitre for the bishop, and the trade emblem for the merchant are examples. The shield of arms or achievement of arms with inscription may be regarded as a form of emblematical memorial, and are by far the most numerous. Other emblems signify mortality or piety. The skull symbolizes death; the rose represents the transience of life or devotion to the Virgin. The heart has several meanings of which redemption or the Sacred Heart of Jesus are the most usual (Fig. 237). The cross symbol of the Christian faith is essentially an emblematic device, and plain, decorated or inscribed crosses are properly considered in this category of brass (Fig. 238). Many of these emblems are found incorporated within larger compositions, but their significance in design is primarily as memorials in their own right.

CROSSES

Cross and bracket brasses form an interesting group. Both designs include figures which are depicted within the open heads of floriated crosses, or upon brackets. They appear to be an English speciality and are possibly of common origin. An early English form of tomb represents the deceased in half or quarter effigy at the head of the slab, while most of the lower surface is decorated with a pattern of foliage or flowers, branching from a central stem. Alice de Ridleigh (*c*. 1350) at St. John's, Chester, is a late example. Several early indents of cross brasses show the half-effigy set above a cross and not within it.[14] By *c*. 1320 it was an established design to set the half- or full-figure within the head of the cross (Fig. 126). The meaning of this arrangement may be the protection afforded to the deceased by the Christian faith. A cross (*c*. 1320), at Chinnor, Oxon., represents a priest's head and hands appearing with the cross head. The foliated stems of most cross brasses reflect the influence of the earlier decorative motif.

BRACKETS

The bracket brass was most probably of similar derivation. A tabernacle supported by a bracket replaced the crosshead. A traditional stone example in low relief (*c*. 1320) is at Bredon, Worcs., and there is evidence of an early fourteenth century bracket indent at Linwood, Lincs.[15] These tall shafted designs are clearly in a different category from the small corbel placed beneath the feet of William de Aldeburgh, Aldborough, Yorks. It is difficult to grasp the significance of the bracket brass in its most common form, in which the deceased is shown as elevated on a pedestal (Fig. 63). In examples where the top position is filled by a sacred representation the intention is clear, but such designs are an elaborated form of votive compositions. The prevalence of canopied brackets in English churches for wall decorations and the housing of images clearly influenced the designers. The meaning of the design is obscure and it may be doubted whether it was entirely clear to the engravers. The great length and grace of the bracket may have ensured its popularity.

Special designs

A few brasses were designed by special order and have a significance of their own. By far the most original is that at Salisbury Cathedral to Bishop Robert Wyvil (1375) (Fig. 62). During his forty-five years of administration, Bishop Wyvil recovered the castle of Sherborne and the Chase of Bere for the Church in a lawsuit against the Earl of Salisbury, which nearly ended in a trial by battle. The brass commemorates this achievement and the half-effigy of the Bishop is the only conventional feature of it. Bishop Wyvil is shown in prayer looking out of a great castle window, turrets arising around and above him, while his champion stands at the main gate, armed with a shield and war hammer. Rabbits and hares running in the foreground represent the Chase. It is tempting to associate this design with the romantic mediaeval subject of the beleaguered lady. A fine painting (*c*. 1400) in the Alhambra, Granada, Spain, depicts the battle of two contestants before a castle gate. The half-figure of a lady in prayer appears in the open window of the keep, and animals are in the foreground.[16] This type of composition possibly inspired the draughtsman in making this special brass design.

The influence of realism and the Renaissance

Mediaeval patterns were so well established that they survived both realist and Renaissance influences. The meaning of conventions became forgotten yet the conventions themselves persisted especially in England and Flanders. Important changes are discernible by 1450 notably in German brasses. Many figures are shown in half profile as standing within a vaulted room. Certain backgrounds are carefully defined, and floors are drawn in exaggerated perspective. By 1520 the interior of a room was an established form of representation in both Germany (Fig. 196) and Flanders. Not only are these compositions more vital and pictorial in conception, but simulated shading and detailed definition impart a convincing naturalism to the figures. This naturalism is not strictly portraiture, but gives a strong impression of personality. The Pownder brass (1525), at the Christchurch Mansion museum, Ipswich, is an exquisite brass monument, in which little of the Gothic influence remains (Fig. 65). Flemish and German brasses reflect much Renaissance influence after 1550 in the form of antique ornament, classical canopies and an approach to true portraits. Piety of motive may be recorded in the inscription but it is not necessarily revealed in the design. In England brasses are occasionally found which depict the deceased in acts of daily life such as hunting or preaching (Fig. 255).

Nevertheless, the persistence of old designs is remarkable, especially in England. Modifications were considerable but conventional patterns were rarely discarded. The brasses of Nicholas Wadham, Esq., and wife (1609), Ilminster, Somerset, deserve study (Fig. 64). The main figures stand on circular bases facing each other. The treatment of costume and armour is naturalistic, and the faces are probably portraits. Yet flying scrolls rise from their mouths bearing texts. Between the heads of the figures is an achievement of arms, which clearly takes the place of a religious representation, to which in earlier times prayer scrolls would have been directed. The heads of knights and other notables are shown resting on helmets to the end of the sixteenth century. The prayerful pose persists. Archbishop Harsnett's brass (1631), Chigwell, Essex, displays the four Evangelists at the corners of the marginal inscription. Similar conventions are notable in Flemish brasses.

Votive compositions reflect similar changes. Kneeling figures become more realistic, their backgrounds acquire the impression of depth, and in England religious figures or symbols give way to armorial bearings. Yet the traditional arrangement is retained. Shroud and skeleton brasses are found well into the eighteenth century. Some types of emblem survive including hearts and mitres. There are few designs which break away entirely from the conventions of the Middle Ages, and most of those that do were produced by craftsmen other than monumental specialists.

The influence of late fifteenth century realism, of classical designs and of humanist and protestant thought in the sixteenth century, was important in moulding the aspect and meaning of memorial brasses. Yet conservatism in monumental art was strong, and while conventions lost their original significance, their forms survived with remarkable consistency. Brass design was created in the Middle Ages. New thoughts served mainly to adapt what had been established.

The engraver's ideal

The interpretation given is of course incomplete. The intrinsic beauty of a design cannot be explained in terms of iconography, derivation or evolution. The good craftsman was proud of the quality of his work, and the aesthetic aspects of art were important to him. Mediaeval standards of beauty in this context are not recorded in any known treatise but as J. A. Goodall has noted, 'the references to beauty in the writings of the schoolmen on metaphysics provide a key to the qualities looked for in a work of art. That is to say, the work should be pleasing to the sight and this was sought for in three qualities. That it should be well drawn or made, with brightness and splendour of colour, and due proportion of harmony, which was found in numerical progressions, geometrical forms and symmetry, or in the relation of the parts to the whole. Not all works of art made then measured up to the requirements; mediocre or downright bad artists have always existed, but, in the best work these qualities were amply fulfilled.'[17] The splendour of a brass of merit, bright in its gilding, rich in its colourful inlays, satisfying in its proportions and faultless in its execution, was not only the product of the current modes and influences. It was equally the achievement of craftsmen in pursuit of a recognized ideal.

7 · The engravers

Monumental brasses were by their very nature the interest of a wide range of craftsmen. Marblers or sculptors were concerned with their preparation as decorators of memorial stones. Latteners and bronze casters were equally involved in their manufacture as workers of cast and engraved metal. Goldsmiths applied their skill to a medium receptive of delicate engraving. In contrast, casters of heavy ecclesiastical and military articles—the bell-founders and cannon-founders—also participated, as their foundries could be applied to the casting of the plate. In addition, craftsmen in other media, such as glaziers, were involved through a common trade in preparing memorials. As products highly adaptable in size and cost, brasses offered a regular source of work according to the needs of the maker. Brass engravers were not exclusive specialists. The extent to which this particular craft employed them was related to the market.

Marblers and sculptors

The association of brass engraving with the preparation of stone monuments is conclusively proved by English, Flemish and Silesian evidence. There is little doubt that the majority of English brasses were made by the London marblers, whose workshops were situated in the city, especially around the graveyards of St. Paul's Cathedral and the monastic houses of the Blackfriars and Greyfriars, though their form of organization or 'mystery' in the fourteenth and early fifteenth centuries is not known. The Guild of Marblers in London was enfranchised on 31 August 1486, and accorded the right to elect two wardens, who had powers of inspection and of the seizure of work 'not sufficiently wrought'. The wardens' authority extended to 'every persone occupying the said Crafte within the Fraunchise of the said Citee that maketh any Stonewerk of marbyll, laton' werke or coper werke belonging or perteynyng to the same Crafte'.[1] In addition to this general direction the details of certain wills associate the marblers with brasses beyond any doubt. Judge Roucliffe, in his will of 1494, requested James Reames or Remus, marbler of St. Paul's Yard, to make an epitaph for him in the Temple.[2] There is every reason in this case to presume this marbler was also responsible for the important brass to the judge and his wife at Cowthorpe, Yorks. According to the will of John Lorymer, Citizen and Marbler (d. 1499), Henry Lorymer was to complete and sell 'such marbylle stonys and laten wurke thereto belonging whiche I have within the precincte of the blacke Fryers'.[3] The will of Thomas Salter, Chantry priest (d. 1558), specified that his portrait should be 'graven in copper of a cunynge m[ar]bler that dwellithe in sancte Dunstons p[ar]ishe in the west agaynste the south side of the church'.[4] A provincial marbler, John Hippis of Newark, Notts., agreed on 6 April 1515 to prepare a brass and canopied high tomb for John Willughby Esq. (see p. 97). It may be deduced from this evidence that the crafts of the tomb-makers were very closely associated, whether engaged in the preparation of brasses, incised slabs or certain types of high tomb.

The connection between brass engraving and the work of the midland alabasterers is far less clear. An apparently relevant record, a contract of c. 1510[5] in which Henry Harpur

6

and William Moorecock of Burton-on-Trent agreed to supply an alabaster tomb with cover and brasses to commemorate Henry Foljambe Esq., is less conclusive on investigation as the cover slab is of Purbeck marble, probably obtained from London with brass inlays. Only one recorded alabaster incised slab, at Stanford-on-Soar, Notts. (1498), bears the indents of subsidiary brass details. There is inadequate evidence as yet to associate brass engraving with the alabaster carvers. The carvers were primarily situated at Chellaston and later at Burton. Brasses are known to have been made at Newark and were probably made at Coventry.

The trade of the London marblers was assumed during the reign of Elizabeth I by a number of immigrant and local sculptors whose work has been satisfactorily identified. The role of the sculptor as a carver in marble and engraver in brass is proved from several sources. The Royal Master Masons, Nicholas Stone and Edward Marshall, both engraved brasses in addition to their notable work as monumental sculptors. The details of the cost of an inscription and arms to Cecily Puckering at St. Mary, Warwick, as recorded in Stone's account book for July, 1636, have already been described. Marshall's signature appears on the brass of Edward Filmer and family (1629) at East Sutton, Kent. The Flemish *émigré* sculptor Gerard Johnson (d. 1612), who was employed to make and erect two of the tombs of the Dukes of Rutland at Bottesford, Leics., engraved a considerable series of brasses at his Southwark workshop. His cartoons for two brasses to the Gage family at West Firle, Sussex, still survive. The remarkable English sculptor Epiphany Evesham signed the brass of Edmund West (1618) at Marsworth, Bucks. The signature of Francis Grigs, another London sculptor, is found on the brass of Richard Cressett and family (1640), at Monk Hopton, Shropshire, and on others in Essex and Yorkshire.

There are indications that two of the mediaeval master masons retained an interest in this craft. The great Henry Yevele, Royal Master Mason at Westminster, in his will of 1400 referred to a lease of tenements in St. Paul's Churchyard with 'omnis bona mea mamoria et de latoun ac instrumenta mea ibidem'. William Hyndeley (d. 1505), Master Mason in 1472 at York Minster, left to William Gilmyn his tools for 'gravying in plaite'.[6]

Continental evidence reveals a similar association of crafts. In Gent by the fifteenth century the brass engravers were members of the guild of stone cutters (*Steenhauwere*). Masters of the guild were allowed to engrave stone or metal at choice, though carvers of effigies in the round had a separate organization—namely the 'Beeldemaker' guild.[7] The most eminent known Gent marblers, the families of van Meyere, Goethals and Dedelinc, were famous for incised slabs as well as brasses. Among the *tombiers* of Tournai the families of d'Escamaing and Hanette worked freely in both media.[8] The most celebrated *tombier* of the fifteenth century, Alard Génois, was styled 'ouvrier de marbre et de sépulture de keuvre'. Jodok Tawchen, a respectable brass engraver of Wrocław, Poland, was described as 'Lapicida' in the Sprowa agreement (p. 96).

Latteners and bronze casters

The second class of craftsmen, the latteners and bronze casters, were greatly involved in this business. The separation of latteners from marblers in England is a dangerous distinction, as they shared the same guild by the fifteenth century and often shared the same skills. Nevertheless, there were clearly some craftsmen who were regarded as specialists such as the lattener John Orchard, almost certainly the master responsible under Henry Yevele for the metal work of the tombs of King Edward III, and his eldest son Prince Edward, the coppersmiths Broker and Prest, who were employed in the making of the tomb of King Richard II, and Thomas Stevyns, coppersmith, one of the contractors for the superb effigy of Richard Beauchamp, Earl of Warwick (d. 1439) at St. Mary, Warwick, and responsible for the engraved latten marginal inscriptions. It may be presumed that such masters engraved brasses. The supreme examples of craftsmen, who worked almost exclusively in bronze and whose fame is based on their sepulchral work, were the Vischer family of Nürnberg.[9] Hermann the Elder established the family business by casting fonts and monumental relief plates. His son Peter made a brilliant reputation for his monumental craft, ably assisted by his sons Hermann, Peter and the less gifted Hans. The shrine at St. Sebald at Nürnberg, in which Peter, Hermann and the younger Peter all participated, is a masterpiece reflecting the genius of the family. The brasses engraved by the Vischers at Bamberg, Erfurt, Kraków and Meissen (Figs. 195, 196) are among the finest of their period.

Goldsmiths

Among the third group the goldsmiths were a particularly important and influential body, and many master goldsmiths were skilled in the use of inferior metals. Their title was a supreme qualification. It is accordingly difficult to distinguish between the master craftsman or even financier who was a goldsmith and the practising gold worker. William Torel, the craftsman responsible for the casting of the latten effigies at Westminster to King Henry III and Queen Eleanor, was a goldsmith. Similarly, Richard Brasyer the younger, an outstanding Norwich bell-founder, was also a goldsmith. Documentary evidence of the sixteenth and seventeenth centuries records the participation of goldsmiths in brass memorial engraving. James Gray, a Scottish goldsmith, was paid £20 for engraving the inscription and devices for the brass of the Earl of Moray at St. Giles' Cathedral, Edinburgh.[10] According to the accounts of the Bishop of Durham, 32 shillings were paid 'to the goldsmythe at Yorke for a plate to set over Mrs. Barnes'.[11] Her curious rectangular memorial bearing a cross and floral decoration and dated 1581 is at Auckland St. Andrew, Durham. Sylvanus Crue, goldsmith of Wrexham, signed the brass at Llanrwst, Denbigh, to Lady Mary Mostyn (1658), and several others in the west of England. In Flanders Frederik Malders of Maaseik, Belgium, whose signature appears on the brass of Canon Roland Thienen (1616) at Sittard, Holland, was certainly a goldsmith. Gaspard Bruy-degoms of the Antwerpen Mint, engraver of the brass at Aberdeen to Dr. Duncan Liddel (engr. *c.* 1619) was most probably a goldsmith by profession. At Köln the uncompleted works of the engraver Willem Loeman were finished by a goldsmith[12] (Fig. 202), and in Saxony a goldsmith is recorded as having assisted in the engraving of the Freiberg brasses. In addition to these proved examples, there are several earlier brasses which show a delicacy of treatment consistent with the practice of a worker in fine metal. Most out-standing is the remarkable gilt and enamelled plate to Sir Thomas Sellynger and his wife Anne (d. 1475, engr. *c.* 1495) at St. George's Chapel, Windsor, Berks. (Fig. 66). Another is the large palimpsest fragment at Great Berkhamsted, Herts., to Thomas Humphre of London, goldsmith (*c.* 1500), the inscription of which is exceptionally fine. Thomas Hevenyngham, Esq. (1499) and family at Ketteringham, Norfolk (Fig. 227), and John Croke, Alderman of London (1477), and family at All Hallows-by-the-Tower, London, are also especially well engraved on surprisingly thin plate. It would, however, be specula-tive to press such deductions far.

The bell- and cannon-founders

The casting of bells and of cannon were closely associated, not only on account of common foundry facilities, but also the similarity of the casting process. Bell metal, an alloy of copper and tin, was used in both articles, and could be further used for casting monumental plates. The manufacture of fine bells and cannon required much decorative skill. Some bells were beautifully inscribed, while decoration was lavished on cannon. In 1572 Wolf Hilliger cast cannon for Duke Wilhelm the younger of Braunschweig in the shape of dragons. One was engraved with the prophet Daniel seated in the lions' den, and another with the prophet Jonah being cast up by the whale.[13] There was little difficulty in applying such decorative ingenuity to monuments.

The noted Hilliger family of Freiberg are by far the best recorded engravers of this group. The family established themselves as founders in the fifteenth century and secured an outstanding reputation by 1560. Wolfgang Hilliger was appointed cannon-founder to the Elector in 1567, and his eldest son Martin, who succeeded him in 1576, was equally notable. He was succeeded by his third son Hans who in 1640 was succeeded by Hans Wilhelm. All these members of the family were famous for their cannon, bells and memorial brasses. Twenty-eight of their brasses, all representing members of the Ducal and Electoral houses of Saxony, lie on the floor of the mortuary chapel in Freiberg Cathedral (Figs. 67, 105, 245 and 246).

Other established bell-founders have left records, or signatures or initials on brasses. Matthias Benning, cannon-founder to the Council of Lübeck, was commissioned in 1562 to make a brass in memory of Bishop Tydeman. The initials 'E.K.' for Eckhard Kucher, a Thuringian bell-founder, are found on the brass of Eobanus Zcigeler, (engr. 1561), at Erfurt Cathedral.[14] A famous Bohemian bell-founder, Brykcy of Zinnberg, is recorded as the maker of the inscription of Nykodem Kostelniczek (1583) at Kostel sv Jindřicha, Praha (Prague), Czechoslovakia.[15] A seventeenth century English bell-founder, William Cockey of Wincanton, Somerset, signed an inscription dated 1691 to the Bennet family at South Brewham, Somerset, and several other inscriptions in the West Country. Earlier and more important English bell-founders were the East Anglian families of Brasyer and Chirche, both of which were perhaps involved in brass engraving at Norwich and Bury St. Edmunds.

Glaziers

The participation of glaziers at least in the sphere of design may be suspected from the similarity of kneeling votive groups in stained glass and in brasses. This conjecture is fortunately supported by documentary references. On 2 October (1445) Richard Stephen, glazier, acknowledged an indenture dated 9 June (1445), whereby Richard Ronge, glazier, and Alice, conveyed to the said Richard their right to the seven years' tenancy (of the logge between the Carmelite church and Fleet Street) which contained a provision that within a month of the decease of Richard or Alice, his or her executors should charge a citizen and marbler, and Richard Stephen should appoint another, to value all stones and utensils belonging to the craft of marbler.[16] It is of considerable interest that the craft of marbler should be practised by or under the direct supervision of a glazier, and that slabs, etc., should be retained on the glazier's premises. In further support of this agreement, the marbler and engraver James Reames was referred to as a glazier.[17] Thomas Stevyns of the Beauchamp contract similarly combined these skills. In Norwich, an important glazier, William Heyward, has been shown by Greenwood to have received an order for a brass in 1503, a transaction further discussed in *The Memorials*.

Other crafts

An unusual form of decoration or design could involve the skill of further craftsmen. Glass mosaic was used as background to an early cross brass at Westminster Abbey, and was probably carried out under Italian supervision (Fig. 68).[18] The taste in seventeenth century England for brasses decorated with elaborate allegorical subjects attracted the participation of book plate engravers. Such intricate compositions were well suited to their skill, and the mural position of such brasses did not expose their fine engraving to wear. Several allegorical plates were the work of Richard Haydocke, engraver and Fellow of New College, Oxford (Fig. 256), some bearing his initials or name. The engravers Robert and William Vaughan made at least two of the brasses at Llanrwst, one of which is signed by William (Fig. 262), while letters refer to the preparation of another. Mrs. A. J. K. Esdaile suggests that William Marshall, illustrator of *Quarles Emblems* in 1635, was also the engraver of the brass to William Button, Esq. (*c.* 1620), at Alton Priors, Wilts.[19]

Guilds

The organizations and regulations governing brass engravers can be derived from a variety of incomplete sources which only apply to certain groups. The London marblers by their enfranchisement were authorized to elect two wardens who were required to be sworn before the Mayor and Aldermen of the city. They possessed powers of investigation and seizure of poor-quality work, which was required to be bought 'into the chambre of this citie'. Half of the forfeiture was to be used to the benefit of the Chamber and half to the Craft Guild. The forfeiture consisted of the fourth part of 'every stone so forfaited after the rate of the price that it coste as the byer thereof shall confesse', and four pence for every pound of latten. Furthermore no craft member was allowed to 'take uppon hym to sett on werke any manner foreyn in the said crafte within this citie' on pain of a fine of ten shillings.

The Guild of Rotgiesser in Nürnberg, to which the Vischer family belonged, was extremely powerful in that city and jealous of any kind of competition. Sons of masters were granted privileges within the guild and incentives to carry on the family craft. Attempts by craftsmen to take their skill elsewhere were strongly opposed and masters were required to undertake to abandon their business before leaving the city. Hans Vischer made such an undertaking before leaving for Eichstätt. Participation by craftsmen of other guilds in the trade was persistently resisted.[20]

Certain regulations concerning the latten workers of Tournai have been preserved. The latteners were required to respect Holy days, forbidden to work at night, and restricted in the number of apprentices dependent upon them to three only.[21]

The guild organizations were clearly concerned to maintain a high standard of product, and most mediaeval brasses are of good quality. One substantial error could apparently lead to the rejection of a plate. An interesting example is the inscription of Robert Symson (d. 1497) who is described as 'deacanus ac magister domus seu hospitalis Sancti Jacobi iuxta Northampton'. Symson was in fact Dean of Darlington and Master of the Hospital of St. James at Northallerton. His inscription was re-engraved for Walter Pope and wife (1502), at Cowley, Middx., and it is reasonable to assume that the mistake made it waste. On the other hand several curious examples were apparently accepted. At Barking, Essex, the name of Richard Malet, priest (1485), was omitted on the inscription but was added on the vestments of the figure. Richard Chernok (*c.* 1490) at Shapwick, Dorset, displays the peculiar imposition of a scarf upon a rosary. Particularly absurd is the small figure of Richard Blakysley (1493), Lillingstone Dayrell, Bucks., who shows only one end of his stole (Fig. 69). More surprising are the incorrect cutting and joining of several accomplished brasses, such as those at Chartham, Kent (Figs 120,. 121), and Lubiąż, Poland (Figs. 113, 115), and the laying of unfinished memorials as at Kues, West Germany (Fig. 94). It is probable that the demands of the customer were more effective in maintaining quality than guild inspection. The goldsmiths, who were especially concerned with the purity and excellence of their articles, enjoyed only a limited success in controlling unscrupulous members of the craft and interlopers. It is unlikely that the discipline of the marblers was as exacting, especially in provincial centres.

Engravers' marks

It was clearly not the custom for mediaeval craftsmen to sign or mark effigies, incised slabs or brasses to identify the maker. Gaignières records three French exceptions, one on a brass at Evreux (1281) inscribed 'GUILLAUME DE PLALLI ME FECIT' (Fig. 106). The second, in the Abbey of Preuilly, to Bishop Jehan de Chanlay, Bishop of Le Mans (1291), bore the statement 'MAIST G. PALU ME FEIS', probably being a variation of the first. The third example at Beauvais has already been mentioned on p. 48. The earliest possible English 'signature' is at Adlingfleet, Yorks., on an inscription of 1569, which concludes 'HOC·OPUS·FIERI·FECIT·JOHES·SKERNE·DE·ESTOFFT', though John most probably only paid for the memorial. Engravers' names occur in substantial numbers during the seventeenth century but are even then unusual. Only the Yorkshire engravers Phineas Briggs and Thomas and Joshua Mann signed with apparent consistency.

Engravers' marks are very rare. The most published is that at Westley Waterless, Cambs., on the Creke brass (*c.* 1330–40). This represents a mallet, a crescent and a star arranged around the letter 'N' (Fig. 70). Waller, as a conjecture, associated this with the seal of one Walter 'le Masun' on which the symbols but not the letter are present. This mark is unique in England for its detail and clarity. Its irregular depth is nevertheless more consistent with a stamp than an engraved device, and it almost certainly relates to the caster. It is also significant that grass lines are cut into the mark, in part obscuring its design, suggesting an interest to disown it. A form of the letter 'N' is cut on the base of the dexter canopy shaft on the Camoys brass (1421), at Trotton, Sussex (Fig. 178). It is properly engraved and may be genuine, but the possibility exists that it is of no significance. Three initials unconnected with the figure are cut on the vestments of a priest (*c.* 1530) at Somersham, Hunts., but are presumably a later addition. Probably more significant than any of these is the oak-leaf device inserted within the initial capital of several English inscriptions, all belonging to a pattern series designated 'A', and dating from the closing years of the fourteenth century and the beginning of the fifteenth. This ornament is associated on certain marginal inscriptions with an elongated dragon, used to mark the end of the text. Brasses at Wymington, Beds. (1391) and Wanlip, Leics. (1393) are good examples. These details appear to be more than conventional ornament.

No certain Flemish mark is known to the author, though a small head engraved *within* a fold line on the brass of Margareta Wenemaer (d. 1352) at the Museum de Bijloke, Gent, Belgium, has every appearance of being one. It may, nevertheless, be objected that in its original state this detail would have been totally obscured by inlay. A curious shield forming part of a fourteenth century Flemish reverse of an inscription from Trunch, Norfolk, now preserved in the British Museum, has been suspected of being a maker's mark. This contains the crescent and star emblems of the Westley Waterless mark associated with the letter 'W'. Unfortunately an illustrated drawing published by Boutell gives the shield a false appearance. The letter and devices are crudely cut and asymmetrical. It is not entirely impossible that a shield left blank on the original was subsequently decorated after the piece came into private possession.[22] Furthermore, even if the shield is genuine, its position in the border would almost certainly refer to the commemorated rather than the engraver.

One brass of the Vischer *atelier* to Canon Georg von Lewenstein (1464) at Bamberg, West Germany, bears clear marks. There are the usual Vischer 'pennon' and a punning fish (Fig. 71b). A small shield bearing a crossed 'Z' mark appears on the sinister canopy shaft of a brass to a canon of the Bockstorf family (*c.* 1465) at Zeitz, East Germany (Fig. 71a). A well-executed shield and mark appear on the upper sinister side of the canopy to Archbishop Jakub (1480) at Gniezno, Poland (Fig. 71c).

The inclusion of such marks was exceptional. The engraver of the Gniezno brass may have regarded his work as of special distinction but the Bamberg brass is by no means an outstanding Vischer plate. There is no satisfactory explanation for these examples which arose from the whim of the makers or unknown circumstances connected with the work.

This summary of those who can be proved to have engraved brasses gives support to certain conclusions. The mediaeval craftsman was very versatile, and brass engraving was not the preserve of any particular craft. The marblers appear the most important group involved but clearly had no monopoly. Brasses accordingly reflect in their conception and execution a wide variety of skills. Much of this diversity may be traced to their manufacture, and a full appreciation of their presentation can only be obtained through comparisons with other associated arts. The marblers' brasses cannot be dissociated from incised slabs and high tombs. Similarly, brasses cannot be dissociated from stained glass design. The examination of Vischer brasses without reference to Vischer relief casts is grossly limiting. Brasses may rarely be claimed to be among the finest work of mediaeval, Renaissance or classical monumental art. But their interest as the product of a variety of crafts is in no way diminished by this. They remain a potentially rich source of information on the practice of the craftsmen.

Furthermore, the development of brass design and arrangement was not solely influenced by the diverse skills of the engravers. The engravers were not always the designers and were often dependent on the patterns of others, some of whom were draughtsmen and painters. Finally, the customer exerted a powerful influence which is easily overlooked. Monumental engraving was a business, and the pleasure of the purchaser could not be ignored. The form of brasses can only be appreciated if the control of executors and patrons is understood.

8 · The interest of the purchaser

The manuscript miniatures in the British Museum, depicting the incising of a slab, show in both pictures the widow and presumably her children discussing progress with the Master Craftsman (Figs. 9, 10). They appear to be inspecting the work in the course of execution. The directions of the purchaser were often a controlling factor in the making of a brass, and peculiarities of design may frequently be traced to the personal wishes of the commemorated or his executors. These wishes are found expressed in wills, or agreements actually drawn up with the engraver. The available evidence is revealing, though continuing research will undoubtedly provide a clearer view of the relationship, and disclose much interesting detail of the foibles of particular families and individuals. There were a number of engravers from whom to choose and many purchasers clearly exercised this choice. London and provincial work is found side by side in many churches. Two of the three great Cromwell brasses at Tattershall, Lincs., are of London design but the third, to Lady Joan, is on stylistic evidence a Norwich product. Imported brasses widened the possible selection. Engravers secured good and bad reputations. Thomas Salter specified the 'cunynge marbler' by St. Dunstan's in the West to engrave his brass. In contrast, Edmund Paston wrote in 1489 concerning the tomb of John Paston 'that ye will remember my brotheris ston, so that it myth be mad er I cumm ageyn, and that it be klenly wrowgth. It is told me that the man at Sent Bridis is no klenly portrayer; [the] r for I wold fayn it myth be portrayed by sum odir man, and he to grave it up.'[1] The zeal with which the purchaser took care over the execution, and imposed detailed requirements on the engraver, must have depended on personality, status, the expense of the undertaking and the extent to which brasses were engraved as individual commissions, rather than the routine products of prolific workshops. It is in this last respect that the craft in England differed markedly from that in other European centres. Small-scale memorials for unimportant people were presumably sought for their cheapness rather than their quality.

The stock figure

The engraving of memorial brasses anticipating specific orders, facing the purchaser with a ready prepared article, seems on first consideration an improbable practice. Such preparation required an outlay of capital on the craftsman's part, whereas there is evidence of advances being required for the execution of important contracts, as on page 95. There is nevertheless in England circumstantial and more positive evidence that stock figures were made, especially at the close of the fifteenth and in the early years of the sixteenth centuries.

There are several cases where figures appear distinctly earlier than their inscriptions, and there are no grounds to suspect appropriations. The brass at Faringdon, Berks., of Thomas Faryndon Esq., with wife and daughter, dated 1443, is a striking example, and Richard Grey at Eton College Chapel, Bucks., dated 1521, is another. Lawrence Stone strongly supports the view of Dr. J. P. C. Kent in suspecting such figures to have been made without commissions, and used conveniently at a later date. Stone writes 'Even before this [1460], however, there is evidence to suggest that at least one workshop was turning out standard products in anticipation of customer's orders; in this particular case the orders seem to have been slow in coming in, with the result that some very similar brasses bear dates ranging over twenty-five years.'[2] The evidence is open to other interpretations such as conservatism in design or a specified copy. Stone's suspicion is nevertheless reinforced by the close of the fifteenth century, not only by the small size and standard presentation of figures, but by the terms of the will of John Lorymer, marbler, dated 28 May 1499.[3] The author is particularly indebted to J. A. Goodall, F.S.A., for the transcription of this will, which is of great interest in this context.

> Lorymer requested, 'I will that Henry lorymer my brother shall haue
> of my goodys after my decease to the value of x li. to be delyuered
> vnto hym vnder the Maner Forme and condicion herafter folowing that
> is to sey that iff the said Henry lorymer wele truly and effectually
> Doe his diligence and labour to vtter and make Full sale of suche
> marbylle stonys and laten werke thereto belonging whiche I haue
> within the precinte of the blacke Fryers aforseyd to the vse and
> behooffe of Johan my wyff she being of knowledge to every suche Bargayn
> and the seid Harry to take and haue for his Daily and wekely wages for
> the workmanshipp [sic] of the same Stones and laten wurkes and of euery
> ij stones and wurkes soo to be sold the seid Johan my wyff shall haue
> the hoole mony of the sale of them the wurkmanshipp of them to be
> abatyd and deductyd and euery thirde stone that the said Henry shall
> wurke and putt to sale the same Henry shall haue all the money and
> gaynes cummyng of the same thirde stone and laten wurkes to his owne
> vse Proffett and behooff as in party of paymentt of the said x li.
> sterling. And so consequently to selle ij stones to the vse of the
> seid Johan my wyff and the thirde to the vse and behoof of hym selff
> in the Fourme a forsaid vnto the tyme that he be full contente and
> paid of the seid summe of x li. sterlinges . . .'

The impression created is that John Lorymer at his death left a large quantity of slabs inlaid with latten, which in due course his brother as a marbler was to finish off, to the extent that the latter profited by £10. Henry was to be paid for all his craftsmanship as a matter of course, but the complete monuments were to be divided between him and John's widow on a basis of one to two, until his share was met. It is self evident from the arrangement envisaged that a great deal had been provided by John, as otherwise the £10 could have been achieved by the sale of a few monuments. It seems highly unlikely that John would have hoarded incomplete commissions. In the opinion of both Goodall and the author John Lorymer had made the slabs ready with figures, and even perhaps plain inscription plates. Only the wording, arms, merchants' marks, children, etc., then needed to be added. Such practice would fully explain not only incongruity of design between some figures and their accessories, but the cramped presentation of some inscriptions and inconsistency of abbreviations in their text.

Stock products, which are presumably an English peculiarity in this connection, reflect the lowest level of the purchaser's participation. Such arrangements can have only been effective as the standards of the craft declined, and the remainder of the chapter is concerned with the impact of a positive control.

The evidence of wills

Most English references to this subject have been derived from wills. The detail given where tombs are specified is usually limited. The will of Agnes Wybarne of Ticehurst, Sussex (1502), directed her executors 'to bye a convenient Stone to laye upon my husband John Wybarne's grave and myne'.[4] These vague directions were apparently treated literally, and an existing brass and stone of *c*. 1380 were re-used with very curious effect. Slightly more specific were the directions in 1475 of Thomas Tyrrell of East Horndon, Essex. He wished a brass to be laid to himself and his wife according 'honestly for oure degree'.[5] The surviving part of this brass of modest size but good execution was recently stolen by vandals. The specification is interesting, indicating that the richness of a brass was related to the standing as well as to the means of the commemorated.

Far more substantial are the particulars given by the will of Sir Thomas Stathum of Morley, Derbyshire (1470), whose brass is still in excellent condition (Fig. 72). Thomas apparently based his specifications on the existing brass to John Stathum, Esq., at Morley. 'Corpus meum sepeliendum in the south side of the chauncell in the kirke of Morley at saint Nicholas Auter ende undir the lowe wall, the said Wall to be taken downe and ther upon me leyde a stone of marble with iij ymages of laton oon ymage maade aftir me and th othir ij aftir both my wifis we all knelyng on our kneys with eche on of us a rolle in our handis unto our Lady saint Marye and to saint Christophore over our heedis with iiij scochons of myn armes and both my wifis armes quarterly to gedir and to ware on the said stone vj marcs.'[6] The brass answers this description in most respects. The main difference is that the figures are shown recumbent, and an additional figure of St. Anne balances the upper part of the composition. From this example it seems the will was not obeyed in every detail.

The Stathum will described the form and arrangement of the brass. The will of Thomas Muschamp, 1472, a citizen and mercer of London, left little discretion to the engraver in content or detail. It states:

'I woll that I have a marble stone to be laid upon my body with myn Armes and my Marke. And I woll, that upon the said stone be made with a sware [sic] bordure of laton of iiij unches brode and at ij Corners therof myn Armes and my wyves Armes departed And at the othir ij Corners my saide Marke, with this scripture written uppon the said stone "Miseremini mei miseremini mei saltem vos amici mei quia manus domini tetigita me" With an Image for me an other for my wife and Images for my Children, And over the Image for me a Rolle with this scriptur: Credo quod Redemptor meus vivit. And over the Image of my wife: Credo quod in novissimo die de terra surrectura sum. And vii Images of my vij sonnes to be apon the same stone with a Rolle commyng over their hedes havying this scriptur: Credo quod in carne mea videbo deum salvatorem meum. And vij ymages of my vij doughters to be upon the same stone and a Rolle to be over their hedes of this scriptur. Credo videre bona domini in terra viventium. And under the fete of the Images of me and of my wife aforesaid I woll that their be sett this scriptur: Orate pro animabus Thome Muschamp Civis et Merceri ac nuper vicecomitis Civitatis London, qui objit tale die et tale Anno & Matild' uxoris eius que objit tale die et tali Anno.'[7]

Thomas Muschamp was buried at St. Mary Magdalen, Milk Street, London, and the brass was destroyed, possibly in the Great Fire. There is little difficulty, however, in reconstructing it in its main essentials. The precise statement of the inscriptions is a particularly important feature. The personal quality of certain inscriptions has already been noted by Haines, in particular that at Wheathampstead, Herts., to Hugh Bostock and wife (*c*. 1450), which was probably composed by the son of the deceased, the distinguished Abbot Wheathampstead of St. Albans.[8] The will of John Annsell, merchant taylor of

London (d. 1516), is as detailed as that of Muschamp but adds very precise instructions concerning the representations to be included. He required that above the figures should be placed 'A pictour of the holy Lambe, with a little scriptour under his foote saying the holy Lambe, with a picture of the pellycane saying at his foote in a lytle scripture the goostly burde, saying in a scripture from the mannes heede the ij Johannis pray for the thirde'.[9]

Arms and merchants' marks were objects of particular note. John Annsell required 'the Armes of myn occupacion and the Armes of London'. Robert Fabyan, draper of London (d. 1511), willed, 'I will be sett iv platts graven with iv scochens of the Drapers armes, and at the foot myn own armes, and my merchant Marke.'[10] Specifications concerning the figures themselves, other than the general requirement to be armed or heraldically dressed, are rare. Sir Thomas Ughtred (d. 1398), ordered a stone 'cum duabus ymaginibus patris mei et matris meae de laton, sculptis in armis meis, et in armis de les Burdons'.[11] Sir John de Foxle, whose brass is at Bray, Berks. (Fig. 174), specified that he and his wives should be shown in their appropriate arms.[12] The will of Thomas Salter is unusual in requiring a chalice and rayed wafer to be held in the hands, and the eyes closed as in death.

The evidence of contracts

While wills are a valuable record of the specifications given to engravers, the actual contracts drawn up and signed are of greatest importance. Only one such English contract has been published, though there are several Flemish, German and Silesian examples of outstanding interest. The most important of these contracts have been printed in full as appendices to this chapter. Their salient points require mention. The earliest group of contracts were preserved until 1940 in the Civic Archives of Tournai. These are summarized in Chapter Four of *The Memorials* which is concerned with fourteenth-century Tournai and Flemish brasses. One, however, is a most detailed record, drawn up on 8 September 1301 or 1311, between the executors of Jean du Mur, formerly Archdeacon of Gent, and an engraver Jacques Couvès of Tournai. According to its clauses the engraver is required to provide a stone and brass as good as that commemorating Henri of Gent, a former Archdeacon and Canon of Tournai, and to follow specifications of which he has a copy. The size and fixture of the brass plates is prescribed in detail. The figure of the Archdeacon is to be executed in a manner pleasing to the executors with the face, hands and alb all inlaid in fine alabaster. The form of the canopy with its tabernacle and masonry is specified, and is required to comply in all respects with a pattern in the hands of the executors. The background of the plate is to be filled with a decoration of the executor's choice. The border inscription is to be similar to that of Henri of Gent and to be engraved with verses provided by the executors. The preparation of the stone, brass and colour inlays is to be of excellent quality. The agreed price of 150 Tournai livres is stated.

This contract is of particular interest in prescribing the engraving of the most elaborate type of Flemish brass, enriched with colour and the inlay of alabaster details. The features most notable in the context of this chapter are the detail of the specifications, the items to be provided by the executors in the form of patterns and verses to be selected by them, and above all the direction to base the design and standard of the memorial on one already existing in Tournai. Similar references to local monuments are included in the other Tournai contracts. A comparable dependence on the executors is revealed in a Gent contract of 1418 between Simon de Formelis and Jan van Meyere *tombier*.[13] Van Meyere was required to engrave a brass ten feet long and five feet broad for Madam de Lovendeghem, to be placed in St. Michiel, Gent, the brass costing fourteen livres. A pattern of the figure and heraldry would be provided and the monument as a whole was to be similar to that of Jan Daens in front of the altar of St. Nicholas in the same church. Another contract of Jan van Meyere dated 1423 required him to make a brass to the Van de Moure family for the church of St. John at Gent, in the fashion of the tombs of Willem van Ravenscot, Bloc van Steelant and Daniel van den Holle.[14]

Inter-relationship of brasses created by executors' specifications is further illustrated by two contracts from Gent and the Silesian contract of 1462 between Jodok Tawchen *lapicida* and the delegates of the Archbishop of Gnieznó. The earlier of the Gent contracts is of 1442, and required the *tombier* Hughe or Hugo Goethals to make a brass to Sir Wouter van Mullem to be placed in St. Jacques at Gent.[15] The effigies of a knight and wife were to comply with a pattern provided, and nine medallions were to be included as on the brass of Simon Clocman. The other contract of 1482 was made with the Gent *tombier*, Jan Dedelinc, and concerned the engraving of a brass to the Borluut family.[16] It was to be like that of Simon Clocman at St. Nicholas, 'save that the persons, except for the child placed between them, should be represented in death robes'. The Clocman brass, apparently a specially good one, is quoted as a model for two entirely independent undertakings.

The Tawchen contract is another document of great interest and is reproduced in full (p. 96). The construction and design of a brass to Archbishop Jan of Sprowa is defined in detail. The metallic inlays of the pallium and arms are described and particular attention is given to the correct joining of plates, so that the overall effect of one plate might be achieved. The price of 172 Hungarian florins is stated at the end. The models on which the brass is to be designed are the brasses of Archbishops Wojciech (Adalbert) Jastrzambiecz and Mikołaj Traba in Gnienzó Cathedral, well known to Tawchen who engraved the latter. The importance of this contract is greatly enhanced by the existence of earlier documentary references to the Jastrzambiecz and Traba brasses. In the Acts of the Chapter of Gnieznó for 1426 is recorded a meeting in which Archbishop Jastrzambiecz ordered a brass to be engraved for his deceased predecessor Mikołaj Traba who died in 1422. The work was to be given to Tawchen. Jastrzambiecz incidentally referred to the preparation of his own memorial which he stated had been made ready at Bruges at the cost of four hundred guilders. He described it as a monument modelled on that of Jan Zuchywilk, a prelate who died in 1382 and was commemorated at Gnieznó. The actual record reads 'Lapis iam paratur in Brugis . . . qui lapis ornatus aurichalco ad instar lapidis Johannis Arepi Zuchywilk'. It is known that Zuchywilk's brass was also of Flemish origin, and so inspired the distant and expensive order of Jastrzambiecz.[17] These records take a stage further the process proved at Gent. The copies are not based on one original as with the Clocman brass, but the first copy is used as a model for a second. It will be shown that this extended form of derivation produced interesting artistic consequences, for which the customer was predominantly responsible. Imitation was furthermore a factor common to the production of monuments throughout northern Europe. To the abundant Continental examples may be added the directions of the will of John Smyth (1500). Smyth willed to be buried in the Greyfriars at Coventry and that his memorial be made 'lyke to a tombe in the Greyfreres of London made and sett ther for William Maryner and his wiff and lyke scripture and ymagery as ther is in everything'.[18]

The record of an agreement made in 1457 with the celebrated Tournai engraver Alard Génois by Jean Robert, Abbot of St. Aubert at Cambrai, concerned the making of a brass for the Abbot's father and mother. This agreement is included as Appendix III to this chapter. The design was to show the family kneeling with a crucifix, the Blessed Virgin and St. John as a centre-piece. The wording of this inscription was provided, together with invocatory scrolls of the figures. It was stipulated that the brass should be similar to that of Jacques le Fuselier, and designed 'en le forme et manière que je l'enay baillet un patron en papier'. It is likely that this paper was a cartoon of the brass drawn by an independent draughtsman.

Another brass of invocatory type with kneeling figures and representations of the Blessed Virgin, St. John the Baptist and St. Anne is described in an agreement of 1515 between John Willughby, Esq., and John Hippis, marbler, included as Appendix IV to this chapter. This English agreement is in many respects comparable to that of Génois. The heraldic brasses and canopied high tombs are fully described, with the terms of payment and completion included. It is specified that the tomb should be made 'of the same stonne that my Lord Phitzhugh is of' and that 'this tomb to be made after a patron drawne in parchment'. However this does not necessarily infer that an exact drawing was submitted. The style of contemporary patrons may be appreciated from a surviving example of *c.* 1485, submitted to a glazier for or by Thomas Froxmere and wife (Fig. 73).[19] This was intended for a window depicting kneeling donors, but its subject, crude draughtsmanship and inserted written requirements relating to arms, are probably typical of directions given at this time to English engravers. The emphasis was on overall arrangement and correct representation of details important to the family.

Equally precise in description is another early sixteenth century contract drawn up for the Sandys family with a *tombier* of Artois, to prepare two high tombs to be laid at Basingstoke, Hants., the tops to be inlaid with crosses of white or yellow copper.[20]

Further and more intimate proof of the purchaser's influence comes from late sixteenth- and seventeenth-century documents. The commission given to Matthias Benning of Lübeck by the executors of the Lutheran Bishop Johann Tydeman in 1562 is a valuable document, especially as the brass itself survives and can be compared with the directions.[21] This is included as Appendix V to this chapter. More surprising are two lots of English correspondence, the first concerning the Gage tombs at West Firle, Sussex, and the second concerning the Wynn brasses at Llanrwst, Denbigh.

The evidence of correspondence

The correspondence between John Gage, Esq., of Firle and the Southwark sculptor and engraver Gerard Johnson is a most fortunate survival. Among the muniments of Viscount Gage are two cartoons of brasses drawn up by Johnson, probably between 1585 and 1590, and sent for approval to John Gage. One shows the high tomb and brasses intended for the commemoration of Sir Edward Gage (Fig. 12), the other shows the brasses for John Gage, Esq., and his two wives (Fig. 74). Around the margins of this second cartoon are notes from both Johnson and Gage. Johnson wrote 'This Stone to be of Marble enlayed, the pictures and Stouchions [sic] wth the epitaphe to be of Brasse'. Gage was quite critical of the design, especially of the representation of his wives. He commented 'Where you have sett owte my two wyves wth longe heare wyered, my request is that they shall be bothe attired wth frenche hoodes and cornetts som*m*e heare shewed under the cornetts, the pattren of the cornett I have sent y*o*u by this berer in a boxe bowed & dressed as it should stand uppon their heades. their gownes to be made lose and not girded wth no girdle w^thowt vardingales and close before and to be so longe as may cover some *p*arte of their feete'.[22] Gage made further stipulations about the size of the stone, to which Johnson replied. The brasses at Firle are in excellent condition and prove that Johnson altered his proposals to comply with his patron's wishes (Fig. 75). The design of Sir Edward's tomb was also modified. The full face figures of the cartoon are shown in half profile in the actual brass. The wife's wired hair is replaced by a French hood.

The Johnson correspondence is famous. The letters concerning Vaughan have apparently passed with little serious notice, though preserved among the Wynn papers in the National Library of Wales. Three of the papers refer to the engraving of a copper plate and a brass by the book engraver, Robert Vaughan.[23] The first was written by Vaughan on 22 June 1650, to Sir Owen Wynne at Gwydir complaining that two copper plates on which he had begun to engrave the pedigree of the Wynn family had been embezzled together with the drafts. He asks for further heraldic information, and points out that he is at his own fancy for the faces until he comes to Sir John Wynn, as there are no true pictures extant of the earlier members of the family. On 5 September 1661, Henry Bodvel wrote from London on Vaughan's behalf to Maurice Wynn, Receiver General for North Wales. His letter concerns the engraving of the brass to Sir Owen Wynne, which is one of the choicest at Llanrwst (Fig. 76); and asks to know 'with all ye speed you can, whither you will have Sr Owen engraven'd with a face new trym'd as Sr Richard is; or with a bushie beard. as I remember hee had when I was both times in his Countie for hee allwayes wore it Careless; They have begunn uppon the face & head but the beard I have Commanded them not to touch till they heare from mee, ffor if it bee made according to Sr Richards face, it will not bee like Sr Owens' (Fig. 77). This extract from the engraver's communication is most revealing. Vaughan was clearly troubled whether to attempt a recognizable likeness, which his fine technique allowed, or produce a fashionable representation palpably unlike the deceased. The brass shows Sir Owen in a neat 'imperial'-type beard (Fig. 76) from which it may be presumed that the second alternative was preferred. The third letter, also from Henry Bodvel to Maurice Wynn, records among other matters that 'I have sent downe Sr Owen Wynnes effigis by one Will' Harrison Carrier, . . . the direction is, it should bee left wth Mr Ralph Burroughs. The engravening cost [£]5. &[£]2 16s the brasse came. This enclosed letter is from Mr. Vaughan.' Unfortunately the enclosure is lost with the engraver's final observations. This correspondence is particularly valuable as a supplement to that of John Gage, as Gage's interest lay in the dress depicted and questions of portraiture did not arise.

These glimpses of the relationships between customer and craftsman over a period of three hundred and fifty years show conclusively the control exercised at times by the former. Often the engraver was required to comply with detailed specifications, and on occasion his drafts were subjected to considerable alteration. Most important is the evidence that patterns drawn up independently were submitted for the guidance of the engraver, and other earlier memorials were named as models for the work in hand. The engraver's discretion in the design of a brass could be highly qualified.

APPENDIX I

An agreement of 1311 between the executors of Jean du Mur, Archdeacon of Gent, and Jacques Couvès of Tournai for making a monumental brass of the deceased archdeacon

Know all men by these presents that Jacques Couvès agreed with the executors of Master Jean du Mur, formerly archdeacon of Gand [Gent], whom God absolve, to deliver well and properly made, and to lay over the body of the aforesaid master Jean, a memorial plate worked in the following manner: Firstly the stone must be as long and as wide, and be as good and in every way as suitable as the stone which lies over master Henri de Gand, formerly canon and archdeacon of Tournai; and on this stone there must lie, well and properly set, a sheet of latten plate of the same size as the stone shall be, [but] rebated eight inches on each side for the border; and this sheet must be of fine pure latten, as good and suitable in every way as is the latten on the tomb of the former master Henri of Gand, it being understood that there must be as much space [on it] as the executors require for the patterns, of which the said Jacques has the sample; and this sheet of latten must consist of three pieces soldered together, the three [pieces] well and properly soldered with white solder, and at each joint of the three pieces of latten attached to the stone by four rivets, and laid straight and pierced and rivetted from above well and neatly. And the three pieces of latten joined and attached together in the aforesaid manner must be well and sufficiently set upon the stone with good cement; and that on this latten there must be an image of the [Arch]deacon, portrayed by whatever hand shall please the executors, and the adornment of the vestments [shall be] suitable in the view of the executors and the face and hands of the [Arch]deacon and the white of the alb must be in good alabaster as shall appear suitable to the executors; and between the border and the image of the [Arch]deacon there must be a column on each side, richly ornamented in true representation of masonry, bordered below and above with low reliefs and mouldings as they may appear on the parchment which the executors have, and above these two columns there shall be a fine tabernacle as good in all respects as those tabernacles on parchment which the executors have. And let it be known that upon the latten between the image of the [Arch]deacon and the columns, each side must be decorated in such a way as shall satisfy the executors. And upon the border of eight inches of stone remaining round the latten, there must be a border of bands of latten comparable to that which shall be chosen of the two which are on the former master Henri de Gand['s tomb], and in this border there must be verses such as the executors shall provide, and the latten in this border must be of the same standard in every way as that of the image. Also let it be known that the cutting of the said stone, and of the latten when it shall be engraved, must be well and cleanly engraved without a mistake, and all the colours thereon must be fine, hard and made of good oil and resin; and for the bedding of the latten in the stone and the application of the colours to the latten, the consent of the executors must be sought.

All the above said work, well and satisfactorily [completed], Jacques Couvès has engaged to make and deliver at his cost and expense at his peril, over the body of Master Jean du Mur formerly canon of Tournai and archdeacon of Gand, for one hundred and fifty Tournai livres, of which he acknowledges himself paid one hundred livres by the executors, who have advanced it to him in order that he should work well and make haste in the manner aforesaid; it being understood that these works must be made before the month of May next which we are awaiting and thereupon he must be paid fifty Tournai livres. And if it should happen, which heaven forbid, that Jacques make less than is set down, or he make it worse than the contents herein written, the executors shall accept nothing; but if he makes more or better than may be set down, he shall be recompensed according to the judgement of craftsmen, provided he made it with the consent of the executors or of one of them, or whoever they shall have put in charge to supervise the work.

And if Jacques Couvès should default in the aforesaid covenants, and the executors should be put to cost or expense or suffer wrong, or any one of them, he shall bring what is written in order to render account where the truth lies between him and Jacques Couvès; he shall bring what is written without changing the aforesaid covenants on pain of punishment to him and all the goods and chattels which he has and shall have. To these covenants and estimates was Jean de Haluin sworn witness and Jakemes de Douai was another man; and these were the parties [to the agreement] and this was written in the year of the incarnation 1311, the day of our lady, in September.

Translated from the old French, as recorded from the parchment (destroyed 1940) by Adolphe Hocquet in *Le Rayonnement de l'Art Tournaisien*, Tournai, 1924, pp. 25–7. It should be noted that Professor Léo Verriest gives a different reading of the date, namely 1301; see *Annales du Cercle Archéologique de Mons*, 1939, pp. 182–3.

APPENDIX II

A recorded agreement of 1462 between Jodok Tawchen of Wrocław and the Chapter of Gnieznó for making a monumental brass to Archbishop Jan Sprowa

We, the counsellors of the state of Wratislava by the contents of these documents have declared to everyone, that in our presence and during our session, the said craftsman Jodok Tawchen, marbler [*lapidica*], our fellow citizen, has declared and promised under this agreement and contract to make a certain stone or funeral epitaph for the most Reverend Father in Christ and Lord, Lord Jan, Archbishop of Gnieznó, our noble Lord. In the making of which to the Reverend Archbishop, if he should incur our dissatisfaction, or if any defect should arise, he has himself promised to change and perfect it in accordance with the form detailed below.

First he has promised that he will freshly cast a figure whole and entire from the mitre to the base in good, whole, and clean plates and to cast the plates of a sufficient and lasting thickness, neither jutting out or projecting more than any other plates. And he will draw and engrave an image on these same plates, and he will delineate the face well, with short hair plainly portrayed. The hands and feet are to be like the figure depicted on the stone of the Lord Archbishop Mikołaj, lying in the church at Gnieznó and seen by him, and the cross and pallium are to be the same size as those of the tomb of the Lord Jastrzam-biecz in the same church. And he will join stone to stone so that the join is not apparent, whether he will do this strongly by iron, pitch or lead, so that it will rather appear one stone which is whole.*

He will also ensure that the metal or plate of the figure, together with the two parts of the arms adjoining the image should be made freshly and correct, and without any noticeable division, just as on the tomb of Lord Jastrzambiecz. He will also integrate all the pieces and plates, and cast the metals perfectly, so as to last. He will also make the pallium in a cast of silver mixed with copper. He will also make the coats of arms of the said Reverend Archbishop thicker and more beautiful, just like the arms shown to him in the said places, and those under the feet are to be of a greater size and quality made from a durable metal viz., silver mixed with copper, and he will cast it so that it adheres strongly to the stone. And he promises to do this work as here set out, together with fixing the tomb in its place, by the next feast day of John the Baptist.

There were present with us the venerable father Skoda, Canon of the honourable Lord Jan of the Church of Wratislava, and Lord Zebisch, Chaplain of the aforesaid Reverend Father and Lord, Lord Jan the Archbishop; and in the name of the same Reverend Father, they have promised Master Jodok that they will abide by this principal agreement, and, in accordance with the pleasure of their Reverend Father, to grant him a bonus. And Master Jodok has declared that as a payment and reward for fulfilling this principal contract and agreement, he will receive 172 Hungarian florins.

Translated from the Latin as recorded in *De vita atque operibus magistri Jodici Tauchen lapicidae wratislaviensis seculo XV*[ts] *florentis*, by Alwin Schulz, Breslau, 1864.

---

* It is not clear whether this item refers to stones forming the indent for the brass, or to the plates constituting the brass. The term *lapis*, here translated as stone, is often used in the sense of memorial generally and may refer to the plates. The sentence is meaningful in either context. It is, however, note-worthy that *tabula* is used elsewhere in the contract for describing the plate.

APPENDIX III

Record of an agreement made in 1457 between Jean Robert, Abbot of Cambrai and the Tournai marbler, Alard Génois

On Thursday 25th August [14]57, I negotiated with Alardin Génois, craftsman in marble and latten memorials of Tournai, in the great church of this place, the Prior being present, to make a tablet of copper or latten, inset in a tablet of marble, in the very same manner as the tablet of Jacques le Fuselier is; and to make it in such form and manner as I have provided on a pattern on paper. The tablet is to be eleven feet long or wide, and eleven and a half feet high. Within there must be engraved a crucifix, Our Lady, Saint John, my father and mother kneeling, and fourteen brothers and sisters; and written below that which is ordered; and a scroll issuing from the hands of my father and mother, whom God absolve, on which shall be written 'Respice, Domine, in servos tuos et in opera tua et dirige filios eorum'. And he is to enamel it well and richly, and deliver it to our house in Valenciennes at about the beginning of next March, and to have for it seven gold crowns.

Translated from the old French as cited by Grange and Cloquet (p. 321, *Études sur l'Art à Tournai et sur les Anciens Artistes de cette ville*, Tournai, 1887) who themselves recorded from V. Dinaux, *Archives du Nord de la France et du Midi de la Belgique*, p. 319). The enormous size of the memorial stipulated is inconsistent with this type of composition, and while the translation of the transcript is correct the meaning is questionable. The measurements may apply to the stone setting of the plate.

APPENDIX IV

An agreement made in 1515 between John Willughby, Esq., and John Hippis, marbler of Lincoln, for a tomb and brasses

This indenture made at Wollaton' the sixt day of aprill' in the vj yere of the reigne of our soverayne lord kyng Henry the viij[th] wyttnessith and recordith that John' Willughby Esquiar on the on party hath cownaunde and Bargaynyd with John' Hippis of Lyncoln' marbolar on the othir party That the said John' Hippis shall make or cause to be made a Tumbe of the same stonne that my lorde Phitzhugh is of of vj fott in lenght and vij foote hight of the grounde to the upart part therof and in the backe stonne undur the vavyt to be made an ymage of a gentilman in his Coyt armye of copar and gylt and an othir ymage of a gentilwoman in hur mantill and Cyrcuyt of copar and gilt with an ymage of our lady over ther heddis with othir ymagis on of saynt John' Baptiste and a othir of saynte Anne ethir of them a peticioner And over yche of them a Scucion over ther heedis of ther armys with a scripture undur ther fett and by the sidis iiij Scucions of ther armys of Copar and gylt And this Tumb to be made aftur a patron drawne in parchment by the fest of saynt Anne or within xiiij dais aftur And the said John' Hippis shall bryng the said Tumbe and set it up in the church of Wollaton' at his propur cost and charge upon the payne and forfetting of x li And the said John' Willughby shall pay or cause to be paid unto the said John' Hippis for makyng therof vli vjs viijd wherof the said John' Hippis hath reycayvid at the makyng of thes presentes xxvjs viijd in party of payment therof And the residue to be paid at makyng and fynnyshyng of the said Tumbe undur the payne and fforfettyng of x li And the said John' shall bryng a stonne to lye from the wall to the stepp

7

and in breid from the awtur to the tumbe In wytnesse wherof ethir party Interchin' ablie hath set to ther sealis Yevyn the day yeer and Place above specified

per me John' Hypps

Published in the Thoroton Society Record Series, 1962, pp. 1–2.

APPENDIX V

Text of a commission of 1562 for the casting and engraving of a brass to Bishop Johann Tydeman of Lübeck given to Matthias Benning of Lübeck

On 8 March 1562, the executors of the Bishop commissioned 'from the worthy Matthias Benning, cannon-founder to the Council of Lübeck and in residence on the Lastaien, a memorial brass for the tomb in the Cathedral of the esteemed Bishop Johann of honourable memory, the said brass to measure eleven feet long by nine feet wide and to be cast and shaped in the said pure metal without any fissures, blemishes or pits whatsoever, as cleanly as it can and may conceivably be done in view of the nature and material of the work, to be paid at the rate of 140 Lübeck marks for every pound when the brass is cast and complete. In addition the aforementioned Matthias shall for the same money be pledged and in duty bound to engrave on the brass a bishop's portrait with mitre, staff and priestly vestments, together with the four Evangelists at the corners of the brass plate, the shield or coat of arms of His Grace, and the inscription appointed on the instructions of a patron also to be depicted, the which the executors do likewise offer to have engraved at their expense with his advice and foreknowledge. When the memorial brass has been decently prepared, polished and worked, the same Matthias shall at his own risk and expense and to the satisfaction and convenience of the executors deliver it whole and undamaged to the Cathedral at Lübeck and install it ready and complete on the tomb of the aforementioned Lord Johann.

Translated from the German as recorded in *Bau und Kunstdenkmäler der Freien und Hansastadt Lübeck*, J. Baltzer and F. Bruns, Lübeck, 1920, Band III, p. 260.

9 · The sources of designs

It will be apparent from the evidence given in previous chapters that the design of a brass could originate from several different types of source. The engraver might make the pattern according to his own precedents. Alternatively he might copy other available material of his own choice, copy some memorial or detail specified by the purchaser, or reproduce in entirety a pattern drawn up by an independent draughtsman. It is fortunate that the different origins of design, indicated by documentary sources, are illustrated in the brasses engraved and cast by the Vischers.

Three great quadrangular brasses from Poznań, Poland, all looted during the Nazi occupation and now presumed to have been destroyed, were undoubtedly products of Peter Vischer the Elder's foundry. The brass of Feliks Padniewski (1488), formerly in the Dominican church, was a typical early work of the master in elaborate late gothic style. The rendering of the knight's face and hands, the arrangement of drapery, canopy and curtain background were only consistent with designs of this workshop. Furthermore, details of the decoration, such as the grotesque gargoyles upon the canopy shafts, were apparent copies from Peter Vischer's 1488 draft of the shrine of St. Sebald in Nürnberg. Similarly the very rich plate of Bishop Uriel of Górka at the cathedral was a highly important Vischer brass, though derivative and slightly archaic in arrangement. Whereas the canopy shafts were based on an earlier Flemish model, certain of the apostles within them were copies from the St. Sebald shrine design (Figs. 78, 79). The third brass representing Uriel's father Łukasz Palatine of Poznań had a different character (Fig. 80). The splendid armed figure in recessed relief, and the embroidered curtain background, were in typical Vischer style of that period. In contrast the canopy work with its tabernacles and apostle-filled shafts was in characteristic Flemish style of the fourteenth century. Here again certain of the apostles were derived from the St. Sebald shrine draft. This archaic impression was further enhanced by a border fillet decorated with the flowers and stops of the fourteenth century Flemish convention. The model of this design was undoubtedly the Flemish rectangular brass of Bishop Andrzej Bninski which was also in the Poznań cathedral (Fig. 81). The Bishop's brass was itself a late fifteenth century copy of some earlier monument. The similarity of the canopy work in all details between the designs of Andrzej and Łukasz is so exact that Creeny believed both monuments to be the work of one engraver. The copy must have been specified, most probably by Bishop Uriel, who is believed to have ordered his father's brass as well as his own.[1]

Even his great reputation did not save Peter the Elder entirely from the prepared patterns of his contemporaries. While he cast the low-relief bronze figure of Georg II, Bishop of Bamberg, the drawing for it was prepared at Bamberg by the provincial German artist, Wolfgang Katzheimer. In the Bamberg Chapter accounts for the year 1505 is recorded '*Drei Pfund Meister Wolfgang Mahler von einer Visierung zum Güss über Bischof Georges Leichenstein*'.[2]

Peter Vischer the Elder was an unwilling user of other draughtsmen's ideas. His son Hermann sought outside inspiration and copied Dürer extensively. The representations of Saints Albert and Stanislaus depicted on the brass of Cardinal Fryderyk at Kraków Cathedral are a very close copy of two figures from the Dürer woodcut of Saints Nicholas,

Ulrich and Erasmus. St. Stanislaus is an almost exact reproduction of Erasmus, only a windlass being omitted and some small details altered (Figs. 82, 83, 84). It is interesting to note that the figure of Abbot David von Winkelsheim (1526), at Radolfzell near Konstanz, Germany,[3] is an adapted copy of the St. Ulrich figure, though possibly engraved by a South German craftsman. The Madonna and Christchild cast in low relief at the end of the Cardinal's tomb is also a copy of a Dürer design of 1510. Several of the cast military figures ascribed to Hermann, such as Piotr Kmitas at St. Mary's, Kraków and Count Hermann VIII at Römhild, East Germany, were strongly influenced by Dürer designs as most fully expressed in the St. George and St. Eustace panels of the Paumgärtner altarpiece in Münich.

These examples from the great Nürnberg workshop can be matched by other similar English, Flemish and German designs. The main limitation on the comparisons has been the small measure of research on the material available.

Workshop designs

It is evident that the majority of English and Flemish brasses were designed within the workshops of the engravers by the masters themselves or by draughtsmen on whom they depended. The extremely large number of brasses made, the consistency of style within recognizable groups, and the gradual adaptation of patterns, make the former existence of workshop designs a certainty. Only the Johnson cartoons and Wilhem Loeman's drawing have so far been traced as proof of the engraver's preparations, but there is every reason to expect from a comparable mediaeval practice that patterns were handed on from one master to his successor. The York glass painter, Robert Petty, inherited all his 'toels and scroes' from his elder brother, and Thomas Shirley bequeathed to his son 'all my drawings, appliances and necessaries . . . belonging in any way to my craft'.[4]

Dr. J. P. C. Kent's important study on English military brasses from *c.* 1360 to 1490, traces in a convincing manner the development and divergence of certain designs.[5] The slight, gradual but important adaptation of patterns is most easily traced in the fifteenth century within a series he classifies as 'B'. The transition of the armed representation from a figure at Ulcombe, Kent (1442) (Fig. 85), through others at Etchingham, Sussex (1444), Little Waltham, Essex (1447), Marston Mortaine, Beds. (1451) (Fig. 88) and Barham, Kent (*c.* 1456) (Fig. 86) to Hildersham, Cambs. (1466) (Fig. 87) is very striking, and supported by a substantial number of examples. Similarly the kneeling armed figure of John Ruggewyn (1412), Standon, Herts. (Fig. 90), and John Stathum, Esq. (1454), Morley, Derbyshire (Fig. 89), afford a revealing comparison. The poses, arrangement and other subsidiary detail of both figures are identical, while their armour reflects considerable change. Certain groups of Flemish brasses, especially those of the fourteenth century, exhibit a similar relationship, though detailed comparisons are made difficult both by the inadequate number of examples and the complexity of the compositions. There seems no reason to dispute Dr. Kent's general analysis. While his study was restricted to military figures the development of particular series can be traced covering civilian and ecclesiastical representations as well. It can hardly be doubted that the designer of Paul Dayrell (1491), Lillingstone Dayrell, Bucks. (Fig. 92), also drew the pattern of the civilian Nicholas Deen (d. 1479), Barrowby, Lincs. (Fig. 91). Similarly, Sir John de Wyngefeld (1389), Letheringham, Suffolk; a civilian and wife (*c.* 1390), now at the Archaeological Museum, Northampton; and the priest John de Swynstede (1395), Edlesborough, Bucks., were clearly drawn by one or closely associated artists. Consistency, numbers, and a gradual change indicate that the creation and modification of these patterns was carried on within or in close connection with the workshops. Their evolution is the key to a systematic typology and dating of brasses. Identified series in Britain are indicated on the illustration captions, summarized in the appendix to this chapter, and discussed in more detail in *The Memorials*.

Whether more can be soundly deduced from the information available is controversial. Dr. Kent argues that development of distinct series of brasses reflected the existence of 'several unconnected firms. Each had its own tradition of design, and its effigies developed along lines independent of those of its competitors.' This interpretation of the situation is attractive. It nevertheless infers an exclusive possession of designs and an independence of outside influence that would not be inferred from documentary evidence.

The term 'firm' requires precise definition, as its usual association with closely integrated organization may well be inappropriate. The exclusive character of designs can prove deceptive when representation was influenced by a great variety of conventions, pattern makers were not necessarily full-time employees, and the execution of a brass required technical competence without demanding individual treatment. It is significant that Gough considered the great fourteenth century Flemish brasses to have been the work of one artist, a 'Cellini of the fourteenth century'. Macklin attributed them to two workshops, as their designs exhibited the influence of two master minds. The irrefutable evidence of contracts from Tournai indicates that a considerable number of marblers were involved in this craft, who were able to contract as individuals though combining on occasions to undertake some particular task. Dr. Kent rejects the 'London school' as suggested by Druitt, and proposes a series of firms. The author supports this interpretation but is of the opinion that the situation was even more complex. There were evidently a fair number of craftsmen in London and the great Flemish centres who were sufficiently skilled to engrave brasses. It would seem, however, that a few masters obtained a specially high reputation in this particular work, which was maintained by their family successors. It is suggested that these leading engravers established the patterns which were followed as required by other craft members. The integrity of certain London workshops is beyond serious doubt, especially that which produced the series of 'Fermour' figures of Queen Mary's reign (Fig. 213). This particular series is distinguished, not only by consistency of design but also by excellence of execution. Furthermore, an increasing number of examples are being found to have been re-engraved on the reverse of the same earlier brasses. In contrast, earlier series connected with these show marked variation of quality even though figure designs are comparable. Page-Phillips has shown that different types of script occur with similar figure patterns, and proposes that the script rather than the figure itself reveals the work of a particular craftsman.[6] It is appropriate to regard all this related work as produced by a 'workshop', provided that the term is understood to embrace not only a master craftsman with his assistants and apprentices, but possibly other associated though independent businesses, following the same range of designs. The London workshops engaged in brass engraving appear to have included the private shops of important masters such as John Essex and Henry Yevele, and small family businesses where wives such as Joan Lorymer, had 'knowledge to every suche Bargayn', (see p. 89). Such businesses would not necessarily have developed their own patterns, especially when cited evidence indicates that goldsmiths occasionally engraved brasses, using externally prepared designs. The brass of Thomas Hevenyngham (Fig. 227) is distinguished for its gilding, execution and thinness of plate; its design belongs to an established Norwich series. Under such circumstances the connection between similar plates may not always be as close as Dr. Kent suggests.

Exceptional examples challenge the exclusive nature of designs. Four early fifteenth century military brasses in Lincolnshire, of which that at Spilsby (*c.* 1405) is the most outstanding,[7] are classified by Kent as of a London series 'C'. Their classification is logical on the basis of pattern. Yet the wife of the Spilsby figure is quite unlike any London figure, having peculiarities which associate her most strongly with other north-eastern provincial brasses. The stone matrix itself appears to be an imported stone, and certainly not Purbeck. There is much reason to suspect a London model was being adapted by engravers in York or Lincoln.[8] By the close of the fifteenth century brasses in the Stamford area are even more confusing, and it is difficult to avoid the conclusion that perceptive imitators were working in the town. It is possible that some London copies may be exposed by a detailed analysis of inscription lettering.

How far design is a conclusive identification of a workshop is a difficult problem which may ultimately be resolved by documentary proof. Dr. Kent's main conclusions concerning the multiplicity of workshops and the development of patterns appear most adequately substantiated. The compactness and exclusiveness of his firms give cause for qualification.

Imitation of earlier patterns

Patterns in current use were set aside by the requirements of the deceased or his executors. The use of ancient and often foreign models may be traced from many sources. Two examples from the Vischer workshop have been described. The brass of Archbishop Jakub Szienienski (1480), Gniezn ó, Poland, is a particularly complex monument of this type (Fig. 93). The origin of the brass is baffling on account of its inconsistencies. The only detailed analysis made by a Polish scholar reached no definite conclusion.[9] In the author's view this brass was made in Wrocław. The design is executed in a grandiose manner with a lack of concern for exact detail which is characteristic of Silesian plates. The extensive use of recessed relief is frequently found in Wrocław work. Furthermore, the chapter of Gniezn ó established a connection with the Wrocław marbler Tawchen for the representation of archbishops. Nevertheless the canopy work and flowered background is an elaborate if clumsy copy of a fourteenth century Flemish model. The figure is even more peculiar. The pose is twisted and the proportions of the body distorted. The great shield below the feet is a German rather than Polish or Flemish feature. The documentary record of Archbishop Sprowa's brass fortunately shows that memorial to have been a Silesian copy of a fifteenth-century Flemish copy of a fourteenth century Flemish original. The same may be concluded of Archbishop Jakub's grand but curious brass.[10]

The secondary memorial of Cardinal Nicholas de Cusa (engr. 1488), at the Hospital of St. Nicholas, Kues, West Germany (Fig. 94), is based on the pattern of the Cardinal's incised slab at St. Peter-ad-Vincula, Roma. The Cardinal's heart was buried in the hospital founded by him in his birthplace. The slab at Rome is a dignified and graceful design, undoubtedly the work of Italian craftsmen (Fig. 95). The brass at Kues is almost certainly of Rhenish work. Though copying the Italian pattern in its essentials the German engraver unfortunately coarsened the Cardinal's features and created a heavy and unbalanced design. The brass was made on the initiative of a Dean of Aachen, who presumably obtained the original pattern from Rome.[11]

The Lübeck engravers imitated Flemish masterpieces available for their study. The graceless brass of Bishop Bertram Cremen (d. 1377) in Lübeck Cathedral contains detail of Flemish derivation. More notable is the lovely memorial of Johann Luneborch (*c.* 1470), at the Katherinenkirche (Fig. 96). Much of the detail of the brass has been worked in the Flemish manner, though the bold letters of the border inscription are typically German. Many fourteenth century Flemish motifs are combined in the background (Fig. 199), and the Tree of Jesse border framing the composition is a copy of this design on the Flemish Clingenberg brass (1356), formerly at the Petrikirche (Fig. 97).

The retention of fourteenth century motifs and conventions by the Flemish engravers themselves is amply illustrated. The great quadrangular plates of St. Henry of Finland at Nousisainen and Bishop Andrzej, formerly at Poznań, are excellent examples. In neither case were the fifteenth century conventions allowed to influence the design except in minor decorative detail. The large and over-elaborate figure of Johann Rode (1477), Bremen Cathedral, is probably another such copy, though the excellence of the Lune-borch imitation raises slight doubts. Jacob Bave and wife (1464), St. Jacques, Bruges, is a particularly valuable case as the composition includes two shrouded figures under canopies of fourteenth century type with saints and prophets copied from early patterns. Similar features are revealed in the Gaillard drawing of Nicolaus Lancbaerd, priest (1471), formerly at St. Walburge, Bruges. A number of palimpsest fragments of Flemish origin, though now in England, were cut from similar memorials. These include portions of ecclesiastical figures at Bayford, Herts.; Marsworth, Bucks.; Paston, Norfolk; and Up-minster, Essex. The brass of Branca de Vilhana (*c.* 1490), Evora, Portugal, exhibits a canopy of adapted fourteenth century style, though the lady herself, the background and subsidiary figures are portrayed in a manner contemporary with the brass.

A few English brasses clearly reflect the imitation of earlier patterns. There are others which appear to have been inspired by earlier memorials, though the exact connection cannot be established. The Garneys brasses at Kenton and Ringsfield, Suffolk, are an interesting pair. John Garneys, Esq. and family (1524), at Kenton (Fig. 98), was closely copied in the early seventeenth century for Nicholas Garneys and family (Fig. 99). The later work is very shallow in its engraving, but is a careful reproduction. The most signifi-cant changes are the substitution of an achievement of arms for a crucifix above the figures, and the addition of a moustache to the knight. The curious brass of Peter Rede (1568), St. Peter Mancroft, Norwich, and Anthony Darcy, Esq. (1540), Tolleshunt Darcy, Essex, were both copied from fifteenth century models. The first is a perceptive imitation of an East Anglian provincial knight in a sallet of *c.* 1470 (Fig. 100). There is an indent of just such a figure on the floor of the south ambulatory of Norwich Cathedral, similar in outline and size except for an animal at the feet. The Tolleshunt Darcy brass is quite possibly an imitation of John de Boys (*c.* 1420) in the same church. The armour represented is a curious mixture of fifteenth and sixteenth century styles. The famous brass of Sir Robert and Sir Thomas Swynborne at Little Horkesley, Essex, was designed with reference to an earlier workshop pattern or memorial. The father's figure is armed appropriately to his date of decease in 1391, while his son beside him is shown in armour of 1412 (Fig. 177).

The incongruities of these brasses are unmistakable. The peculiarities of some others are equally interesting. The cross brass of Britell Avenel (1408), Buxted, Sussex, is early in form and may have been influenced by that of John de Lewes (*c.* 1330), the indent of which is still in the church. There are important similarities between the triple canopied brasses with pendant shields of Eleanor de Bohun (1399), Westminster Abbey (Fig. 173); Lady Joyce Tiptoft (engr. *c.* 1475), Enfield, Middx., and the destroyed brass of Agnes, Duchess of Norfolk (1545), formerly at St. Mary, Lambeth, which might be explained by the executors' specifications.[12] The great canopied brasses at Wivenhoe, Essex, formerly flanked by saint-filled side-shafts, were probably inspired by earlier models. It is tempting to relate the brass of Sir Roger le Strange (1506), Hunstanton, Norfolk, to that of Sir Hugh Hastyngs at Elsing (Fig. 129). Comparisons can be drawn at Hereford be-tween the large brasses of Canon Rudhale (1476) and Dean Frowsetoure (1529).[13] Not only in both brasses are the figures shown in rich copes, wearing the *pileus*, but the form and content of their elaborate canopies have much similarity. An unusual feature of the Rudhale canopy is the slim shafts set as flying buttresses outside the tiers of niches supporting the canopy. This arrangement is modified in the Frowsetoure brass by replacing the outer shafts with decorative bands. Especially noteworthy are some large canopy fragments at the east end of the nave at Boston, Lincs. These, though badly worn, are still strikingly foreign in appearance and datable at a glance to the early fifteenth century. The remaining indent, however, shows they belonged to an English composition of *c.* 1480. The abundant Tournai memorials in this church most probably influenced the specifications.

It is appropriate to mention other brasses which are deliberately retrospective in design though not necessarily based on some particular monument. John Saye and family, St. Peter, Colchester, Essex, is an unusual quadrangular wall brass probably engraved *c.* 1570. The kneeling figures are represented in pseudo fifteenth century costume, a girl wearing a butterfly head-dress. One wife of Arthur Dericote (1562), Hackney, Middx., wears a pedimental head-dress in contrast to the French hoods of her companions.[14] Such care for detail is found on a few fifteenth century memorials. William West (d. 1390) at Sudborough, Northants., wears the characteristic hood of the late fourteenth century, yet his wife's head-dress is in the fashion of *c.* 1440. William Whappelode the elder (d. 1393), Chalfont St. Peter, Bucks., displays the outmoded detail of large circular besagews on his brass of 1446. The deliberate seventeenth century forgeries at Pluckley, Kent, are clever imitations, possibly made from discarded originals. Most unexpected of late incongruities is the figure of Sir William Molineux (*c.* 1570), Sefton, Lancs. (Fig. 101). This particular brass has caused considerable speculation. Sir William is shown in late Tudor armour, but wearing a hood of mail and a curious form of 'SS' collar. The brass as a whole is unusual in design. The reason for including such antique equipment cannot be easily explained. Sir William distinguished himself at Flodden Field, where he captured Scottish standards displayed on the brass. It is possible that he desired to be represented as armed on that occasion. The engraver set out to create an impression of old armour, and wished to make a contrast with the figure of Sir William's son, Sir Richard (d. 1568), commemorated close by.

It is highly probable that the majority of brasses designed on existing memorials reveal no features inappropriate to their date. The overall effect of this influence was to impose a conservatism of presentation, encouraging the reproduction of conventional patterns without substantial change from one generation to the next. Only in exceptional cases are the directions in such matters evidently reflected in inconsistencies.

Use of materials from outside the workshops

The engraver's third major source of design—illustrated material from outside the workshop—has still to be analysed. The use of Dürer woodcuts has already been described. There are many valuable comparisons yet to be made. Most craftsmen had references to aid them in their work. The glass painter Robert Preston left his apprentice 'all my bookes that is fitte for one prentesse of his craffte to lerne by',[15] and there were undoubtedly many books of patterns and motifs available to the engravers. The howling monster designs, commonly found on fourteenth century Flemish brasses, are found also in painted glass, sculpture and textiles. Pattern books of saints could be used equally on the embroidery of vestments or the representation monumentally of the same robes. Bestiaries were a useful source for decoration and foot-rests. J. A. Goodall has identified the fishes at the base of a cross at Grainthorpe, Lincs., as probably based on a common pattern with those in 'the creation of the Fishes' page of Queen Mary's psalter some eighty years earlier in date. Late fifteenth-century prints of a catechetical and religious nature were another probable source. The strongly Germanic presentation of the armour in several brasses of the York workshops was probably derived from prints rather than any direct foreign influence. There can be little doubt that the remarkable inscription at Leça do Balio, Portugal, was inspired by an illuminated manuscript.[16]

Sculptured tomb design was a significant influence on the engravers. The famous Elsing brass is a clear rearrangement of the tomb of Edmund Crouchback, Earl of Lancaster, at Westminster. The early military brasses at Lubiaz closely follow the arrangement and detail of the Silesian sculptured effigies of Duke Bolko I (d. 1301) at Krzeszów and Duke Henryk IV (d. 1290) at Wrocław.[17] Brass design as a whole reflected the trends of sculptured monuments.

Glass painting and the decorative features of ornamental metal work were further sources. Some glass painters were also marblers. The kneeling heraldic groups of brass and glass bear close comparison. The affinity between the small panels of military figures in the Ely Lady Chapel glass and the subsidiary figures of the Elsing brass seem too close to be accidental (Figs. 102, 103). The decorative fillet on the brass of Mikołaj Tomicki (engr. 1524) at Tomice, Poland, reproduces many motifs engraved on the metal grills of the Sigismund chapel in Kraków Cathedral.

The participation of painters

The fourth source of design, the participation of painters employed to draw up the composition, is the most interesting. A report of 1594 by Gaspar Tryller, treasurer to the Elector of Saxony, gives a valuable insight into the proceedings connected with the preparation of important brasses. The report was concerned with the engraving of five brasses by Martin Hilliger of Freiberg. According to the treasurer the contract for the casting and working of the brasses was so drawn up by him with the collaboration of Paul Buchner, armourer and Johann Maria Nosseni, architect, that Hilliger was not only to cast the brasses but also 'to have the portraits, coats of arms, settings and other appropriate decoration designed and hatched. Similarly to have the inscriptions nobly engraved and everything most cleanly prepared by painter and goldsmith for 15 florins and 15 groschen for each hundred-weight.'[18] The caster appears as the head of a team including an eminent architect, an expert armourer, a painter and a goldsmith. The designs were apparently those of the painter, advised by Buchner and Nosseni, while the goldsmith dealt with the detail of the engraving. Such a combination of talent would only be available to the most eminent employers. The professional painter alone was not so rare a participator in the presentation of monumental brass designs.

The evidence relating to Flemish painters is scanty, but their influence may be surmised. A Scottish bishop of Dunkeld, George Crichton, arranged in 1537 at Antwerpen for the preparation of a monument, requiring the services of Jan Mandijns, a reputable painter of that city, for the 'painting and portrayal on a copper plate'.[19] The pattern appears once as a separate item of expense in the Halyburton Ledger and documentary references to patterns in the hands of executors may indicate the work of a specially paid artist. Some family compositions as that of Thomas Pownder (1525), now in the Christchurch Mansion Museum, Ipswich, Suffolk (Fig. 65), convey the impression of a painter's draft, and it is tempting to attribute the design of Margaret Hornebolt's brass (1529), Fulham, Middx., to her painter husband Gerard, who was employed by King Henry VIII. The source of design has to date been traced for only two Flemish brasses, namely those at Emden, West

Germany (1507) and Basel, Switzerland (*c.* 1450). Goodall has recognized the first as being based on the 1473 Augsburg woodcut *Salvator Mundi.* The other was certainly copied from a painting, possibly by the master Roger van der Weyden, though only a seventeenth-century copy now exists (Figs. 149 and 150).[20] Both cases are further discussed in *The Memorials,* and the Emden connection illustrated.

No specific painter has been identified as participating in the design of an English brass, though in this connection the Bullen brass at Hever, Kent, deserves special comment. The figure of Sir Thomas Bullen, K.G. (1538), is exceptionally well drawn for its period, and cannot be related to other Tudor brasses (Fig. 212). The inscription is in fine Roman capitals and framed as on an antique tablet. The features of the figure are carefully defined, and the perspective of the feet is most competently rendered. It is certain that an unusually skilled draughtsman made the pattern. The two Flemings—Gerard and Lucas Hornebolt, court painters to Henry VIII, received special patronage from the Boleyn family.[21] A connection with these artists is conjectural but deserves further investigation.

German and Polish authorities, faced with a high proportion of brasses based on special designs, have been more enterprising in identifying the probable artists involved. Three of the most important brasses in Lübeck are of such unusual treatment that stylistic comparisons are meaningful. Hermann Hutterock and wife (1505) in the Marienkirche (Fig. 198) are original in treatment. The shrouded figures are engraved with a remarkable richness of line, and their draperies are arranged in complex, branch-like forms. Dr. Walter Paatz demonstrates convincingly that this brass was one of the last works of the versatile North German painter Bernt Notke.[22] Two of this artist's famous paintings, the *Mass of St. Gregory* and the *Dance of Death,* were destroyed in the burning of the Marienkirche. His great wood carvings, the rood group from Lübeck Cathedral and the St. George in Stockholm Cathedral still exist. Both Dr. Hans Eichler and Dr. Paatz ascribe the design of the figure of Johann Luneborch (Figs. 96, 199) to Hermen Rode, a celebrated North German artist whose works are found in several of the Baltic cities.[23] The exquisite brass of Bartolomäus Heisegger, from the Marienkirche (Fig. 200), has been attributed by Paatz to Jacob van Utrecht, an immigrant painter, who was working in Lübeck in 1519. The mark on the knife of St. Bartholomew on this brass may well be the painter's.[24]

Turning to the Nürnberg workshops, it is not yet proved whether some of the brasses at Meissen engraved by the Vischer atelier were merely designed in the manner of Dürer, or were drawn by that master in person as specially commissioned works. The distinguished East German art historian Dr. E. H. Lemper has recently favoured the latter alternative, most especially in the case of Duchess Zedena (Fig. 196).[25]

Two painters concerned with the preparation of the Freiberg brasses have been identified with certainty. Both were employed by the Dukes of Saxony as Court painters. The earlier and by far the more important was Lukas Cranach the Elder, whose portrait of Duke Heinrich 'the Pious' was used with little change for the Duke's brass (Figs. 104, 105). Whether the design of the figure was copied from the portrait or from a preliminary drawing is a matter for conjecture. The brass is a magnificent example of attempted portraiture in the modern sense of the term, and simulates the colour contrasts of the painting, the striped effect of the hose being interpreted by series of pounced dots. It is probable that the designs of Cranach's contemporary, the Court painter Hans Krell, were used for the Meissen brasses to Duke Johann (1537) and Duke Friedrich (1539).[26] The second certain artist, Andreas Götting, was employed in the drafting of several of the early seventeenth century Freiberg brasses, and in designing ornaments for bronze cannon.

Valuable research on a far earlier brass has been completed by Magister K. Wróblewska of Olsztyn, Poland.[27] Her study shows that the remarkable plate at Nowemiasto, Poland, to the Teutonic knight, Sir Kuno von Liebensteyn (1391) (Fig. 160), was designed by Peter of the Marienburg, court artist to the Grand Master of the Teutonic Order. Peter was appointed to the court of the Grand Master Conrad von Jungingen until 1407. He was in charge of a series of wall paintings in the castle of Lochstedt, the church of Juditten and the cathedral of Kwidzyn (Marienwerder). The peculiarities of the military figures and helms at the first two places (Fig. 159), and of the angels at Kwidzyn, leave little doubt that the same master was concerned with the Nowemiasto brass. The foundry at the Marienburg was at that time in the charge of Ludwison of Bremen, who presumably cast the plates.

It is regrettable, in view of the variety of pattern sources revealed, that so little attention has been paid to this aspect of brasses or indeed of monumental effigies. This neglect is in part explained by an unbalanced interest in costume and heraldic aspects of memorials, but also by an assumption that brasses were an exclusive business, divorced from the attention of important painters. This is a misguided impression. The greatest artists of the Middle Ages and the Renaissance frequently accepted monumental commissions. It is, therefore, not surprising that occasionally, within the wide range of monumental brass designs, the work or influence of men of genius can now be recognized. A failure to investigate has for too long assured the designers' anonymity.

APPENDIX

Pattern series of English monumental brasses *c.* 1350–*c.* 1610

The following tables present the apparent sequence of series, though only as a provisional statement. The situation before *c.* 1350 is too uncertain to illustrate. Series have been included in which at least four figure brasses have survived. Some unusual brasses are not covered by the tables, including a few provincial examples from the West Country, the Stamford area and the North. The characteristics of each series may be seen by reference to the illustration captions. The development of each is discussed in *The Memorials*.

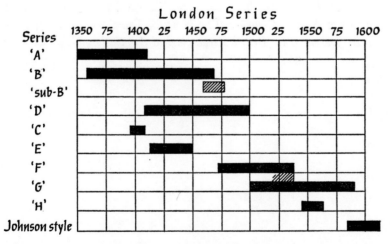

'Sub-B' appears to consist of hybrid products with affinities to both 'B' and 'D'. The relationship of the London 'F' and 'G' series is very confused in the early years of the sixteenth century. The indicated merger of these series around 1530 was preceded by much copying, and wives of one series are occasionally found with husbands of the other.

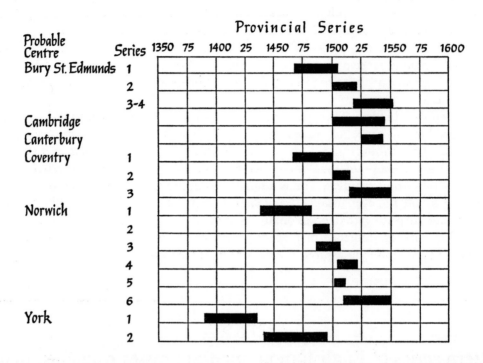

It is not clear whether the Bury St. Edmunds third series is one with a variation in script, or two closely related series, the fourth starting *c.* 1535. A seventh series at Norwich, of short duration between 1495 and 1500, is not shown as only two figure brasses exist though inscriptions are more numerous. Workshops in Norwich and York continued to make brasses into the seventeenth century, but series have not been established.

For readings on styles and series see:

S. Badham, J. Blair and R. Emmerson, *Specimens of Lettering from English Monumental Brasses*, Phillips and Page, London, 1976.

J. R. Greenwood in *Trans Mon. Brass Soc.*, vol. XI, pub. 1971, *Mon. Brass Soc. bulletin 4*, 1973; and *Brasses of Norfolk Churches*, The Norfolk Trust, Woodbridge, 1976.

J. R. C. Kent in *Journal of the British Archaeological Association*, New Series 12, 1949.

Conclusion

As the subjects in these nine chapters are varied and widespread in scope only certain aspects of them can be presented, and, despite the documentary evidence cited for the views advanced, many of the conclusions drawn are necessarily qualified.

It has been shown that brass engraving was an integral part of the work of the marblers, but also attracted the skills of many other types of craftsmen. Similarly the designs of brasses, while generally reflecting technical competence, range from very ordinary or poor work to fine art. The nature of brass engraving as a form of business and commerce has been emphasized. The purchaser as well as the engraver and designer influenced both the style and arrangement of these monuments. The analysis of the meaning of brasses and the motives of those who sought such commemoration is little more than an introduction to a vast subject, but indicates the qualities of brasses as expressions of mediaeval thought and belief. The outline of the distribution of brasses both socially and geographically demonstrates the popularity and the European character of this type of monument.

All these aspects of the study have received inadequate attention in the past, and require more investigation. Their consideration is nevertheless an essential preparation for the complementary study—the chronological description of the development and variations of these memorials.

Notes

Introduction (pages 23 to 27)

1 Published in *Sussex Record Society*, vol. XLV: *Sussex Wills*, vol. IV, 1940, p. 110.

2 Caution is necessary in this respect. In many cases brasses were prepared in the lifetime of the deceased or long after death. Furthermore there is a conservatism in monumental art which may be misleading if applied to other art forms. Notwithstanding, the value of brasses in this context should be considerable, especially in relation to the study of stained glass.

3 Now preserved in the British Museum. These consist of pressings, made by applying damp paper to the brass, the lines having first been flooded with printer's ink. The design is accordingly reversed. While these constitute the oldest surviving collection, the seventeenth-century paintings of the Dutch artist Hendrik van Vliet depict children rubbing brasses or slabs, and isolated English rubbings survive dating from the first half of the eighteenth century.

Chapter 1: The origin of monumental brasses (pages 29 to 31)

1 Described in *The Memorial Slabs of Clonmacnois* by R. A. S. Macalister, Dublin, 1909.

2 Illustrated and discussed in *Tomb Sculpture*, London, 1964. Especially noteworthy are the inlaid figures of William Count of Flanders (1109) at the Museum, St. Omer, France—plate 191—and Bishop Frumald of Arras (1184) at the Museum, Arras, France—plate 194.

3 It would appear that until the twelfth century burials within the church were generally restricted to saints, heads of religious houses and founders of churches. The Emperor Charlemagne was buried in Aachen Cathedral, West Germany, in A.D. 814. By the thirteenth century the donations and legacies of the wealthy had entirely changed the situation. Church authorities vied with each other to grant a last resting place. Mathew Paris wrote in 1243 of the Franciscans: 'It is only twenty-four years since they built their first Houses in England . . . and now, if a rich man is like to die, they take care to crowd in, to the injury and slight of the clergy.' Disputes over internment between rival interests caused a brawl in Gloucester in 1285 (see p. 85 in *The Franciscans in England* by E. Hutton, Plymouth, 1926).

4 See for example the slabs of St. Piat (*c.* 1150) at Seclin, France, and of St. Helena (*c.* 1180) at Forét, Belgium, illustrated by W. F. Creeny in *Illustrations of Incised Slabs on the Continent of Europe*, Norwich, 1891, plates 1 and 4 respectively.

5 An excellent example of such inlays being the slab of Perone wife of Gilles van Lerinne (1247), at the Musées Royaux d'Art et d'Histoire, Bruxelles, Belgium, illustrated W. F. Creeny op. cit., plate 6.

6 Note particularly the quadrangular plates representing Blanche de France (d. 1243) and Jean de France (d. 1247), children of Louis IX, King of France, at the Abbey of Royaumont. Both drawings are in the Bodleian collection, Oxford, and illustrated as figs. 189 and 190, in *Les Tombeaux de la Collection Gaignières*, by J. Adhémar, vol. I, Paris, 1974.

7 Illustrated by E. Panofsky, op. cit., plate 190; also, as a prime source in the history of heraldry, in *Historic Heraldry*, King Penguin reprint 1970. A plaque of similar type, drawn by Gaignières, represented Ulger, Bishop of Angers (d. 1149), and was placed in St. Maurice, Angers, France.

8 See Dr. H. K. Cameron, 'Technical Aspects of Medieval Monumental Brasses' in *The Archaeological Journal*, vol. 131, 1974, p. 219. Cameron concludes that it was the greater ease with which the plate could be produced thin, together with certain colour advantages, that gave latten its importance.

9 This extraordinary arrangement is described on p. 385 in *Die Bau und Kunstdenkmäler der Freien und Hansestadt Lübeck*, vol. II by F. Hirsch, G. Shaumann and F. Bruns, Lübeck, 1920.

10 The term 'conventional' has been used to differentiate this from some earlier memorials, such as the Le Mans plaque and the St. Ulrich coffin plate at Augsburg, which, through the peculiarities of their execution or situation, do not have all the main characteristics associated with monumental brasses.

11 Illustrated by J. Adhémar, op. cit., p. 28, fig. 106.

12 The author is indebted to Dr. and Mrs. M. Tennenhaus for information concerning this interesting plate, which was revealed for less than three years. A full description has been published in *Trans. Mon. Brass Soc.*, vol. XI, 1972 (pub. 1974), pp. 262–4.

13 H. H. Trivick, *The Craft and Design of Monumental Brasses*, London, 1969, p. 24.

14 The whole slab of Heinrich Gassman is illustrated, fig. 78, in *Brass Rubbing* by M. W. Norris, London, 1965, p. 66.

Chapter 2: The manufacture of brasses (pages 32 to 43)

1 Published from the Walpole Society Records in *Trans. Mon. Brass Soc.*, vol. VIII, 1944, p. 49.

2 The subject is fully discussed by G. Dru Drury in 'The Use of Purbeck Marble in Mediaeval Times', *Proceedings of the Dorset Natural History and Archaeological Society*, vol. 70, 1948, pp. 74–98.

3 Described by S. E. Rigold in 'Petrology as an Aid to Classification of Brasses', *Trans. Mon. Brass Soc.*, vol. X, 1966, pp. 285–6.

4 Antoing stone is occasionally specified in Flemish contracts either as Antoing or Tournai stone. A notable case of its use by English craftsmen is for the large heraldic inlay at Lytchett Matravers, Dorset, for Sir John Maltravers (1364). Here the dark stone provided an appropriate field for the arms—*sable, a fret or,* i.e. black with a gold fret. (See article by P. I. McQueen, *Trans. Mon. Brass Soc.*, vol. X, 1966, pp. 244–8.)

5 Published by L. Verriest in 'Un Fonds D'Archives D'un intérêt exceptionnel . . .'; article in *Annales du Cercle Archéologique de Mons*, 1939, contract no. XLVI, p. 189.

6 A particularly interesting example of such treatment is at Laughton, Lincs., where the appropriated and slightly altered brass of a knight (*c.* 1400) has been reset in the original slab after resurfacing. A strip of the slab was for some curious reason left at its original level, still retaining the matrix and rivet holes.

7 Published in *Testamenta Cantiana, East Kent*, by A. Hussey, London, 1907, p. 5. The recorded text here is that corrected by R. H. D'Elboux.

8 'Latten. An Etymological Note', *Trans. Mon. Brass Soc.*, vol. X, 1965, pp. 167–8.

9 Published in *The Archaeological Journal*, vol. 131, 1974, pp. 215–37. This is a revision of his earlier important paper 'The Metals used in Monumental Brasses', *Trans. Mon. Brass Soc.*, vol. VIII, 1946, pp. 109–30.

10 Albertus Magnus records in Book IV of his treatise on minerals, 'But those who carry on much work with copper in our region—that is, in Paris and Cologne and other places where I have been and seen this tested by experience—convert copper into brass by means of the powder of a stone called calamina.' He further describes the addition of small quantities of tin to change the colour, and the inclusion of 'oil of glass' to achieve brilliance. This valuable record is available in translation: *Albertus Magnus, Book of Minerals* translated by D. Wyckoff, Oxford, 1967. The quotation is from p. 224.

11 Details of many of the analyses listed have been published in *Trans. Mon. Brass Soc.*, as follows: Kings Lynn, Tattershall, Luton, The Victoria and Albert Museum and the Cambridge Museum of Archaeology and Ethnology in vol. VIII, 1946, p. 123; Somerton in vol. IX, 1954, p. 103; Oxford in vol. IX, 1954, p. 201; Penn in vol. IX, 1955, p. 281; Easton Neston in vol. IX, 1952, p. 57; Edlesborough in vol. IX, 1958, p. 308 and Peckleton in vol. X, 1965, p. 196. The remainder are cited from the article 'Technical Aspects of Medieval Monumental Brasses' op. cit. by Dr. H. K. Cameron, Table I of which lists eighty-two samples.

12 The details of an examination by W. E. Gawthorp, together with a photograph, are published in *Trans. Mon. Brass Soc.*, vol. VIII, 1935, p. 84.

13 Described by R. H. D'Elboux in *The Antiquaries Journal*, vol. XXIX, 1949, p. 185.

14 Recorded by J. Schmidt in 'Die Glocken—und Stückgiesserfamilie Hilliger', *Mitteilungen des Freiberger Alterthumsvereins*, vol. XXXI, 1865, p. 354.

15 Recorded by J. Schmidt, op. cit., p. 358.

16 13 June 1453, 'A hearse of latten over the image, to bear a covering to be ordeyned; the large plate to be made of the finest and thickest cullen plate', etc.

17 *The Early English Customs System*, by N. S. B. Gras, 1918, Harvard, p. 507.

18 *The Brasses of England*, London, 1907, p. 2.

19 See article by C. C. Oman, 'Mediaeval Brass Lecterns in England' in *The Archaeological Journal*, vol. LXXXVII, 1930, published 1931, pp. 117–149. Casting discussed pp. 121–3.

20 The British Museum references for these illustrations are for fig. 9—Brit. Mus. Add. M.S.10292. fo.55b; and for fig. 10—Brit. Mus. M.S. Royal. 14E iii fo.66.

21 Illustrated by H. Huth in *Künstler and Werkstatt der Spätgotik*, Augsburg, 1923, plate I.

22 Comparison of tracings of these figures reveals a degree of similarity between the major lines which is far too close to be circumstantial.

23 See *The Brasses of our Homeland Churches*, London, 1923, p. 21.

24 Recorded in *English Industries in the Middle Ages*, L. F. Salzmann, Oxford, 1931, p. 362.

25 Exposed when the brass of Sir Humphrey Stafford (1548) and wife was removed for repair.

26 A study on methods of fixing is made by H. F. Owen Evans, 'The Fixing of Brasses', *Trans. Mon. Brass Soc.*, vol. X, 1964, pp. 58–62.

27 An analysis has been made by the Scientific Department of the National Gallery, London, of the remaining inlays of the brass of Canon Oskens (1535), believed to have come from Nippes, near Köln, now in the Victoria and Albert Museum, London. This analysis is of unusual interest and is recorded here in full with kind permission of the Department of Metalwork of the Victoria and Albert Museum.

'Four separate samples were supplied. Each of these was found to consist of a single thick layer of a slightly glossy, rather granular, pigmented wax coating. The main binding component in each case is wax, and extraction of a little of this with hot organic solvents suggested that it is beeswax (the honey-like smell of the extracted wax is still perceptible on warming). In each sample, however, a certain amount of resinous material is also present and can be extracted as a clear, hard, resinous ring by means of alcohol. The strong, turpentine-like smell suggests rosin. Addition of rosin would serve to make the wax a little harder and a little more adhesive. The pigments present in the four samples were as follows.

1. *Dark green sample* a bluish-green copper carbonate pigment. The irregular size and shape of the fairly large particles and the presence of some iron oxide particles as an impurity suggests the natural form, the copper carbonate mineral *malachite*.

2. *Dark red-brown sample* (from centre part)
The main pigment present is *vermilion* (red mercuric sulphide), though some red-brown ferric oxide (ochre) is also present. It is not possible to say whether the vermilion is the natural or synthetic variety, since these are often indistinguishable, and in any case both have been used concurrently since antiquity.

3. *Blue-green sample* (from top left-hand column)
A blue copper carbonate pigment was present, and again the irregularity of particle size and shape and the presence of occasional particles of red-brown iron oxide indicates the natural mineral form, *azurite* (the latter often occurs with its green counterpart, malachite, in mineral deposits).

4. *Dark green sample* (from inscription at bottom of plaque)
The main pigment present was *malachite* as in

Sample 1. In addition, however, there are a number of coarse, glossy black particles. These proved to be hard bituminous material which melted at a higher temperature than the wax and resin mixture surrounding it.

28 The head is illustrated in *Trans. Mon. Brass Soc.*, vol. IV, 1901, p. 157.
29 The originality of this head, unlike that of the king which is a restoration, is proved by the drawing of the brass made prior to restoration, published by H. Hansen, J. J. A. Worsaae and C. F. Herbst in *Kongegravene i Ringsted Kirke*, Copenhagen, 1858.
30 The inlaid head when still in fair condition is illustrated as plate LI, *The Antiquaries Journal*, vol. XIV, 1934, opp. p. 280. However, a rubbing of 1801 is preserved at the Bodleian Library, Oxford, showing the original latten head, which was at that time loose in the Armorie at New College. See 'A Regency Collection of Brass Rubbings', by J. Bertram, *Trans. Mon. Brass Soc.* vol. XII, 1975 (pub. '76), p. 98 and Fig. 3.
31 Accounts preserved in Felbrigg House, reference in the guide *Church of St. Margaret Felbrigg*, 3rd revised edn., p. 19. Acknowledgement to J. R. Greenwood.
32 The Belvoir Household Accounts in these matters are published in a Historical Manuscripts Commission volume, *The Manuscripts of His Grace the Duke of Rutland, K.G.*, vol. IV, 1905, especially pp. 398–9.
33 This matter and others relating to costs of transport by road and water are described by J. E. Thorold-Rodgers in *History of Agriculture and Prices in England* vol. I, Oxford, 1866, pp. 658ff.
34 Letter 2312 of the Wynn Papers, preserved in the Welsh National Library, Aberystwyth. According to letter 2329 of 12 December 1661, the brass was set in its stone by Roger Piers.

Chapter 3: The geographical distribution of brasses (pages 44 to 57)

1 The paucity of engraved brasses in Italy indicates most strongly that there were no workshops concerned with this type of memorial, though casters or goldsmiths apparently met the rare order. Furthermore the absence of imported figure-brasses supports the conclusion that there was no clientele, inlaid marble decoration being preferred. There are no grounds to suspect selective destruction. A few brasses have been recorded. The engraved altar-piece at Susa is evidently a Flemish import. A very large composition, consisting of arms and a cardinal's hat, flanked by two female allegorical figures, an inscription in separately inlaid letters and a decorative border, commemorates Cardinal Pio di Savoia (d. 1689), at the church del Gesù at Roma (Rome). This is certainly Italian work. At S. Giorgio dei Greci in Venezia (Venice) are fragments of three inscriptions, two with shields

and one with a heart, of the sixteenth and seventeenth centuries.
   J. A. Goodall has noted early inscription indents, dating from the eleventh century in the crypt church of Hosios Lucas in Phocis, Greece, which are discussed by R. W. Schultz and S. H. Barnsley in *The Monastery of Saint Luke of Stiris in Phocis*, 1901, pp. 7 and 34–5.
   There is evidence to support the view that a few brasses were engraved in Spain, but Flemish imports were clearly favoured there. It would appear also that in France the major concentrations of brasses were in the northern and central towns.
   No figure brasses have been noted east of Poland. Such memorials would not have been welcomed by the Eastern Church, but might have been laid in Hansa churches in Russia.
2 The existence of brass engravers in Ireland

8

cannot be entirely discounted, even though not one established instance of their work exists. Many incised slabs were made, some bearing figures as at the cathedral of Kilkenny and the abbeys of Athassel and Jerpoint, and engraved brass processional crosses of Irish workmanship have been preserved. The slab at Old Leighlin is undoubtedly Irish. It is nevertheless most likely that the brass was prepared elsewhere and set in a local slab, in the manner of Wenllan Moreton (1427) at Llandough-next-Cowbridge, Glamorgan, Wales.

3 These indents may be of brasses of Tournai workmanship but their form is decidedly unusual. They are described by S. E. Rigold, *Trans. Mon. Brass Soc.*, vol. X, 1966, pp. 275–82.

4 'The ledger of Andrew Halyburton' by F. A. Greenhill, *Trans. Mon. Brass Soc.*, vol. IX, 1954, pp. 184–90.

5 Full details of this reference are given in Chapter Eight (p. 92), and in the notes following.

6 By far the most comprehensive analysis of the distribution of brasses of Tournai and the Flemish Centres, is that given by Dr. H. K. Cameron in *Trans. Mon. Brass Soc.*, vol. XI, part II, 1970 (pub. 1972), pp. 50–81. This article includes not only lists and descriptions of destroyed and existing plates, but also illustrations of some destroyed memorials at Altenberg, Bruges, Ribe and Roskilde.

7 Possibly Sir George Yeardley (d. 1627). The indent is in good condition showing an armed figure with helmet, foot inscription, marginal inscription, scroll and shield. Illustrated and described by H. K. Cameron in *Trans. Mon. Brass Soc.*, vol. X, 1967 (pub. 1969), pp. 369–70.

Chapter 4: The social distribution of brasses (pages 52 to 58)

1 The Sandys Contract is published in full with comment by F. A. Greenhill in *Trans. Mon. Brass Soc.*, vol. IX, 1960, pp. 354–61.

2 The Liddel account is published in full with comment by C. T. Davies in *Trans. Mon. Brass Soc.*, vol. III, 1898, pp. 183–6.

3 An analysis of costs derived from wills in England is made by R. H. D'Elboux in 'Testamentary Brasses', *The Antiquaries Journal*, vol. XXIX, 1949, pp. 188–91.

4 Both contracts with others are summarized by F. H. Crossley in *English Church Monuments, A.D. 1150–1550*, London, 1921, pp. 30–1.

5 Although many figures are depicted in armour, and are accordingly referred to as military brasses, it is necessary to note that this was done out of respect for their status and not with regard to their occupation. It is probable that the majority of Tudor gentlemen shown in armour never had cause to wear it.

6 The indent, supposedly that of the Queen, lies in the south transept of Westminster Abbey, but is now too worn to interpret. See *The Brasses of Westminster Abbey* by J. S. N. Wright, John Baker, London, 1969, p. 43.

7 A drawing of this curious memorial is published by A. B. Connor in *The Proceedings of the Somerset Archaeological and Natural History Society*, vol. LXXXII, 1936, 'Monumental Brasses in Somerset', part VI, plate XII: and reproduced in the reprint *Monumental Brasses in Somerset*, 1970, as Plate XXXVIII.

8 This fragment has some peculiarities that appear consistent with the Sandford illustration (Fig. 20), but the heavy covering of the indent has prevented comparison at the time of writing.

9 Other indents of brasses which probably commemorated nobility are at King's Langley, Herts., and Fotheringay, Northants. The first has been attributed to Isabella of Castile (d. 1393), wife of Edmund of Langley, Duke of York, the second to Edward Duke of York

(d. 1415). The latter, an exceedingly elaborate indent, is mostly covered by a Tudor monument. The brass of Edmund Tudor, Earl of Richmond (d. 1456) at St. David's Cathedral, Pembrokeshire, Wales, was restored in the nineteenth century.

10 'The Cat, the Rat, and Lovell our Dog, rule all England under an Hog.' A scurrilous couplet composed and publicized by William Colyngbourne. See *Richard the Third* by P. M. Kendall, London, 1955, p. 301.

11 As a result of the Hundred Years War the French bourgeoisie and country people were impoverished, and the effects of this on their patronage of the arts is examined by J. Evans in *Art of Mediaeval France*, London, 1948. Gaignières illustrates a sufficient number of brasses to people of little consequence to refute the conclusion that he ignored such monuments.

12 Another earlier brass to a herald, John Mowbray, Clarenceaux (1428) formerly of St. Olave, Hart Street, London, is reproduced in *Trans. Mon. Brass Soc.*, vol. IX, 1958, opp. p. 301, in an article by H. Stanford, London.

13 For a fuller list of these officials see *Church Brasses* by A. C. Bouquet, London, 1956, p. 173.

14 The whistle worn by this unusual figure may be compared with those carved on Castle Hedingham church tower, connected with John de Vere, Earl of Oxford as Lord High Admiral. The brass is illustrated in *The Memorials*, Fig. 209.

15 J. Weever, *Ancient Funeral Monuments*, 1631, p. 536. 'Her portraiture is in brasse with a milke pale upon her head; she was [by relation] a liberall benefactor to this church.'

16 This immense composition measuring about 4.75 metres by 2.90 metres is illustrated in the *Portfolio Mon. Brass Soc.*, vol. I, part 6, plate 6, and reproduced by H. Macklin in *The Brasses of England*, p. 314.

Chapter 5: The importance of motive in commemoration (pages 58 to 67)

1 Published as a note in *Trans. Mon. Brass Soc.*, vol. VI, 1912, p. 252.

2 The space was sometimes completed, e.g. Nicholas Leveson and wife, first date 1539, second 1560, at St. Andrew Undershaft, London.

3 Other similar duplications are of Henry and Joan Bradschawe shown at Halton, Bucks. (1553), and again with Joan's second husband at Noke, Oxon. (1598), and also William Roberts and wife shown at Digswell, Herts. (1484), and again at Little Braxted, Essex (1508).

4 Others duplicated in the same church are Anne Hobart (1530 and 1561 (effigies now lost)), Loddon, Norfolk; Peter Frechwell, Esq. (*c.* 1480 and 1503), Stavely, Derbyshire, and Edward Goodman (1560 and 1583), Ruthin, Denbigh.

5 This translation from the Latin is given in *A Book of Facsimiles of Monumental Brasses on the Continent of Europe* by W. F. Creeny, London, 1884, p. 29. A very long inscription of thirty-six lines at the Hôpital Notre Dame, Ypres, Belgium, records benefactions and foundations of masses by Pieter Lansaem and wife (1467) and another at the Museum van Zeeuwsch Genootschap, Middelburg, Holland, records foundations of masses for the Ysenbaert family (1509).

6 Recorded in *Schlesische Fürstenbilder des Mittelalters* by H. Luchs, Breslau, 1872 (no page series but a section is devoted to this memorial).

7 *Surrey Archaeological Collections*, vol. II, 1864, p. 169.

8 Published in *The Monumental Brasses of Gloucestershire*, C. T. Davis, London, 1899, p. 10.

9 This complicated matter is well discussed by G. McN. Rushforth in 'The Kirkham Monument in Paignton Church', *Transaction of the Exeter Diocesan Architectural and Archaeological Society*, 1927, 3rd series, vol. IV, pp. 1–37, and by H. Thurston in *The Memory of Our Dead*, London, 1915, p. 165.

10 Joan Brokes (1487) has both a mural and a floor brass at Peper-Harow, Surrey; a kneeling figure with Holy Trinity (restored) is on the wall and a small cross in the floor.

11 These inscriptions are at Chigwell, East Ham, Low Leyton, Waltham Abbey, Walthamstow and Woodford all in Essex, and at Enfield, Middlesex. A further inscription has been lost from Chingford, Essex.

12 Published in *Sussex Record Society*, vol. XLII, 1937, p. 210.

13 This little-known brass is not recorded by Mill Stephenson and is set round the edges of the font. It is illustrated in *An Historical Survey of Torquay*, by A. C. Ellis, 1930, p. 101.

14 This indent is illustrated and described by M. Christy and W. W. Porteous in *Transactions of the Essex Archaeological Society*, new series, vol. VII, 1900, p. 244.

15 An altar was, for instance, made at one end of the monument to William, ninth Earl of Arundel (d. 1480) in the Fitzalan chapel at Arundel, Sussex.

16 Recorded by R. H. D'Elboux in 'Testamentary Brasses', *The Antiquaries Journal*, vol. XXIX, 1949. Another but more doubtful case was on the door at Biggleswade, Beds., to John Tadelowe and wife. This is discussed in *Trans. Mon. Brass Soc.*, vol. IX, 1955, pp. 284–5, by K. W. Kuhlicke.

17 Recorded in *Monumenta Medii Aevi Historia res gestas Poloniae illustrantia*, Tom 13, ed. B. Ulanowski, Kraków, 1894, p. 666. It is unlikely that this refers to the splendid figure-plate of the bishop illustrated as Fig. 81, but to another less elaborate brass of which a seventeenth-century record exists.

18 Published by C. G. R. Birch in *Trans. Mon. Brass Soc.*, vol. II, 1895, pp. 223–4.

19 Described by C. T. Davis in *The Monumental Brasses of Gloucestershire*, 1899, p. 218.

20 A similar point is made by R. Griffin and M. Stephenson in *A List of Monumental Brasses Remaining in the County of Kent in 1922*, London, 1923, p. 86. At Cobham, Kent, both the brasses of Sir Reginald Braybrok (d. 1405) and Sir Nicholas Hawberk (d. 1407) refer to Joan Cobham as Dame Joan, Lady of Cobham and heir of John de Cobham founder of this college. The founder did not die until 1408, and the description could not have been properly applied until after that date. The brasses were presumably made *c.* 1410.

21 Fully described and illustrated by R. H. D'Elboux in 'The Dering Brasses', *The Antiquaries Journal*, vol. XXVII, 1947, pp. 11–23.

22 Noted by R. H. D'Elboux in 'Testamentary Brasses', op. cit.

23 External brasses have been listed and described by R. H. D'Elboux in *Trans. Mon. Brass Soc.*, vol. VIII, 1946, pp. 150–7 and 1949, pp. 208–19.

24 These plates are fully described, together with others at Oudenarde, Sluis and Tournai, by F. Van Molle, in 'Koperen Koppen en vuisten in het oude vlaamse Strafrecht', *Artium Minorum Folia Lovaniensia*, XV, 1974.

Chapter 6: The interpretation of monumental brass design (pages 68 to 80)

1 *Tomb Sculpture*, London, 1964, p. 26.

2 The tombs of Edmund, Earl of Lancaster (d. 1296) and Aymer de Valence (d. 1326) are illustrated on pages 54 and 60 respectively of *English Church Monuments, 1150–1550* by F. H. Crossley, London, 1921.

3 E. H. Kantorowicz, *The King's Two Bodies*, 1957, Princeton, with especial reference to monuments on pp. 431–7.

4 The case for portraiture in mediaeval brasses has recently been presented by H. H. Trivick in *The Craft and Design of Monumental Brasses*,

London, 1969, and the reader is referred to his arguments and conclusions especially on pages 69–71. In general Trivick admits the existence of many brasses which were in no sense portraits, but claims that many others bore a recognizable and deliberately created likeness to the deceased —far more so in fact than has been accepted in the past or would be conceded by the present writer. The impact of his argument is blunted by his use of the word 'portrait', by which he means no more than a representation having character, possibly without resemblance to the commemorated, and it is not clear when an actual likeness is being asserted. It is further compromised by admitting that the brasses of such notables as the Earl of Warwick are conventional representations, while claiming that the faces of modest half-effigy priests are 'portraits'.

5 A drawing among the Surrenden Manuscripts, dated 1628, of the brass before serious mutilation is published in *Archaeologia Cantiana*, vol. I, 1858, following p. 80.

6 A poor rubbing of this brass is preserved in the collection of the Society of Antiquaries, London. This rubbing formed the basis of a rather uncertain illustration in H. Haines, A *Manual of Monumental Brasses*, Oxford, 1861, p. cxxxii.

7 Amusing examples of these faces are at Acton Burnell, Shropshire (1382); Mapledurham, Oxon. (1395), Shottesbrooke, Berks., (1401) and Worstead, Norfolk (1440). Two decorate the inscription of William and John Wyot (1410), Langley Marsh, Bucks.

8 See J. Franklyn, *Brasses*, London, 1964, p. 31.

9 For a detailed description of this arrangement in mediaeval art see *The Imagery of British Churches* by M. D. Anderson, London, 1955, p. 189.

10 An alternative origin may be found in Ezekiel I: 5–13 (Douay version) in which four winged creatures each bearing the faces of a man, an ox, a lion and an eagle are described.

11 'For all those souls that have gone forth believing in the four gospels, which hold up all Christendom at the four corners; Grant them, O merciful Lord, the four marriage portions in Heaven', from *The Ancrene Riwle*, trans. M. B. Salu with introduction by G. Sitwell, Welwyn, 1955, p. 12.

12 The reader is referred to *Idealism and Realism* by Henriette s'Jacob, Leyden, 1954, for a fuller analysis of these problems in relation to mediaeval art.

13 Some Flemish painted panels were themselves used as memorials. See *Dutch and Flemish Painters*, being a translation of *Het Schilderborck*, 1604, of Carel van Mander, by C. van der Wall, 1936, especially pages 44 and 178. A panel painted by the important painter Van der Goes commemorated Wouter Gautier at St. James' Church, Gent.

14 Examples of indents with crosses and half-effigies above are at Dorchester, Oxon. (*c.* 1320), Hornchurch, Essex (*c.* 1320), Ramsbury, Wilts (*c.* 1325) and Brasted, Kent (1330).

15 This brass commemorated Sir Henry de Bayous (*c.* 1332), and consisted of a small full-length figure in armour resting on a long stemmed bracket. This appears to be the earliest evidence of this type of design, though brackets were incorporated into elaborate canopies at an earlier date, as on the Haselshaw indent (1308), at Wells Cathedral, Somerset.

16 Very well illustrated in *Spain—a History in Art*, by B. Smith, Simon and Schuster, New York, 1966, pp. 100–101. In spite of its situation the painting is essentially Christian in inspiration, and includes a battle between a knight and a wodehowse.

17 Published as part of the introduction to a guide to an exhibition of brass rubbing at Hampstead. See *An Introduction to the Metaphysics of St. Thomas Aquinas*, by J. F. Anderson, Chicago, 1953, in particular chap. IX, pp. 88–98.

Chapter 7: The engravers (pages 81 to 87)

1 *Calendar of Letter-Books preserved among the archives of the Corporation of the City of London*, ed. R. R. Sharpe, London, 1910, Book L, p. 233.

2 Roucliffe's will is published in *Testamenta Eboracensia*, Surtees Soc., 1868, IV, pp. 102–7, the Reames reference being on p. 104: 'Volo quod Jacobus Remus, marbeler in Poule's Churche Yerde, London, fiat meum epitaphium in templo, . . .'

3 Commissory Court of London. 176. Harvey. See further description on p. 89.

4 Published by J. Challenor Smith in *Trans. Mon. Brass Soc.*, vol. IV, part 3, 1901, p. 136.

5 Published in *Collecteana Topographica et Genealogica*, by J. G. Nichols, vol. I, p. 354, and quoted by Haines, A *Manual of Monumental Brasses*, London, 1861, vol. I, p. lx.

6 The Yevele and Hyndeley references are recorded by J. Harvey in *English Mediaeval Architects*, London, 1954, pp. 318 and 144 respectively.

7 See 'Enquête sur les dalles, lames de cuivre et autres monuments funéraires provenant d'ateliers de Tombiers Gantois XIV-XVI siècle', article by V. van der Haegen in *Annales du XXIIᵉ Congrès de la Fédération Archéologique et Historique de Belgique*, Gand, 1913 pub. 1914, p. 30.

8 This is clear from the contracts cited by A. Hocquet in *Le Rayonnement de l'Art Tournaisien*, Tournai, 1924, especially in preuve II, pp. 16–17 in which an incised slab is to be enriched with elaborate engraved latten inlays.

9 The family workshop and its art are examined in the amply illustrated work *Peter Vischer der Ältere und Seine Werkstatt*, S. Meller, Leipzig, 1925.

10 Published by D. Laing in *Proceedings of the Society of Antiquaries of Scotland*, vol. VI, 1866, p. 53.

11 Published by J. G. Waller in *Archaeologia Aeliana*, vol. XV (new series), 1892, p. 81.
12 Loeman's will of 27 February 1512 left the completion of unfinished work to the goldsmith Lambert, at St. Laurentius, Köln. See R. Scholten, *Zur Geschichte der Stadt Cleve*, Kleve, 1905, p. 169.
13 'Die Glocken und Stückgiesserfamilie Hilliger', by J. Schmidt, article in *Mitteilungen des Freiberges Alterthumsvereins*, 1865, p. 351.
14 *Die Kunstdenkmale der Provinz Sachsen—die Stadt Erfurt*, by K. Becker, M. Brückner, E. Haetge and L. Schürenberg, Burg, 1929, vol. I, p. 354.
15 The author acknowledges the help of Dr. M. Tennenhaus for notice of this brass.
16 See *Calendar of Plea and Memoranda Rolls, 1437–1457, the City of London at the Guildhall*, ed. P. E. Jones, Cambridge, 1954, p. 76.
17 See *Calendar of Close Rolls, 1476–85*, ed. K. H. Ledward, H.M.S.O., London, 1954, p. 279.
18 The work was presumably carried out by the Roman Oderic, who in 1268 was laying mosaic in Westminster Abbey for Abbot Richard de la Ware. See *Westminster Abbey Re-Examined* by W. R. Lethaby, London, 1925, pp. 217–33, especially p. 232.
19 See 'The Sculptor and the Brass', *Trans. Mon. Brass Soc.*, vol. VII, 1935, part 2, p. 56.
20 S. Meller, op. cit., p. 12.
21 See *Études sur l'Art à Tournai et sur les Anciens Artistes de cette ville*, by A. de la Grange and L. Cloquet, Tournai, 1887, p. 291.
22 This fragment is illustrated on p. 149 of Boutell's *Monumental Brasses and Slabs*, 1847. The shield is peculiar. The author is indebted to J. C. Page Phillips for drawing his attention to the poor quality of the execution.

Chapter 8: The interest of the purchaser (pages 88 to 98)

1 *The Paston Letters*, by J. Gairdner, London, 1896, p. 268 (no. 851).
2 *Sculpture in Britain: The Middle Ages*, Pelican History of Art, London and Bungay, 1955, p. 179.
3 Commissary Court of London, f. 176, Harvey.
4 Published in *Sussex Archaeological Collections*, vol. VIII, 1885; Letters of W. Courthorpe, *Somerset Herald*, p. 23.
5 Prerogative Court of Canterbury, 31, Wattys. See also the will of Edmund Mulso Knight, 1458, who required a monument 'after my persone and degre', Prerogative Court of Canterbury, Stokton.
6 Published in *Somerset Archaeological Collections*, vol. II, p. 169.
7 Prerogative Court of Canterbury, 5, Wattys. The Monument was noted by Weever, *Ancient Funerall Monuments*, 1631, p. 695.
8 See article by A. White in *Trans. Mon. Brass Soc.*, vol. VIII, 1943, pp. 8–10. The second line of the inscription 'Pastoris pecorum Prothomartiris angligenarum' is found also on an inscription by Abbot John of Wheathampstead concerning the presentation by him of a manuscript of Valerius Maximus to the University of Oxford. The Bostock inscription furthermore refers to the deceased as Father and Mother.
9 Published by H. C. Andrews in *Trans. Mon. Brass Soc.*, vol. VII, part 2, 1935, p. 77. The original is referenced Prerogative Court of Canterbury, 23, Holden. The published transcription is not entirely accurate, and the author is indebted to J. A. Goodall, F.S.A., for a corrected translation.
10 Published in *Testamenta Vetusta*, by N. H. Nicolas, London, 1826, p. 510.
11 *Testamenta Eboracensia*, part I, Surtees Soc., London, 1836, no. CLXXVII, p. 243.
12 This will is published in full in *The Archaeological Journal*, vol. XV, 1858, pp. 267–77, including discussion of the bequests by A. Way. The directions relating to two brasses are on pp. 168–169.
13 See 'Enquête sur les dalles, lames de cuivre et autres monuments funéraires provenant d'ateliers de tombiers Gantois XIV–XVI Siécle', by V. van der Haegen, in *Annales du XXIIIe Congrès de la Fédération Archéologique et Historique de Belgique*, Gand (1913), pub. 1914, p. 32.
14 V. van der Haegen, op. cit., p. 32.
15 V. van der Haegen, op. cit., p. 37.
16 V. van der Haegen, op. cit., p. 39.
17 This important record is at present kept in the Archdiocesan Archives of Gnieznó, reference Dekretal Kapituly Tom i, Fol. 123(a). It has been published in *Monumenta Medii Aevi-Acta Historica res gestas Poloniae illustrantia*, Tom 13, by H. Ulanowski, Kraków, 1894, p. 339. In view of the importance of the document in strengthening the claim that brasses were engraved in Bruges in the fifteenth century, the text is quoted in full:

'Item praefatus dominus Albertus Arepus deposuit iam actualiter centum marcas gr.latorum Prag. et centum marcas mediorum gr. in cripta seu thesauraria Ecclesie Gnezn. in et ad manus fratrum suorum Capituli Gnezn. pro sepultura sua per ipsos exponendas circa ipsam sepulcuram in Offertorium, in elemosinas ministrorum et pauperum huius Ecclesie ac in cereis et pannis laneis et promittit dare et procurare viginti stamina sericea pro ipsa sepultura, que remaneant in ipsa Ecclesia pro ornatibus et cappis, noluit tamen, quod vicarii sint participes dictorum XX staminum, quia debent contentari de laneis pannis et elemosinis, que tunc ipsis circa sepulturam per fratres de Capitulo/assignabuntur/, in quo consciencias ipsorum fratrum onerat, ne aliter faciant, quam ipse dnus Arepus ordinavit et disposuit testamentaliter et perfecte. Et si secus fecerint, reddent racionem Deo omnipotenti. Et lapis iam paratur in Brugis, super quo exposite sunt iam quadringente marce in moneta prutenicali levis monete per Simonem tenutarium Camyen et procuratorem de pecunia Arepali, nec ultra quidquam restat pro ipso lapide solvendi, qui lapis ornatus auricalco ad instar lapidis Johannis Arepi Zuchywylk, et elegit ac elegit ipse dnus Arepus ante maius altare locum sue sepulture, et dni in Capitulo hoc generali promiserunt solempniter hanc peticionem implere.'

The author is much indebted for information on this matter to the Rev. Wladyslaw Zientarski, Director of the Archdiocesan Archives at Gniezno. According to the Director, Jan of Czarnków, a chronicler contemporary with Jan Zuchywilk, records that Zuchywilk died on 5 April 1382, and was buried in Gniezno, where in the choir he had a tombstone, which during his life he had ordered from Flanders.

18 Prerogative Court of Canterbury, 4, Blamyr.

19 The patron is preserved in the British Museum, Lansdowne 874, folio 191. The author is indebted to Lawrence James for notice of this survival.

20 See 'The Sandys Contract', by F. A. Greenhill, *Trans. Mon. Brass Soc.*, vol. IX, 1960, pp. 354–61.

21 Illustrated in *The Memorials* (Fig. 257) from the plate by W. F. Creeny, *Monumental Brasses on the Continent of Europe*, Norwich, 1884, p. 67.

22 Published as a note with illustration in *Sussex Notes and Queries*, vol. II, May 1929, pp. 175–7.

23 The references are the Wynn Papers nos. 1933, 2310 and 2312, preserved in the National Library of Wales, Aberystwyth. These are briefly summarized in the *Calendar of Wynn (of Gwydir) Papers, 1515–1690*, printed for the National Library, 1924–6. The author is indebted to H. J. B. Allen for drawing his attention to these important records.

Chapter 9: The sources of designs (pages 99 to 109)

1 Illustrations of details from the Sebald shrine draft, compared with details from the brasses of Łukasz and Uriel, are published as plates XXXVII and XXXV in *Der Entwurf von 1488 zum Sebaldusgrab*, Posen, 1915, by F. Detloff. The Sebald shrine was a project of immense importance to Peter Vischer the Elder, and it is most unlikely that he slavishly copied the subsidiary figures from an established pattern book. Their treatment does not indicate such a source. It may accordingly be presumed that both these brasses were influenced by sketches for this draft or the draft itself and cannot be earlier than *c.* 1488. Professor Detloff further shows in *Stosunki Artystyczne Biscupa Poznańskiego Urjela z Górki z Norymberger*, Poznań, 1919, that Uriel was a personal acquaintance of Peter Vischer the Elder. Uriel visited Nürnberg in 1488 and Detloff suggests he ordered his father's memorial and his own at that time.

2 *Peter Vischer der Ältere und Seine Werkstatt*, by S. Meller, Leipzig, 1925, p. 88.

3 Illustrated *Portfolio Mon. Brass Soc.*, vol. VI, 1868, plate 53.

4 *The York School of Glass Painting*, by J. A. Knowles, London, 1936, p. 38. Likewise John Browne, Serjeant Painter, bequeathed 'my great boke of armys, and my boke of trickys of armes, and my boke of armys and badges in my studye' to Richard Bygnalle; see *Archaeologia*, vol. XXXIX, 1963, p. 24.

5 'Monumental Brasses—A New Classification of Military Effigies *c.* 1360–*c.* 1485', in *Journal of the British Archaeological Association*, third series, vol. XIII, 1949, pp. 70–96.

6 *Macklin's Monumental Brasses*, revised by J. C. Page-Phillips, London, 1969, p. 93.

7 Illustrated by M. W. Norris in *Brass Rubbing*, London, 1965, fig. 89.

8 Dr. Kent recognized the difficulty posed by

these brasses but concluded (p. 81) that 'there seems to be nothing distinctly provincial in the style', though he accepts as probable the provincial origin of one at Theddlethorpe All Saints, Lincs. The brasses are discussed more fully in Chapter Seven of *The Memorials*.

9 *Plyta nagrobna Jakuba z Sienna w Katedrze Gnieznienskieg*, by B. Kunzendorf (unpublished), 1955. A copy is in the library of the Art Institute, Poznań, Poland.

10 An alternative, though less probable, source is that of Gdańsk, Poland. The craftsman Hans Brandt, to whom is attributed the brass of Bishop Paulus Legendorf, formerly at Braniewo and now at Olsztyn, is known to have undertaken work for Archbishop Jakub. Such an origin would not alter the complex derivation of the design.

11 See the article 'Cardinal Nicholas de Cusa' by H. F. Owen-Evans, in *Trans. Mon. Brass Soc.*, vol. X, 1963, pp. 25–8.

12 The illustration of Joyce Tiptoft in *The Memorials* (Fig. 166) may be compared with Eleanor de Bohun (Fig. 173) and the lost brass from St. Mary Lambeth as reproduced in *Church Brasses* by A. C. Bouquet, London, 1956, plate 52.

13 The brass of Rudhale is illustrated, p. 2, in *Monumental Brasses in Hereford Cathedral* by A. F. Winnington-Ingram, Hereford, 1956. Frowsetoure is illustrated in *Portfolio Mon. Brass Soc.*, vol. I, 1897, part VIII, plate 5. A sketch of Rudhale before mutilation, made in the seventeenth century by Thomas Dingley, is reproduced in *History from Marble*, Camden Society, 1867, plate CXXXVIII.

14 There are several examples of such treatment, as for example on the retrospectively laid memorials to John Polsted (d. 1540), Cuthbert Blakeden, Esq. (d. 1540) and John Boothe, Esq. (d. 1548), and Robert Smythe (d. 1539), all

with wives, and laid between 1580 and 1588 at Thames Ditton, Surrey.

15 *Testamenta Eboracensia IV*, Surtees Society, vol. LIII, 1866, p. 217.

16 The Leça do Balio composition should be compared with a late fourteenth century Matins page, both illustrated in *The Memorials*, Figs. 48 and 49. The framework of canopied saints and devices occurs on both, though with different detail, and both include a representation of the Annunciation.

17 See *Schlesische Fürstenbilder des Mittelalters*, by H. Luchs, Breslau, 1872, plates 28 and 10a respectively. The similarity to Duke Bolko is exceedingly close except for the position of the shield.

18 'Die Glocken und Stückgiesserfamilie Hilliger', by J. Schmidt in *Mitteilungen des Freiberger Alterthumsvereins*, vol. XXXI, Freiberg, 1865, p. 354.

19 The documents relating to this case are published by F. A. Greenhill in *Trans. Mon. Brass Soc.*, vol. X, 1969, pp. 412–19. The precise character of the work is doubtful, as the size of the copper plate is not stated, and the painter's task is described as '*schilderyen en pourtraituren*'. In all probability it was an engraved plate painted, and the artist may well have supervised the engraving also. A large indent exists at Dunkeld Cathedral, Perthshire, which may have been the setting of this memorial.

20 The attribution is fully discussed by Dr. P. Quarré in 'Plaques de fondations d'Isabelle de Portugal, duchesse de Burgogne, aux Chartreuse de Bâle et de Champmol-les-Dijon', *Jaresbericht 1959 des Historischen Museums*, Basel, 1959.

21 The relationship of the Hornebolts to the Boleyns is described by H. Paget in 'Gerard and Lucas Hornebolt in England', *Burlington Magazine*, Nov. 1959, pp. 396ff; in particular on p. 400. If either were involved it would most probably be Lucas, Gerard having left England about 1532.

22 In *Bernt Notke und Sein Kreis*, Berlin, 1939. The brass and its details are superbly reproduced in vol. II on plates 120–5, vol. I, text, pp. 113–20.

23 Dr. H. Eichler's analysis is published in *Mitteilungen des Vereins für Lübeckische Geschichte und Altertumskunde*, Lübeck, 1930, pp. 39–45. Dr. Eichler compares the figure of Johann both in treatment of head, hands and drapery with the figures on the St. Luke altar in the St. Annen Museum, Lübeck, completed in 1483, and certainly the work of Rode. Eichler concludes 'On the whole it can be said that the figure of Lunerburg, without any attempt at portraiture, represents a prototype, painted by Rode in a great number of variations.' Dr. Paatz agrees with Eichler's attribution.

24 In 'Die Lübeckische Bronzeproduction des 15 und 16 Jahrhunderts', in *Repertorium für Kunstwissenschaft*, Berlin/Leipzig, 1930, p. 85. Dr. Paatz compares the figure of the Virgin on the Lübeck brass with the Virgin on the Schleissheim altarpiece, painted by Jacob van Utrecht.

25 *Das Christliche Denkmal—Der Dom zu Meissen*, Union-Verlag, Berlin, 1967, pp. 56–8.

26 Dr. Ernst Heinz Lemper, op. cit., p. 58.

27 'Gotycka Plyta Nagrobna Kunona von Liebenstein w Nowyn Miescie nad Drweca', by Kamila Wróblewska, in *Kommunikaty Mazursko-Warminskie*, no. 3, 1961.

Bibliography

The following bibliography does not contain all the works referred to in notes within the text, but is included as a select list of publications relating to the subjects covered in *The Craft*. A fuller bibliography, with notes as to the particular value of several of the books and articles mentioned, is included in *The Memorials*.

General monumental background

Boutell, C., *Christian Monuments in England and Wales*, G. Bell, London, 1849.

Creeny, W. F., *Illustrations of Incised Slabs on the Continent of Europe*, Norwich, 1891.

Crossley, F. H., *English Church Monuments*, Batsford, London, 1921.

Esdaile, A. J. K., *English Church Monuments 1510–1840*, Batsford, London, 1946.

Evans, J., *English Art 1307–1461*, Oxford, 1949.

Gough, R., *Sepulchral Monuments of Great Britain*, two vols., J. Nichols, London, 1786–96.

Greenhill, F. A., *Incised Effigial Slabs*, Faber and Faber, London, 1976.

Harvey, J. H., *Henry Yevele*, Batsford, London, 1944. *Mediaeval Craftsmen*, Batsford, London, 1975.

Hollis, T. and G., *Monumental Effigies of Great Britain*, London, 1840–2.

Lethaby, W. R., *Westminster Abbey and the King's Craftsmen*, Duckworth, London, 1906.

Lüer, H. and Creutz, M., *Geschichte der Metallkunst*, Stuttgart, 1909.

Mercer, E., *English Art 1553–1625*, Oxford, 1962.

Müller, T., *Sculpture in the Netherlands, Germany, France and Spain: 1400–1500*, Pelican History of Art, London and Bungay, 1966.

Panofsky, E., *Tomb Sculpture*, Thames and Hudson, London, 1964.

Pevsner, N. B. L., *The Englishness of English Art*, Reith Lectures, BBC, London, 1955.

s'Jacob, H., *Idealism and Realism*, Leyden, 1954.

Stone, L., *Sculpture in Britain—The Middle Ages*, Pelican History of Art, London and Bungay, 1955.

Stothard, C. A., *The Monumental Effigies of Great Britain*, Chatto and Windus, London, 1876 edition.

Weever, J., *Ancient Funerall Monuments within the United Monarchie of Great Britaine and Ireland . . .* , London, 1631.

English brasses—works of general reference

Bertram, J., *Brasses and Brass Rubbing in England*, David & Charles, Newton Abbot, 1970.

Bouquet, A. C., *Church Brasses*, Batsford, London, 1956.

Boutell, C., *Monumental Brasses and Slabs*, G. Bell, London, 1847.

Gawthorpe, W. E., *The Brasses of Our Homeland Churches*, Homeland Pocket Books, London, 1923.

Haines, H., *A Manual of Monumental Brasses*, J. H. and J. Parker, Oxford and London, 1861. Reprinted Adams & Dart, Bath, 1970.

Macklin, H. W., *The Brasses of England*, Methuen, London, 1907.

Mann, J., *Monumental Brasses*, King Penguin, Harmondsworth, 1957.

Norris, M. W., *Brass Rubbing*, Studio Vista, London, 1965, 2nd edn. 1969.

Page-Phillips, J., *Macklin's Monumental Brasses*, George Allen and Unwin, Hemel Hempstead, 1969.

Stephenson, M., *A List of Monumental Brasses in the British Isles*, first printed 1926, and an Appendix by Giuseppi, M. S. and Griffin, R., first printed 1938. The two reprinted together by Headley Bros., Ashford, 1964.

Trivick, H. H., *The Craft and Design of Monumental Brasses*, J. Baker, London, 1969.

Trivick, H. H., *The Picture Book of Brasses in Gilt*, J. Baker, London, 1971.

Victoria and Albert Museum, *Catalogue of Rubbings of Brasses and Incised Slabs*, London, 1929, reprinted 1968.

Waller J. G. and L. A. B., *A Series of Monumental Brasses from the Thirteenth to the Sixteenth Century*, London, 1864. This beautiful volume has been reprinted with additional notes and descriptions by J. A. T. Goodall and J. C. Page-Phillips, by Phillips and Page Ltd., London, 1975.

In addition to the books listed the following periodicals are essential reading:

The Oxford Journal of Monumental Brasses, the journal of the Oxford University Brass Rubbing Society, 1897–1914.

The Oxford Portfolio of Monumental Brasses, the portfolio series of the Oxford University Brass Rubbing Society, 1898–1901, and 1950–5.

The Portfolio of the Monumental Brass Society, the portfolio series of the Monumental Brass Society, 1894–1914, and 1935–(continuing).

Transactions of the Cambridge University Association of Brass Collectors, 1887–93. This association became in 1893 The Monumental Brass Society, and the transactions of the latter are a continuation of the Cambridge series.

Transactions of The Monumental Brass Society, 1893–1914 and 1935–(continuing). Most recent research has been published in these transactions. Further references are made to these transactions under the abbreviation *Trans. Mon. Brass Soc.*

Additional references

The following books and articles are of particular value for special aspects of the study.

Anderson, M. D., *The Imagery of British Churches*, Batsford, London, 1955.

Badham, S., Blair, J. and Emmerson, R., *Specimens of Lettering from English Monumental Brasses*, Phillips and Page Ltd., London, 1976.

Cameron, H. K., 'The Metals Used in Monumental Brasses', *Trans. Mon. Brass Soc.*, vol. VIII, part V, 1946.

Cameron, H. K., 'Technical Aspects of Medieval Monumental Brasses', *The Archaeological Journal*, vol. 131, 1974, pp. 215–37.

D'Elboux, R. H., 'Testamentary Brasses', *Antiquaries Journal*, vol. XXIX, 1949.

Esdaile, A. J. K., 'The Sculptor and the Brass', *Trans. Mon. Brass Soc.*, vol. VII, 1935.

Gadd, M. L., 'English Monumental Brasses of 15th and early 16th centuries, with special reference to the process of their manufacture', *Journal of the British Archaeological Association*, 1937.

Gawthorp, W., 'Ancient and Modern Methods of Engraving Brasses', *Transactions of the St. Paul's Ecclesiological Society*, vol. IX, 1922.

Greenwood, R., and Norris, M., *The Brasses of Norfolk Churches*, The Norfolk Trust, Woodbridge, 1976.

Hamilton, H., *The English Brass and Copper Industry to 1800*, Longmans, London, 1926.

Kent, J. C. P., 'Monumental Brasses—A New Classification of Military Effigies', *Journal of the British Archaeological Association*, Third Series, vol. XII, 1949.

Knowles, J. A., *The York School of Glass Painting*, S.P.C.K., London, 1936.

Page-Phillips, J., *A Sixteenth Century Workshop*. Unpublished, 1958. A copy is retained in the library of the Museum of Archaeology and Ethnology, Cambridge.

Raven, J. J., *The Bells of England*, Methuen and Co., London, 1906.

Wyckoff, D., *Albertus Magnus Book of Minerals*, Translation, Oxford, 1967.

The Continent of Europe

GENERAL

Cameron, H. K., *A List of Monumental Brasses on the Continent of Europe*. The Monumental Brass Society, London, 1970. *Addendum* published 1973.

Creeny, W. F., *A Book of Facsimiles of Monumental Brasses on the Continent of Europe*, privately printed, Norwich, 1884.

The Low Countries

GENERAL

Brehmer, W., 'Lübecks messingene Grabplatten aus vierzehnten Jahrhundert', *Hansiche Geschichtsblätter*, vol. IV, Leipzig, 1884.

Cameron, H. K., 'The 14th-Century School of Flemish Brasses', *Trans. Mon. Brass Soc.*, vol. XI, no. LXXXVII, 1970 (pub. 1972), pp. 50–81.

Collon-Gevaert, S., *Histoire des Arts du Métal en Belgique*, Bruxelles, 1951.

Eichler, H., 'Flandrische gravierte Metallgrabplatten des XIVe Jahrhunderts', *Jahrbuch des preussischen Kunstsammlungen*, vol. LIV, 1933.

Musée de la Byloke, *Exposition Art du Cuivre*, Gand, 1961.

Panofsky, E., *Early Netherlandish Painting*, Harvard, 1953.

Rousseau, H., *Frottis de Tombes Plates—Catalogue Descriptif*, Bruxelles, 1912.

THE BRUGES WORKSHOPS

Greenhill, F. A., 'The Ledger of Andrew Halyburton', *Trans. Mon. Brass Soc.*, vol. IX, 1954.

Ulanowski, B., *Monumenta Medii Aevi Historica res gestas Poloniae illustrantia*, Tom 13, Kraków, 1894. Contains documentary evidence relating to a Flemish brass, formerly at Gnieznó, Poland, supporting the view that engravers worked in Bruges.

THE GENT WORKSHOPS

van de Hagen, V., 'Enquête sur les dalles, lames de cuivres et autres monuments funéraires provenant de tombiers Gantois XIV–XVI Siècle', *Annales du XXIIIe Congrès de la Fédération Archéologique et Historique de Belgique, Gand, 1913*, (pub. 1914).

THE TOURNAI WORKSHOPS

de la Grange, A. and Cloquet, L., *Études sur l'Art à Tournai et sur les Anciens Artistes de cette ville*, Tournai, 1887.

Hoquet, A., *Le Rayonnement de l'Art Tournaisien*, Tournai, 1924.

Verriest, L., 'Un Fonds d'Archives d'un intérêt exceptionnel. Les "Chirographes" de Tournai', *Annales du Cercle Archéologique de Mons*, Mons, 1939, pp. 139–94.

THE ANTWERPEN WORKSHOPS

Op de Beek, R. A. E., 'Flemish Monumental Brasses in Portugal', *Trans. Mon. Brass Soc.*, vol. X, 1965.

MISCELLANEOUS

Borenius, T., 'St. Henry of Finland', the *Archaeological Journal*, vol. LXXXVII, 1930.

Eichler, H., 'A Flemish Brass of 1398', *The Burlington Magazine*, vol. LX, 1932.

Gaillard, J., *Inscriptions Funéraires et Monumentales de la Flandre Occidentale*, Bruges, 1866.

Quarré, P., 'Plaques de Fondations d'Isabelle de Portugal duchesse du Bourgogne, aux Chartreuse de Bâle et de Champmol-les-Dijon', *Jahresbericht 1959 des Historischen Museums*, Basel.

Thome, M., *Les Maîtres Tombiers, Sculptures et Statuaires Liégeois*, Liège, 1909.

Weale, W. H. J., 'Note sur les lames funéraires en cuivre conservées à Bruges', *Bulletin de la Gilde de Saint Thomas et de Saint Luc*, Bruges, 1900.

Germany

GENERAL

Fritz, J. M., *Gestochener Bilder*, Köln, 1966.

Norris, M. W., 'The Schools of Brasses in Germany', *Journal of the British Archaeological Association*, vol. XIX, 1956.

Weimar, W., *Monumental Schriften vergangener Jahrhunderte von ca 1100–1812 an Stein-Bronze und Holzplatten*, Vienna, 1899.

LÜBECK WORKSHOPS

Baltzer J. and Bruns, F., *Die Bau und Kunstdenkmäer der Freien und Hansestadt Lübeck*, Lübeck, 1920.

Cameron, H. K., 'Monumental Brasses on the Continent—Lübeck', *Trans. Mon. Brass Soc.*, vols. VII and X.

Eichler, H., 'Die Messingne Grabplatte des Johann Lüneburg in der Katharinenkirche zu Lübeck', *Mitteilungen des Vereins fur Lübeckische Geschichte und Altertumskunde*, Lübeck, 1930.

Paatz, W., *Bernt Notke und Sein Kreis*, Berlin, 1939.

Paatz, W., 'Die Lübeckische Bronzeproduction des 15 und 16 Jahrhunderts', *Repertorium für Kunstwissenschaft*, Berlin/Leipzig, 1930.

Miscellaneous works relating to brasses from the Baltic regions

Greenhill, F. A., 'Monumental Brasses in Norway', *Trans. Mon. Brass Soc.*, vol. X, 1963.

Hamner, J. W., and Wideén, *Die Grabsteine der Ruinenkirchen in Wisby*, Stockholm.

Wróblewska, K., 'Gotycka Plyta Nagrobna Kunona von Liebenstein w Nowym Miesce nad Drweca', *Kommunikaty Mazursko-Warminskie*, no. 3, 1961.

THE NÜRNBERG WORKSHOPS

Detloff, F., *Der Entwurf von 1488 zum Sebaldusgrab*, Posen, 1915.

Detloff, F., *Stosunki Artystyczne Biscupa Poznańskiego Urjela z Górki z Norymberga*, Poznań, 1919.

Gerlach, H., *Die Mittelalterlichen gravierten messingenen Grabplatten insbesondere in den Domen zu Meissen und Freiberg*, Freiberg, 1866.

Kämpfer, F., *Peter Vischer*, Dresden, 1960.

Kramer, J., *Metallne Grabplatten in Sachsen c. 1390–1510*, Halle, 1912.

Meller, S., *Peter Vischer der Ältere und Seine Werkstatt*, Leipzig, 1925.

Waetzoldt, W., *Dürer*, Phaidon, London, 1950.

THE FREIBERG AND DRESDEN WORKSHOPS

Gerlach, H., *Photographien von Original-Abdrücken mittelalterlicher gravirter messingener Grabplatten*, Freiberg, 1867.

Schmidt, J., 'Die Glocken – und Stückgiesserfamilie Hilliger', article in *Mitteilungen des Freiberger Alterthumsvereins*, vol. XXXI, 1865–6.

THE RHENISH WORKSHOPS

Hilger, H. P., *Die Denkmäler des Rheinlandes. Kreis Kleve. 4*, Düsseldorf, 1967.

Scholten, R., *Zur Geschichte der Stadt Cleve*, Kleve, 1905.

Brasses in Spain

Edleston, R. H., 'The Monumental Brasses of Spain' *Proceedings of the Cambridge Antiquarian Society*, vol. XIX, 1914–15.

Brasses in Switzerland

Cameron, H. K., 'Brasses in Switzerland', *Trans. Mon. Brass Soc.*, vol. X, 1967 (published 1969).

Poland

THE KRAKÓW WORKSHOPS

Czarny, M., 'Poznogotycki malarz Krakówski', *Studia Renesansowe*, Warszawa, 1963, vol. III.

THE WROCŁAW WORKSHOPS

Burgemeister, L. and Grundmann, G., *Die Kunstdenkmäler der Stadt Breslau*, Breslau, 1930.

Kebłowski, J., *Nagrobki Gotyckiena Sląskzu*, Poznań, 1969.

Kunzendorf, B., *Plyta nagrobna Jacuba z Sienna w Katedrze Gnieznienskieg*, 1955, Magister dissertation; unpublished, held by the Art Institute, Poznań.

Luchs, H., *Schlesische Fürstenbilder des Mittelalters*, Breslau, 1872.

Schultz, A., *De Vita atque operibus magistri Jodici Tauchen Lapicidae Wratislaviensis Seculo XV*ᵗˢ *florentis*, Disertatio inauguralis Vratislaviae, Breslau (1864).

Schultz, A., 'Schlesiens Kunstlebe in Fünfzehnten bis achtzehnten Jahrhundert', *Verein fur Geschichte der Bildenden Kunste zu Brezlau*, Breslau, 1872.

The Plates

1. Bronze relief plate to Christoph Ziegler (1517), Meissen Cathedral, East Germany; probably by the Vischer atelier, Nürnberg. Length 0·81m (32½in). Photo by and produced with kind permission of Deutsche Fotothek, Dresden.

2. Inlaid mosaic floor monument to Abbot Gilbert (1152) from the Abbey of Maria Laach, West Germany; now in the Rheinisches Landesmuseum, Bonn. Photo reproduced by kind permission of the Museum Director.

3. Enamelled tomb plate of Jean de France (d.1247), formerly at the Abbey of Royaumont, France. From the drawing of Roger de Gaignières, by kind permission of The Bodleian Library, Oxford.

4. Engraved brass to Phillipe and Jean (engr. c. 1230–50), sons of Louis VIII, King of France; formerly at Notre Dame, Poissy, France. French work. From the drawing illustrated by Montfauçon.

5. General view of the chancel and its brass paved floor, Cobham, Kent. Photo K. & S.

6. Illustration for the smelting and casting of brass (1574) after L. Ercker, reprinted from the *Transactions of the Monumental Brass Society*.

7. (*left*) Engraved coffin plate of St. Ulrich (d. 973), laid in 1187, church of St. Ulrich and St. Afra, Augsburg, West Germany; Swabian work. Length 1·10m (43½in). The plate is now reburied, the illustration being based on a negative rubbing, made by Dr. and Mrs. M. Tennenhaus, and reproduced with their kind permission.
8. (*right*) Bishop Yso von Wölpe (1231), Andreaskirche, Verden, West Germany. German work, length 1·98m (78in). N.R.

9, 10. Incising a monumental slab, manuscript illumination (*c.* 1320).
Photo by kind permission of the Trustees of the British Museum.

11. St. Eligius, patron saint of metal workers, in a workshop (15th C.), German, by the Master of Balaam.
Photo by kind permission of the Prentenkabinet, Amsterdam, Holland.

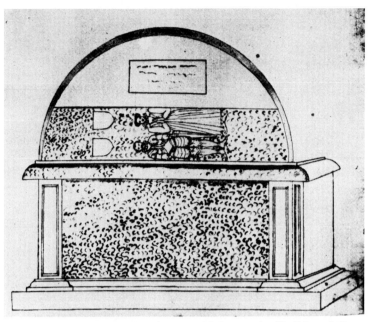

12. Sketch (c. 1585–c. 1590) for tomb with brasses for Sir Edward Gage and wife, at West Firle, Sussex, by Gerard Johnson, sculptor of Southwark. Illustrated by kind permission of Viscount Gage.

13. William Cokyn, Esq. (1527) and two wives, children, etc. omitted, Hatley Cockayne, Beds.; Cambridge work. Length of male effigy 0·72m (28¼in). N.R.

14. John Fysher, Esq. (1528), wife, etc. omitted, Clifton, Beds.; Cambridge work. Length of effigy 0·72m (28¼in). N.R. The full-scale design of Fig. 13 was apparently reused.

15. Johann and Lambert Munten (1559), Aachen Cathedral, West Germany; Rhenish work, probably made in Aachen. Length 0·91m (36in). Photo Münchow.

16. Reverse of plate to Johann and Lambert Munten, Aachen Cathedral; painted with an alternative version of the composition. Photo Münchow.

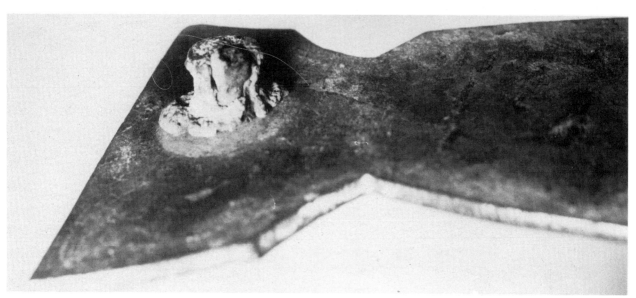

17. Detail—Rivet head from shroud brass (*c.* 1510), still set in original lead plug. Photo Wright.

18. Detail—upper part with inlaid tabard of John Feld, Esq. (1477), Standon, Herts. London work 'F' series. Photo Wright.

19. François Senocq and wife (1552), Musée de la Princerie, Verdun, France; French work heavily painted. Length 0·34m (13½in). Photo Studio-Photo-Cine Bellot-Galloy, by kind permission of the Museum Director.

20. Thomas of Woodstock, Duke of Gloucester (1397), formerly at Westminster Abbey; London work. From the illustration published by F. Sandford in *A Genealogical History of England*, p. 230.

21. Queen Marguerite of France (1295); formerly at the Abbey of St. Denis, France; French work. From the drawing by Roger de Gaignières. By kind permission of The Bodleian Library, Oxford.

22. Archbishop Thomas Cranley (1417),
New College, Oxford, Oxon.; London
work 'B' series. Length of effigy 1·52m
(61in). N.R. Oxford University Portfolio.

23. Duke Friedrich of Saxony (1510), Meissen Cathedral, East Germany;
attributed to Hermann Vischer the Younger, Nürnberg, Germany.
Length 2·31m (96in). Photo by and reproduced with kind permission of
Deutsche Fotothek, Dresden.

24. Detail—Sir Symon Felbrygge, K.G. (1416), Felbrigg, Norfolk;
London work 'B' series. Photo K. & S.

25. Sir George Monox, Lord Mayor of London (1543), wife, shields, etc. omitted, Walthamstow, Essex; London work 'G' series. Length of effigy 0·36m (14in). N.R.

26. Thomas Benolt, Clarenceux King of Arms (1534), and two wives, formerly at St. Helen's, Bishopsgate, London; from drawing in the possession of the Merchant Taylors' Company and reproduced with kind permission of the Master and Wardens of the Company.

27. Griele van Ruwescuere (1410), the Béguinage, Bruges, Belgium; Flemish work. Length 0·43m (17in). N.R.

28. John Borrell, Sergeant-at-Arms (1531), Broxbourne, Herts.; Cambridge work. Feet drawn from a faint rubbing in the Society of Antiquaries. Length of effigy 0·71m (28in). N.R.

29. John Selwyn, gent. (1587) and wife, Walton-upon-Thames, Surrey; Johnson style.
Length of male effigy 0·44m (17½in). Photo K. & S.

30. John Balsam (1410), Blisland, Cornwall; London work?
'A' series. Length of effigy 0·50m (19½in). N.R.

31. John Stonor (1512), Wraysbury, Bucks.; London work
'F' series. Length of effigy 0·31m (12in). N.R.

32. John Reed and wife (1503), Wrangle, Lincs.; London work 'G' series.
Length of male effigy 0·91m (36in). N.R. H. W. Jones.

33. Reginald Spycer (1442) and four wives, Cirencester, Glos.; London work 'B' series. Length of male effigy 0·46m (18in). Photo K. & S.

34. Anne, daughter of Sir Robert Drewry, twice depicted with her two husbands (1572), Depden, Suffolk; London work 'G' series. Length of male effigy 0·28m (11in). Photo K. & S.

35. Composite brass of Richard Covert, Esq. and three wives (engr. *c.* 1525, 1527 and 1547), Slaugham, Sussex; London work 'G' series. Length of male effigy 0·32m (12¾in). Photo K. & S.

36. Tomb with brass of Sir William de Burgate (1409) and wife, Burgate, Suffolk; London work 'B' series. Photo Newell.

37. Latten lectern with engraved brass to Martin Forrester, Friar (*c.* 1460), Yeovil, Somerset; probably London work. Photo K. & S.

38. Detail—Sir John de Cobham holding a representation of Cobham College, which he founded (engr. *c.* 1365), Cobham, Kent; London work 'A' series. Photo K. & S.

39. St. Ethelred, King of the West Saxons (d. 871) (engr. *c.* 1440, inscription 17th C.), Wimborne Minster, Dorset; London work, probably 'B' series. Length of effigy 0·35m (14in). N.R.

40. Three ancestors of Stanislaus Czarnkówski (engr. 1602), Czarnków, Poland; by Walery Kunink of Poznań. Length 2·08m (82in). N.R.

41. (*above*) John Knyvet, Esq. (1417), Mendlesham, Suffolk; London work 'D' series. Length of effigy 1·41m (55½in). N.R. F. A. Greenhill.

43. (*below*) (?) James de Holveston (1378), Blickling, Norfolk; London work 'B' series. Length of effigy 0·25m (9¾in). N.R.

44. Detail—the dog 'Jakke', from lost brass to Sir Brian de Stapilton (1438) and wife, Ingham, Norfolk; London work 'B' series. From the Craven Ord 'pressing' of the original.

45. External high tomb with remains of brass to Stephen Scott (1601), High Halden, Kent. Photo K. & S.

42. (*left*) Bishop Peter Novak (1456), Wrocław
Cathedral, Poland; Wrocław work, possibly
by Jodok Tawchen. Length 2·33m (92in).
Photo by courtesy of the Muzeum Slaskie,
Wrocław, taken prior to damage in the
Second World War.

46. (*left*) William Palmer 'with ye stylt' (1520), Ingoldmells, Lincs.; probably
Bury St. Edmunds work, series 3. Length of effigy 0·51m (20in). N.R.
47. (*right*) An archbishop, probably St. Thomas of Canterbury (*c.* 1520),
Edenham, Lincs.; London work debased 'F' series. Length of effigy 0·45m
(17¾in). N.R. H. F. Owen Evans.

48. Detail—bedesmen at feet of a lady (engr. c.1410), St. Stephen, Norwich; London work. N.R. Society of Antiquaries.

49. Detail—rebus for John Shipwash (1457), Hambledon, Bucks.; London work 'B' series. Length 0·13m (5in). P.R.

50. Margaret Wyllughby, inscription omitted (1483), Raveningham, Norfolk; Norwich work series 1. Length of effigy 0·65m (25½in). N.R.

51. Thomas Salle, Esq. (1422), Stevington, Beds.; London work 'E' series. Length of effigy 0·81m (32in). N.R.

52. Detail—embroidery alluding to the name Walter Pescod (1398), Boston, Lincs. N.R. H. W. Jones. (See Fig. 253.)

53. Abel Porcket (1509), Gruuthuse Museum, Bruges, Belgium; Flemish work. Length 0·81m (32in). N.R. From Creeny.

54. Detail—feet of Edward Cowrtney, Esq. (1509), Landrake, Cornwall; possibly an allusion to the mandrake legend. N.R. Society of Antiquaries.

55. Detail of Margaret Cheyne (1419), Hever, Kent; London work 'B' series. Photo K. & S.

56. Detail of canopy of Canon John Sleford (1401), Balsham, Cambs.; London work 'B' series. Photo Wright.

57. Detail of canopy of Sir Nicholas Hawberk (engr. *c.* 1410), Cobham, Kent; London work 'B' series. Photo K. & S.

58. Albrecht Hövener (1357), Nicolaikirche, Stralsund, East Germany; Flemish work. Length 2.54m (100in). P.R. From Creeny.

59. Edmund Croston (1507), St. Mary-the-Virgin, Oxford; London work 'G' series. Length of effigy 0·23m (9in). N.R. H. F. Owen-Evans.

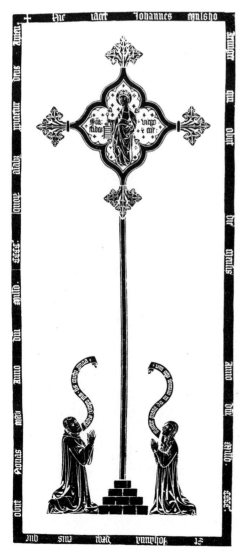

61. Ralph Hamsterley (engr. c. 1515), Oddington, Oxon.; London work 'G' series. Length of effigy 0·74m (29in). N.R. Mon. Brass Soc.

60. John Mulsho, Esq., and wife (1400), Geddington, Northants.; London work 'B' series. Length of male effigy 0·33m (12¾in). N.R. Mon. Brass Soc.

62. Bishop Robert Wyvil (1375),
Salisbury Cathedral, Wilts.; London
work 'A' series. Length of castle
design 2·28m (90in). From Waller.

63. (*left*) Canon Robert
Wyntryngham (1420),
Cotterstock, Northants.;
London work 'D' series.
Length of effigy 0·94m (37in)
N.R. Mon. Brass Soc.

64. (*right*) Nicholas Wadham, Esq. (1609),
and wife, Ilminster, Somerset; probably by
Gerard Johnson of Southwark.
Length of male effigy 1·27m (50in).
N.R. Mon. Brass Soc.

65. Thomas Pownder (1525), and wife, Christchurch Mansion Museum, Ipswich, Suffolk; Flemish work. Length 1·16m (45½in). Photo by kind permission of the Christchurch Mansion Museum.

66. Sir Thomas Sellynger and wife Anne, Duchess of Exeter (d. 1475, engr. *c.* 1495),
St. George's Chapel, Windsor, Berks. London(?) goldsmith's work. Length 0·58m (23in).
Photo K. & S. by kind permission of the Dean and Chapter of St. George's Chapel.

67. View of the floor in the choir, Freiberg Cathedral, East Germany. By courtesy of the director, Stadt Museum, Freiberg.

68. Fragment of a cross and inscription to one of the children of William de Valence, probably Margaret (1276); Westminster Abbey, London. Probably made and inlaid with mosaic by Odoric and the court craftsmen. Length of brass fragment 0·23m (9in). Photo by kind permission of the Dean of Westminster.

69. Richard Blakysley (1493), Lillingstone Dayrell, Bucks.; London work, a variant of 'F' series. Length of effigy 0·27m (10½in). N.R. Presentation of the stole is an engraver's error.

70. Probably a caster's mark (*c.* 1330–40), Westley Waterless, Cambs. Diameter 0·02m (¾in). Photo Wright.

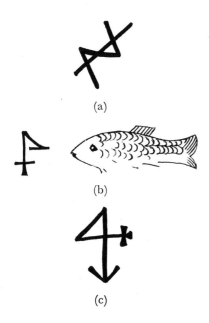

(a)

(b)

(c)

71. Engravers' marks: a) Zeitz, East Germany (*c.* 1465), unknown engraver from (?) Erfurt. b) Bamberg, West Germany (1464), of the Vischer foundry, Nürnberg. c) Gnieznó, Poland (1480) unknown engraver of (?) Wroclaw.

72. Sir Thomas Stathum and two wives (1470), Morley, Derbyshire; London work 'D' series; length of male effigy 0·48m (19in). N.R. H. W. Jones.

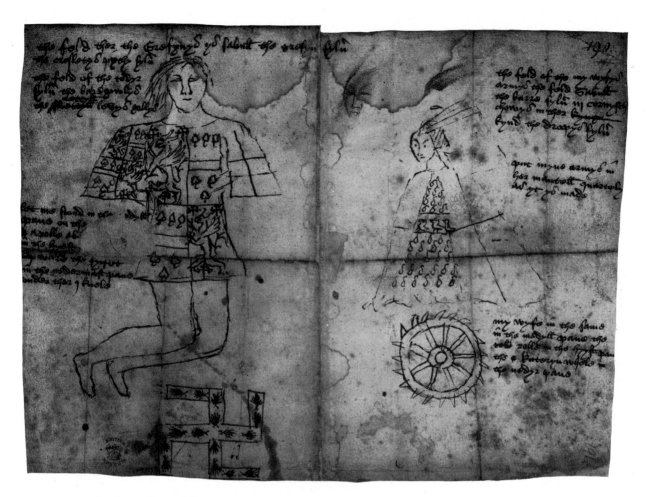

73. Design or 'patron' for figures of the Froxmere family (*c.* 1485). Photo by kind permission of the Trustees of the British Museum.

HIC IACET IOHES GAGE ARMIGER ET
DVÆ VXORES EIVS ELIZABETHA ET MAR
GARETA QVI OBIERVNT ANNO DÑI MILES
MO QVINGENTESIMO NONAGESIMO QVINT
QVORVM ANIMABVS PROPICIETVR DEVS

74. Sketch for the brass of John Gage, Esq., and two wives (c. 1585–c. 1590), by Gerard Johnson of Southwark. Illustrated by kind permission of Viscount Gage.

75. John Gage, Esq. and two wives (c. 1590), West Firle, Sussex, by Gerard Johnson of Southwark. Length of male effigy 0·86m (34in). P.R. I. T. W. Shearman.

76. Sir Owen Wynne (engr. 1661), Llanrwst, Denbigh, Wales, by Robert Vaughan at London. Length 0·50m (19½in). N.R. H. J. B. Allen.

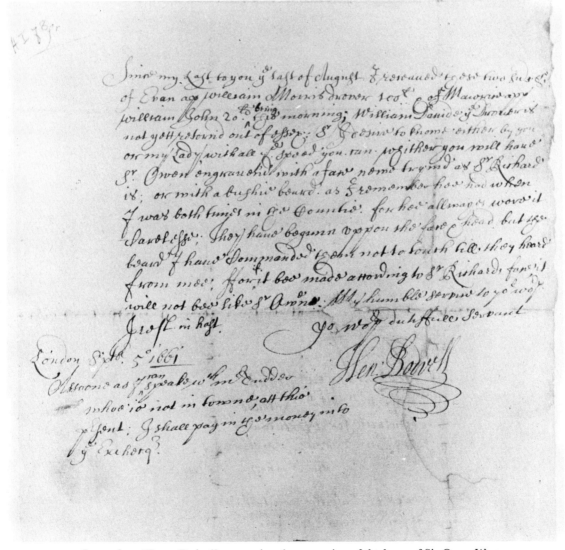

77. Letter from Henry Bodvell concerning the engraving of the brass of Sir Owen Wynne. Photo by kind permission of the National Library of Wales.

78. (*above*) Detail from Peter Vischer the Elder's draft of 1488 from the shrine of St. Sebald. From Detloff.

79. (*below*) Detail from the canopy of Bishop Uriel of Górka (d. 1498, engr. *c.* 1490), formerly at Poznań Cathedral, Poland; by Peter Vischer the Elder of Nürnberg. From Detloff.

80. Łucasz of Górka, Palatine of Poznań (engr. *c.* 1490), formerly at Poznań Cathedral, Poland; by Peter Vischer the Elder of Nürnberg. Length 2·64m (104in). Photo by kind permission of the Instytut Sztuki, Warszawa.

82. Woodcut by Albrecht Dürer of Saints Nicholas, Ulrich and Erasmus.

83. (*left*) Saint Albert, from the canopy of Cardinal Fryderyk (engr. 1510), Kraków Cathedral, Poland; attributed to Hermann Vischer the Younger of Nürnberg. N.R.

84. (*right*) Saint Stanislaus, from the canopy of Cardinal Fryderyk.

81. Bishop Andrzej Bninski (1479); formerly at Poznań Cathedral, Poland. Flemish work. Length 2·51m (99in). P.R. From Creeny.

85. (*left*) (?) John St. Leger (1442), Ulcombe, Kent;
London work 'B' series. Length of male effigy 1·02m
(40in). N.R.

86. (*right*) John Digges (*c.* 1456), wife omitted, Barham,
Kent; London work 'B' series. Length of male effigy
0·91m (36in). N.R.

88. Thomas Reynes, Esq. (1451) and wife, Marston Mortaine, Beds
London work 'B' series. Length of male effigy 0·94m (37in). N.R.

87. Henry Parice, Esq. (1466),
(canopy, inscription, etc.,
omitted), Hildersham, Cambs.;
London work 'B' series.
Length of male effigy 1·09m
(43in). N.R.

89. John Stathum, Esq. (1454) and wife, Morley, Derbyshire; London work 'B' series. Length of male effigy 0·41m (16in). N.R. H. W. Jones.

90. John Ruggewyn, Esq. (1412), Standon, Herts.; London work 'B' series. Length of effigy 0·15m (6in). Photo Wright.

91. Nicholas Deen (d. 1479, engr. *c.* 1490) and
wife, Barrowby, Lincs.; London work 'F'
series. Length of male effigy 0·90m (35¼in).
N.R. H. W. Jones.

92. Paul Dayrell, Esq. (1491) and wife, Lillingstone Dayrell, Bucks.; London
work 'F' series. Length of male effigy 0·69m (27in). Photo K. & S.

93. Archbishop Jakub Szienienski (1480), Gnieznó Cathedral, Poland; (?) Wrocław work.
Length 2·84m (112in). N.R. From Creeny.

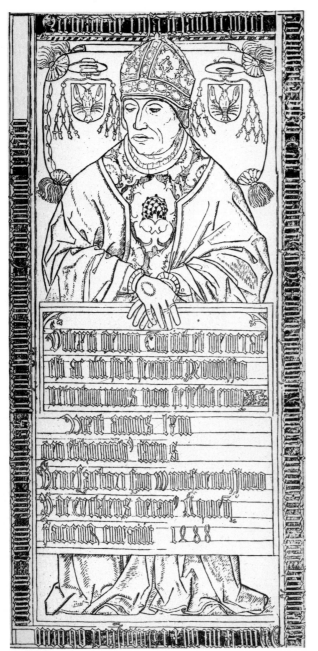

94. Cardinal Nicholas de Cusa (d. 1464, engr. 1488),
Kues, West Germany; Rhenish work; Length 1·99m
(79in). P.R. From Creeny.

95. Cardinal Nicholas de Cusa (d. 1464), incised slab,
St. Peter ad Vincula, Roma (Rome), Italy; Italian
work. Photo Vasari, from Mon. Brass Soc.

96. Johann Lunerborch (engr. *c.* 1470), Katherinenkirche, Lübeck, West Germany; Lübeck work, design attributed to Hermen Rode. Length 2·81m (111in). N.R. Creeny.

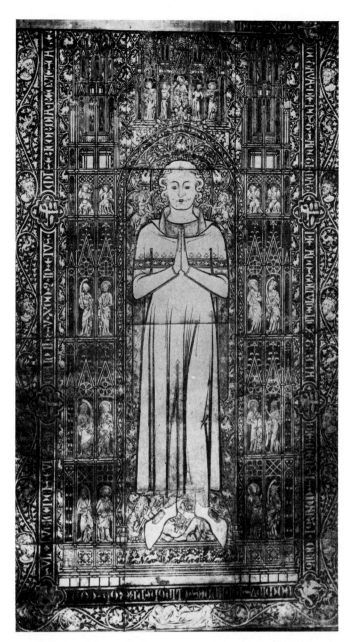

97. Johann Clingenberg (1356), formerly in the Petrikirche, Lübeck, West Germany; Flemish work. Length 2·81m (118in). Photo Castelli.

98. John Garneys, Esq. (1524) and wife, Kenton, Suffolk; London work, debased 'F' series. Length 0·50m (19¾in). Photo Newell.

99. Nicholas Garneys, Esq. and wife (engr. *c.* 1630), Ringsfield, Suffolk; probably Norwich work. Length 0·55m (21½in). Photo Newell.

100. Peter Rede, Esq. (1568), St. Peter Mancroft, Norwich, Norfolk; probably Norwich work. Length 0·85m (33¼in). N.R. H. W. Jones.

101. Sir William Molineux and two wives (engr. c. 1570), Sefton, Lancs.; London work. Length 0·92m (36¼in). From Waller.

103. (*right*) Ralph Lord Stafford, from brass to Sir Hugh Hastyngs (1347), Elsing, Norfolk; London work. Photo K. & S.

102. (*below*) Detail of fourteenth century glass, Ely Cathedral, Cambs. Photo by kind permission of the Courtauld Institute.

104. Duke Heinrich 'The Pious', Duke of
Saxony. Portrait by Lukas Cranach the
Elder, Dresden.

105. Duke Heinrich 'the Pious' (1541), Freiberg Cathedral, East
Germany; caster Martin Hilliger at Dresden; designer Lukas Cranach.
Length 2·54m (99½in). P.R.

106. (*left*) Bishop Philippe de Cahors of Evreux (1281), formerly at the Church of the Jacobins at Evreux, France. French work signed by Guillaume de Plalli. From the drawing of Roger de Gaignières, by kind permission of The Bodleian Library, Oxford.

107. (*centre*) Hervil de Cérizy (?*c.* 1320), formerly at the Abbey of Longpont, France. French or Franco/Flemish work. From the drawing of Roger de Gaignières, Bibliothéque Nationale, Paris.

108. (*right*) Bouchard VI, Count of Vendôme (1343), formerly at St. George, Vendôme, France. French work. From the drawing of Roger de Gaignières, by kind permission of The Bodleian Library, Oxford.

109. (*left*) Figure in armour of the Northwood family, probably Sir John de Northwood (d. 1319), (engr. *c.* 1330), Minster, Isle of Sheppey, Kent; probably French work, legs ascribed to English restoration. Length of effigy 1·72m (68in). N.R. From Belcher.

110. (*right*) Lady, probably Elizabeth, wife of Roger de Northwood (1335), Minster, Isle of Sheppey, Kent; probably French work. Length of effigy 1·57m (62in). N.R. From Belcher.

111. Engraved plate recording the grant of indulgences (*c.* 1285), Halberstadt Cathedral, East Germany; German work. Length 0·41m (16in). Photo Bissinger, by kind permission of Dr. H. Eichler.

112. Bishop Otto von Brunswic (1279), Hidesheim Cathedral, West Germany; German work. Length 1·95m (77in). N.R. From Creeny.

113. Premislaus, Duke of Steinau (d. 1289, engr. *c.* 1305), from Monastery of Lubiaż, Muzeum Slaskie, Wrocław, Poland. Wrocław work. Length of effigy 1·93m (76in). N.R.

114. Boleslaus the Tall, Duke of Silesia (d. 1201, engr. *c.* 1305), from Monastery of Lubiaż, Muzeum Slaskie, Wrocław, Poland; Wrocław work. Length of effigy 1·98m (78in). N.R.

115. Conrad, Duke of Sagan (d. 1304, engr. c. 1305), from Monastery of Lubiaż, Museum Slaskie, Wrocław, Poland; Wrocław work. Length of effigy 1·74m (69in). N.R.

116. Martin Buswoyz (c. 130 from Monastery of Lubiaż, Muzeum Salskie, Wrocław, Poland; Wrocław work. Tot length 1·90m (75in). N.R.

117. Stephan of Lubiaż, Bishop (1345), Holy Cross Church and Diocesan Museum, Wrocław, Poland. Wrocław work. Length of effigy 1·31m (51½in). N.R.

118. Sir John Dabernoun (d. 1277 or
d. 1327, probably engr. *c.* 1320),
Stoke D'Abernon, Surrey; London
work. Length of effigy 1·93m (76in).
From Waller.

119. Detail of Sir John Dabernoun. Photo K. & S.

120. ?Sir William de Setvans (d. 1323).
Chartham, Kent; London work.
Length of effigy 1·88m (74in).
From Waller.

121. Detail of ?Sir William de Setvans. Photo K. & S.

123. Drawing made in 1641 of Sir Gascelin de Marham (c. 1320), canopy indent omitted, formerly at Peterborough Cathedral, Northants. Reproduced by kind permission of the Trustees of the Winchelsea Estate.

122. Sir William Fitzralph (engr. 1325–30), Pebmarsh, Essex. London work. Length of effigy 1·67m (66in). N.R.

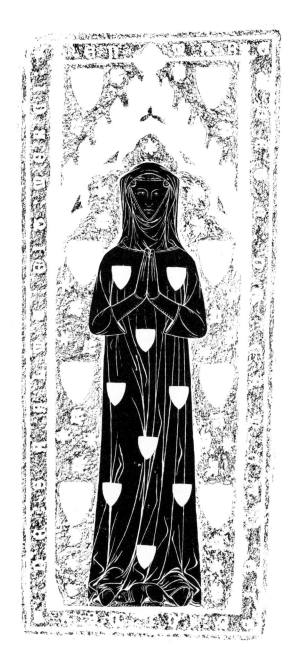

124. (*left*) Margarete de Camoys (*c.* 1315), Trotton, Sussex; London work. Length of effigy 1·60m (63in). N.R. J. R. Greenwood.

125. (*right*) Detail of Lady Joan de Kobeham (engr. *c.* 1320), Cobham, Kent. Photo K. & S.

126. Richard de Hakebourne (1322), Merton College Chapel, Oxford, Oxon.; London work. Length of effigy 0·53m (21in). Photo Hutchins.

127. Sir Richard de Boselyngthorpe, Buslingthorpe, Lincs.; probably North Eastern work.
Though long considered among the earliest English figure brasses, probably engraved
c. 1335–45. Length of effigy 0·44m (17¼in). Photo K. & S.

128. Detail of Sir John Dabernoun the second or third (engr. *c.* 1330–40), Stoke D'Abernon, Surrey; London work. Photo K. & S.

129. Sir Hugh Hastyngs (1347), Elsing, Norfolk; London work. Length of effigy, as remaining, 1·14m (45in). Photo Society of Antiquaries, London.

130. Detail—head of Sir Hugh Hastyngs with angel replaced in 1969. Photo K. & S.

131. Shield, detail of Sir John Gifford (1348),
Bowers Gifford, Essex; London work.
Photo R. Wilmer.

132. Laurence de St. Maur (1337), Higham Ferrers, Northants.
London work. Length of effigy 1·60m (63in). N.R. Mon. Brass Soc.

133. Richard de Beltoun (*c.* 1340), Corringham, Essex;
London work 'A' series. Length of effigy 0·33m
(13in). N.R.

134. Nichol de Gore (1333), Woodchurch, Kent;
London work. Length of effigy 0·32m (12½in).
N.R.

135. King Eric Menved and Queen Ingeborg (1319), Ringsted Cathedral, Denmark; Flemish work, heads of inlaid alabaster. Length 2·83m (112in). P.R. From Creeny.

136. Detail from Bishops Serken and Mul (1350), St. Annen-Museum, Lübeck, West Germany; Flemish work. Photo Castelli.

137. Base panel showing scenes from the life of St. Nicholas, from brass of Bishops Serken and Mul (*c.* 1350), St. Annen-Museum, Lübeck, West Germany; Flemish work. Photo Castelli.

138. Base panel showing scenes from the life of St. Eligius, from brass of Bishops Serken and Mul (1350), St. Annen-Museum, Lübeck, West Germany; Flemish work. Photo Castelli.

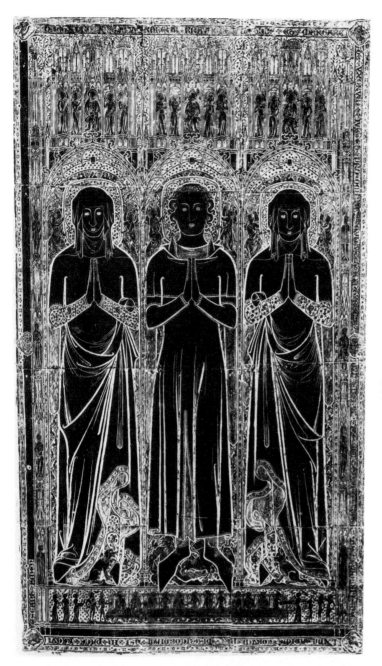

139. Robert Braunche and two wives (1364),
St. Margaret, Kings Lynn, Norfolk;
Flemish work. Length 2·70m (106½in). N.R.

140. Detail of base panel showing a peacock feast, from brass of Robert Braunche (1364),
St. Margaret, Kings Lynn, Norfolk; Flemish work. Photo K. & S.

141. William de Kestevene (1361), North Mimms, Herts.; Flemish work. Length of effigy 0·69m (27in). Photo K. & S.

142. Willem Wenemaer (1325), Museum de Bijloke, Gent, Belgium. Flemish, probably Gent work. Length of effigy 2·05m (81in). N.R.

143. Roger Thornton and wife (1411), St. Nicholas, Newcastle-upon-Tyne, Northumberland; Flemish work. Length 2·26m (89in). Photo Mayo, Newcastle-upon-Tyne.

144. Burial scene, (c. 1370) detail from side panels of St. Henry, Nousisainen, Finland; Flemish work. Length 0·51m (20in). N.R.

145. Battle scene, (c. 1370) detail from side panels of St. Henry, Nousisainen, Finland; Flemish work. Length 0·51m (20in). N.R.

146. Bishops Gottfried and Friedrich von Bülow (1375), Schwerin, East Germany; Flemish work. Length 3·83m (151in). N.R.

147. Joris de Munter and wife (1439), Bruges Cathedral, Belgium; Flemish work. Length 2·47m (97½in). N.R.

148. Sir Maertin van der Capelle (1452), Bruges Cathedral, Belgium; Flemish work. Length 2·41m (95in). N.R.

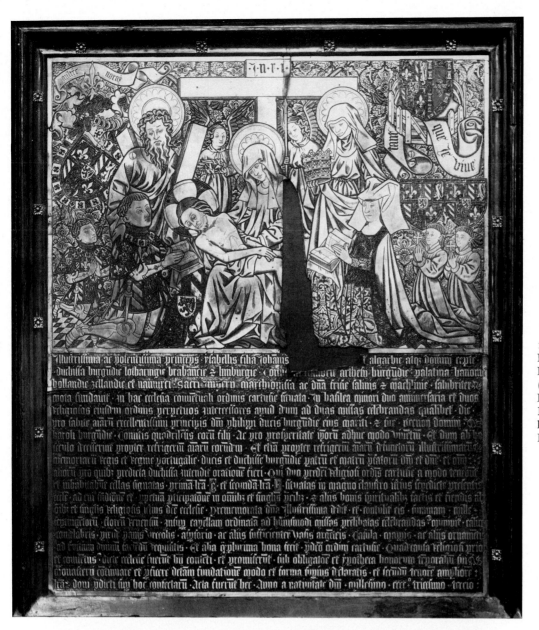

149. Isabella Duchess of Burgundy, Philip Duke of Burgundy and Lord Charles their living son (c .1450), Historisches Museum, Basel, Switzerland; Flemish work. Length 0·99m (39in). Photo by kind permission of the Director, Historisches Museum.

150. Seventeenth century copy of a fifteenth century painting at the Chateau of Montmirey, Jura, France. Photo from Quarré.

151. Abbess Marguerite de Scornay (c. 1460), Nivelles, Belgium; Flemish work. Width 0·81m (32in). Photo by kind permission of Institut Royal du Patrimonie Artistique, Bruxelles. Copyright A.C.L., Bruxelles. The plate is now damaged by fire.

152. Jean Moüen and wife (1453), the Louvre, Paris, France; Flemish work. Width 0·62m (24½in). Photo M. Chuzeville.

153. Detail—Philippe de Mézières (1405); French work.
Photo copyright A. C. L. Bruxelles.

154. Detail—Calvary from brass of Philippe de Mézières.

155. Philippe de Mézières (1405), Mayer van den Bergh Museum,
Antwerpen, Belgium; French work. Length 0·85m (33¼in).
Photo by kind permission of Institut Patrimonie Artistique, Bruxelles.
Copyright A. C. L. Bruxelles.

156. Jacob von Immenhausen (1395), Meyenburg Museum, Nordhausen, East Germany; (?) Thuringian work. Length 0·58m (23in). Photo Bildarchiv Foto, Marburg.

157. Katerina Verter (1397), Mayenburg Museum, Nordhausen, East Germany; (?) Thuringian work. Length 0·59m (23in). Photo Bildarchiv Foto, Marburg.

158. Detail—Heinrich von Werther (1397), Meyenburg Museum, Nordhausen, East Germany.(?) Thuringian work. Photo Bildarchiv Foto, Marburg.

159. Sketches of wall paintings
a) at the castle, Lochstedt;
and b) at the church of
Juditten, U.S.S.R. (formerly
in East Prussia).

160. Sir Kuno von Liebensteyn (1391), Nowemiasto Lubawskie, Poland. Made at the
Marienburg, Malbork, Poland. Length 2·48m (98in). N.R.

162. Thomas de Frevile and wife (1410), Little Shelford, Cambs.; London work 'A' series. Length of male effigy 0·76m (30in). Photo K. & S.

161. Sir John Harsick (1384), and wife, Southacre, Norfolk; London work 'B' series. Length of male effigy 1·55m (61in). Photo K. & S.

163. Thomas de Beauchamp, Earl of Warwick and wife (1406), St. Mary, Warwick, Warwicks.; London work 'B' series. Length of male effigy 1·57m (62in). Photo K. & S.

164. Thomas de Beauchamp and wife (1406), from Waller, showing *pointillé* decoration.

165. Drawing by Dugdale in 1641 of Beauchamp tomb.

166. Richard Hansard and wife (c. 1410), South
Kelsey, Lincs.; North Eastern work,
probably made at York. Length of male
effigy 1·44m (56½in). N.R. H. W. Jones.

167. Roger Keston (1409),
Astwood, Bucks.; London
work 'A' series. Length of
effigy 0·89m (35in). N.R.
H. W. Jones.

168. Raulin and Margaret Brocas (c. 1360), Sherborne St. John, Hants.; London
work 'A' series. Length of male effigy 0·18m (7in). Photo K. & S.

169. (*above*) John Lumbarde (1408), Stone, Kent;
London work 'B' series. Length of effigy 0·36m
(14in). Stem and foot of cross omitted.
Photo K. & S.

170. Detail—Henry de Codyngtoun (1404),
Bottesford, Leics.; London work 'A' series.
Photo K. & S.

171. Detail—canopy of Walter Pescod (1398) and wife (lost), Boston, Lincs.;
London work 'B' series. Photo K. & S.

172. Detail—Eleanor de Bohun, Duchess of Gloucester (1399), Westminster Abbey, London; London work 'B' series. Photo Wright.

173. Eleanor de Bohun, Duchess of Gloucester (1399), Westminster Abbey, London; London work 'B' series. Length of effigy 1·62m (64in). N.R. Victoria and Albert Museum. The right-hand foot of the canopy is here restored.

175. John Strete (1405), Upper Hardres, Kent; London work 'B' series. Total length 1·57m (62in). N.R. H. F. Owen Evans.

174. Sir John de Foxle (1378) and two wives, Bray, Berks.; London work 'B' series. Length of male effigy 0·79m (31in). Photo K. & S.

176. Detail from brass of Sir Robert Swynborne and son Sir Thomas (1412), Little Horkesley, Essex. Photo K. & S.

177. Sir Robert Swynborne and son Sir Thomas (1412), Little Horkesley, Essex; London work 'B' series. Length of Sir Robert's effigy 1·72m (68in). From Waller.

179. Simon Seman (1433), St. Mary's, Barton-on-Humber, Lincs.; London work 'B' series. Length of effigy 1·51m (59½in). N.R. H. W. Jones.

178. Thomas, Baron Camoys (d. 1421 though stated 1419) and wife, Trotton, Sussex; London work 'D' series. Length of male effigy 1·47m (58in). N.R.

180. Agnes Fortey with her two husbands, William Scors, tailor, and Thomas Fortey, woolman (1447), Northleach, Glos.; London work 'E' series. Length of complete Scors effigy 0·87m (34in). Photo K. & S.

  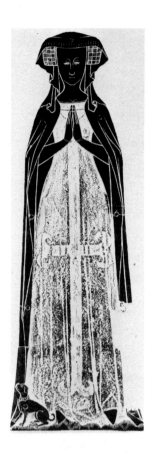

181. (*left*) Agnes Salmon (1430), remains of husband and canopy omitted, Arundel, Sussex; London work 'D' series.
Length of effigy 1·39m (54½in). N.R. 182. (*centre*) Maiden lady of the Clopton family (*c.* 1420), Long Melford, Suffolk; London
work 'D' series. Length of effigy 0·46m (18¼in). Photo Wright. 183. (*right*) Alice Shelton (1424), remains of husband omitted,
Great Snoring, Norfolk; London work 'B' series. Length of effigy 0·93m (36½in). N.R.

184. Detail—Joan Peryent (1415), Digswell, Herts.;
London work 'B' series. Photo K. & S.

185. Priest and students (*c.* 1430), British Museum collection; London work 'B' series. Diameter 0·13m (5¼in). N.R.

186. Detail—children of William West (engr. *c.* 1440), Sudborough, Northants.; London work 'B' series, probably made by the son William who was a London marbler. Length of John West, priest, 0·24m (9½in). Photo K. & S.

187. Detail—the brothers and sisters of Philippe Carreu (1414), Beddington, Surrey; London work. Length of effigy 0·07m (2¾in). Photo Hubbard.

188. Prior Thomas Nelond (1433), Cowfold, Sussex;
London work 'B' series. Length of effigy 1·77m (70in).
From Waller.

189. Robert Staunton, Esq. and wife (1458), Castle
Donnington, Leics. London work 'D' series. Length of
male effigy 0·91m (36in). N.R. H. W. Jones.

190. Lodewijc Cortewille, Esq. (1504) and wife, Victoria and Albert Museum, London—
formerly at Watou, West Vlaanderen, Belgium; Flemish work. Length 2·03m (80in).
P.R.

191. Willem van Gaellen (1539), Breda Cathedral, Holland; Flemish work. Length 2·03m (80in).
Photo by kind permission of Rijkdienst voor de Monumentenzorg, Voorburg, Holland.

192. Guillaume Juvenal des Ursins and (?) son (1472), formerly at Notre Dame Cathedral, Paris, France; French work. From the drawing of Roger de Gaignières, Bibliothèque Nationale, Paris.

194. Nicholas le Brun (1547) and wife, British Museum collection, London, formerly at Jeumont, France; French work. Total length 0·62m (24½in). P.R. H. F. Owen Evans.

193. Charles d'Amboise, Admiral of France, and his son Georges (engr. c. 1525), formerly at the church of the Cordeliers at Amboise, France. French work. From the drawing of Roger de Gaignières. By kind permission of the Bibliothèque Nationale, Paris.

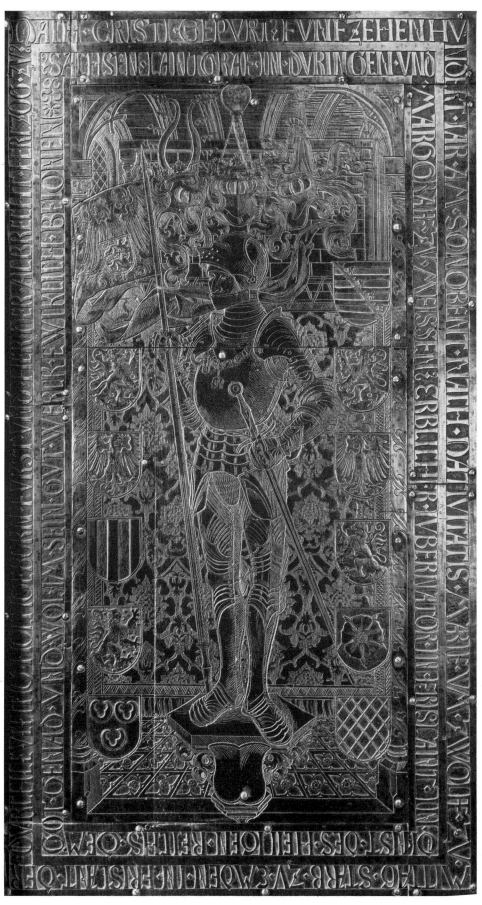

195. Duke Albrecht of Saxony (1500), Meissen Cathedral, East Germany; probably by
Hermann Vischer the Younger, Nürnberg. Length 2·45m (97in).
Photo by, and reproduced with kind permission of, Deutsche Fotothek Dresden.

196. Zedena Duchess of Saxony (1510), Meissen Cathedral, East Germany; probably
by Hermann Vischer the Younger, Nürnberg, and designed by Albrecht Dürer.
Length 2·44m (96½in). Photo by, and reproduced with kind permission of,
Deutsche Fotothek, Dresden.

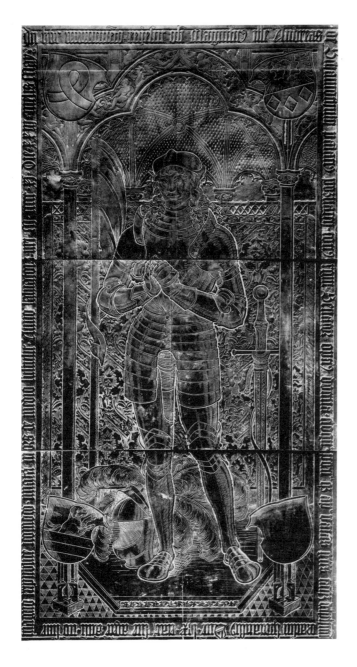

197. Andrzej Szamotułski (1511), formerly at Szamotuły,
Poland; attributed to Hermann Vischer the Younger,
Nürnberg. Length 2·71m (107in). Photo by kind permission
Instytut Sztuki, Warszawa.

198. Hermann Hutterock and wife (1505), Marienkirche,
Lübeck, West Germany; Lübeck work, designed by Bernt
Notke. Length 2·15m (85in). N.R.

199. Detail—Johann Lunerborch (engr. *c.* 1470), Katherinenkirche, Lübeck, West Germany; probably Lübeck work, designed by Hermen Rode. Photo Castelli.

200. Bartolomäus Heisegger (1517), St. Annen-Museum, Lübeck, West Germany; Lübeck work, design attributed to Jacob van Utrecht. Length 0·89m (35in). Photo Castelli.

201. Catherine de Bourbon (d. 1469, engr. c. 1480),
St. Stevenskerk, Nijmegen, Holland; by Willem
Loeman, Köln. Length 1·98m (78in). Photo by
kind permission of Rijkdienst voor de
Monumentenzorg, Voorburg, Holland.

202. Duke Johann II of Kleve and wife (engr. between c. 1510 and c. 1525)
Kleve, West Germany; by Willem Loeman and Lambert a goldsmith,
both of Köln. Length 1·50m (59in). Photo by courtesy of the Landes-
Konservator, Rheinland.

203. Jan Koniekpolski and sons Przedbor and Jan (engr. *c.* 1475), Wielgomłyny, nr. Radomsko, Poland; Kraków work. Length 2·81m (111in). N.R.

204. Sir Walter Mauntell (d. 1487, engr. c. 1495) and wife,
Nether Heyford, Northants.; London work, variation
of 'F' series. Length of male effigy 1·18m (46½in).
N.R. H. W. Jones.

205. Man in armour of (?) the Compton family and wife (c. 1500),
Surrey Archæological Society, Guildford, Surrey; London work 'D'
series. Length 0·50m (19½in). N.R. H. F. Owen Evans.

206. Detail—Roger Dynham, Esq. (1490), Waddesdon, Bucks.; London work 'D' series. Photo K. & S.

209. High tomb of John Tame, Esq. (1500), Fairford, Glos.; London work. Photo K. & S.

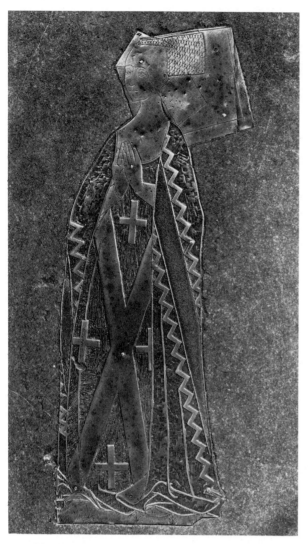

207. (?) Alice Harleston (engr. *c.* 1480), Long Melford, Suffolk; London work 'F' series. Length of effigy 0·92m (36in). Photo Wright.

208. Detail—Bishop Richard Bell (1496), Carlisle Cathedral, Cumberland; London work 'D' series. Photo K. & S.

210. Detail—trade emblems and mark of John Taylour (*c.* 1490), Northleach, Glos.; London work 'D' series. Length 0·16m (6¼in). Photo K. & S.

211. John Tame, Esq. (1500), and wife, Fairford, Glos.; London work 'F' series.
Length of male effigy 0·95m (37½in). Photo K. & S.

212. Detail—Sir Thomas Bullen, K.G. (1538), Hever, Kent; London work with special design. Photo K. & S.

213. Detail—Richard Fermer, Esq.
(1552), Easton Neston, Northants.;
London work 'G' series.
Photo K. & S.

214. Sir John Porte (1557) and wives, Etwall, Derbyshire; London work 'G' series.
Length of male effigy 0·38m (15in). N.R. H. W. Jones.

215. Detail—canopy of Thomas Bushe and wife (1526),
Northleach, Glos.; London work debased 'F' series. Photo K. & S.

216. Thomas Brewse, Esq. (1514) and
wife, Little Wenham, Suffolk;
London work 'G' series. Length of
male effigy 0·71m (28in). N.R.

217. (*left*) Edmund Wayte, gent. (1518), wife and inscription omitted, Renhold, Beds.; London work 'F' series. Length of effigy 0·38m (15in). N.R. Society of Antiquaries.

218. (*centre*) Isabel Gifford (1523), shown in pregnancy gown, inscription omitted, Middle Claydon, Bucks.; London work debased 'F' series. Length of effigy 0·48m (18¾in). N.R.

219. (*right*) Thomas Heron (1517), inscription omitted, Little Ilford, Essex; London work 'G' series. Length of effigy 0·42m (16½in). N.R.

220. Geoffrey Fyche (1537), St. Patrick's Cathedral, Dublin, Ireland; London work 'G' series. Length 0·64m (25in). N.R.

221. (*left*) Thomas Tonge (1472), Beeford, Yorks.; York work series 2. Length of effigy 0·96m (38in). N.R. From Mill Stephenson.
222. (*right*) Sir Robert Demoke (1545), inscription omitted, Scrivelsby, Lincs.; North Eastern work. Length of effigy 0·74m (29¼in). N.R. H. W. Jones.

223. (*left*) Man in armour (*c.* 1470), wife omitted, Great Thurlow, Suffolk; Probably Bury St. Edmunds work series 1. Length of effigy 0·64m (25in). N.R. H. W. Jones.
224. (*centre*) Henry Rochforth, Esq. (1470), inscription and shields omitted, Stoke Rocheford, Lincs.; York work series 2. Length of effigy 0·76m (30in). N.R. H. W. Jones.
225. (*right*) Edmund Clere, Esq. (1488), wife, shields, etc. omitted, Stokesby, Norfolk; Norwich work series 3. Length of effigy 0·67m (26½in). N.R. H. W. Jones.

227. Thomas Hevenyngham, Esq. (1499), wife, shields and scrolls omitted, Ketteringham, Norfolk; Norwich work series 3. Part of the gilding remaining. Length of effigy 0·38m (14¾in). Photo K. & S.

226. Detail—John Wellys, Mayor (1495), St. Laurence Norwich, Norfolk; Norwich work series 3. Photo K. & S.

228. John Terry (1524), and wife, long inscription omitted, St John Maddermarket, Norwich, Norfolk; Norwich work series 6. Total length 0·89m (35in). N.R.

229. Edmund Assheton (1522), Middleton, Lancs.; (?) Northern work. Length of effigy 0·58m (23in). N.R.

231. William Att Wode (1529), wife omitted, Doynton, Glos.; West of England (?Gloucestershire) work. Length of effigy 0·62m (24½in). N.R.

232. John Wyncoll (1544), Little Waldingfield, Suffolk; probably Bury St. Edmunds work series 3 [or 4]. Length of effigy 0·46m (18¼in). N.R.

230. Civilian and wives (c. 1530), Elmdon, Essex; Cambridge work. Length of male effigy 0·74m (29in). N.R.

233. Laurence Saunders, Esq. (1545) and wife, Harrington, Northants.; probably Coventry work series 3. Length of male effigy 0·38m (15in). N.R. H. W. Jones.

234. Raff Brown, Mayor (1522), St. Gregory, Canterbury, Kent; Kentish work, probably made in Canterbury. Length of figure plate 0·26m (10¼in). N.R.

235. Civilian (feet restored) and wife (c. 1480), Lutterworth, Leics.; probably Coventry work series 1. Length of male effigy 0·46m (18¼in). N.R. H. W. Jones.

236. Chalice brass for Edmund Ward (1519), North Walsham, Norfolk; Norwich work series 6. Length of chalice 0·28m (11in). N.R. H. F. Owen Evans.

237. Heart brass for John Merstun (1446), Lillingstone Lovell, Bucks.; London work 'E' series. Length 0·22m (8½in). Photo K. & S.

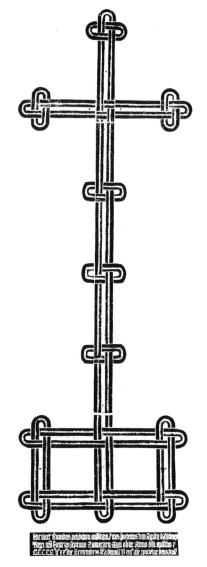

238. Cross for Richard Pendilton (1502) Eversley, Hants.; London work. Total length 1·88m (74½in). N.R. Mon. Brass Soc.

239. Peter Denot, glover (c. 1440), Fletching, Sussex; London work 'B' series. Length of gloves 0·12m (4½in). N.R. H. F. Owen Evans.
Gloves and inscription closer together than in the original.

240. Bernard Brocas, Esq. (1488), Sherborne St. John, Hants.; London work 'F' series. Length of effigy 0·51m (20in). Photo K. & S.

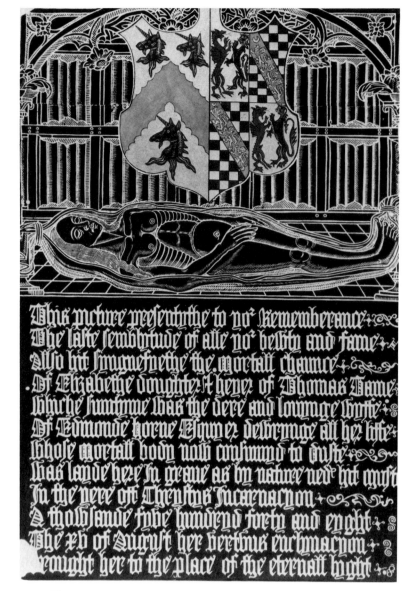

241. Elizabeth Horne (1548), Shipton-under-Wychwood, Oxon.; London work 'G' series. Length 0·66m (26½in). N.R. H. F. Owen Evans.

242. Elyn Bray (1516), Stoke D'Abernon, Surrey; London work 'F' series. Length of effigy 0·30m (12in). N.R.

243. Richard Foxwist, notary (1500), Llanbeblig, Caernarvon, Wales; London work. Length 0·19m (7½in). N.R.

244. Skull, formerly set on tomb of John Deynes (1527) and wife, Beeston Regis, Norfolk; Norwich work. Length 0·30m (12in). N.R. H. W. Owen Evans.

245. Duchess Sybilla Elisabeth (d. 1606),
Freiberg Cathedral, East Germany;
made at Dresden most probably
by Hans Hilliger. Length 2·50m
(98½in). N.R. From Gerlach.

246. Detail—Duchess Dorothea (d. 1617,
engr. c. 1624), Freiberg Cathedral,
East Germany; made at Dresden
by Hans Hilliger. N.R.

247. Iven Reventlow (1569) and two wives and son, Lebrade, Schleswig-Holstein, West
Germany; by Matthias Benning of Lübeck. Total length 1·99m (78½in). P.R., by kind
permission of the Director, Landesamt für Denkmalpfleger Scheswig-Holstein.

248. Francisco de la Puebla and wife (1577), St. Jacques, Bruges, Belgium; Flemish work. Length 2·00m (79in). N.R.

249. Allaine Dister and wife (engr. *c.* 1575), Lavenham, Suffolk; London work 'G' series. Length 0·61m (24in). Photo K. & S.

250. Silvester Lambarde (1587), Lower Halling, Kent; London work 'G' series. Length 0·71m (28in). Photo K. & S.

251. John Cocke, Esq. and daughter (1617), Stagsden, Beds.; London work, Johnson style. Length 0·76m (30in). N.R. H. W. Jones.

252. George Clifton, Esq. (1587) and wife, Clifton, Notts.; London work, Johnson style. Length of male effigy 0·66m (26in). N.R. H. W. Jones.

253. John Fenton (1566), Coleshill, Warwicks.; London work 'G' series. Length of effigy 0·47m (18½in). N.R. H. W. Jones.

254. Anne Boroeghe (1577), Dingley, Northants.; London work 'G' series. Total length 0·40m (15¾in). N.R. H. F. Owen Evans.

255. Alexander Strange (1620), Buntingford, Herts.;? by a London book plate engraver and set in original wooden frame. Length 0·38m (15in). Photo Wright.

256. Bishop Henry Robinson (1616), Carlisle Cathedral, Cumberland; by Richard Haydocke, Oxford. Length 0·57m (22½in). Photo K. & S.

257. John Pen, Esq. (1641) and wife, Penn, Bucks.; London work, attributed to Edward Marshall.
Length of male effigy 0·70m (27½in). Photo K. & S.

258. William Strode, Esq. and wife (1649), Shepton Mallet, Somerset; London work, attributed to Edward Marshall. Width 1·19m (47in). N.R. from Connor.

259. Richard Breton, gent. (1659) and wife, Barwell, Leics.; probably Midlands work. Length 0·53m (31in). N.R. H. W. Jones.

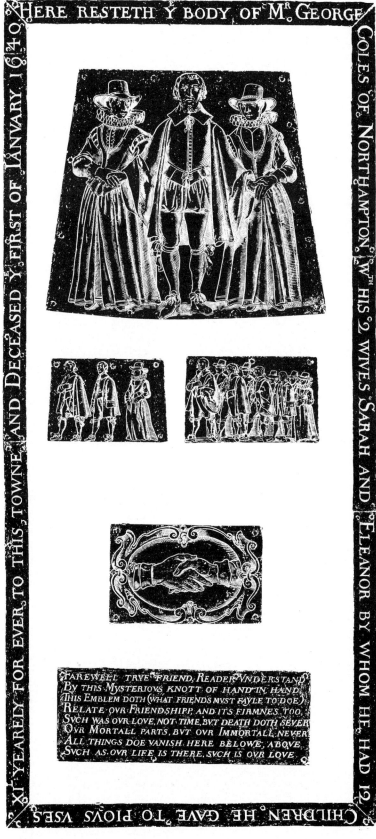

260. George Coles (1640) and wives, St. Sepulchre, Northampton, Northants.; London work. Length of plate with effigies 0·64m (25in). N.R. H. W. Jones.

261. Helen Boteler (1639), Biddenham, Beds.; London work. Length 0·67m (26½in). N.R. H. W. Jones.

Here lyeth the Body of Dame Sarah Wynne wife to the
Honored Sr Richard wynne of Gwyddur Barronet and one
of the Daughters of Sr Thomas Middleton of chirke Castle Knight
shee departed this life the 16th day of Iune 1671

Gul. Vaughan Sculpsit

262. Dame Sarah Wynne (1671), Llanrwst, Denbigh, Wales; by William Vaughan. Length 0·57m (22½in). Photo Hubbard.

263. Brass to the Walsh family (1752), Curry Rivel, Somerset; West Country work. Length 0·38m (15in). Photo Love.

264. (*left*) Mrs. Philadelphia Greenwood (1747), St. Mary Cray, Kent; London work. Length 0·53m (21in). Photo K. & S.

265. (*right*) Benjamin Greenwood, Esq. (1773), St. Mary Cray, Kent; London work. Length 0·53m (21in). Photo K. & S.

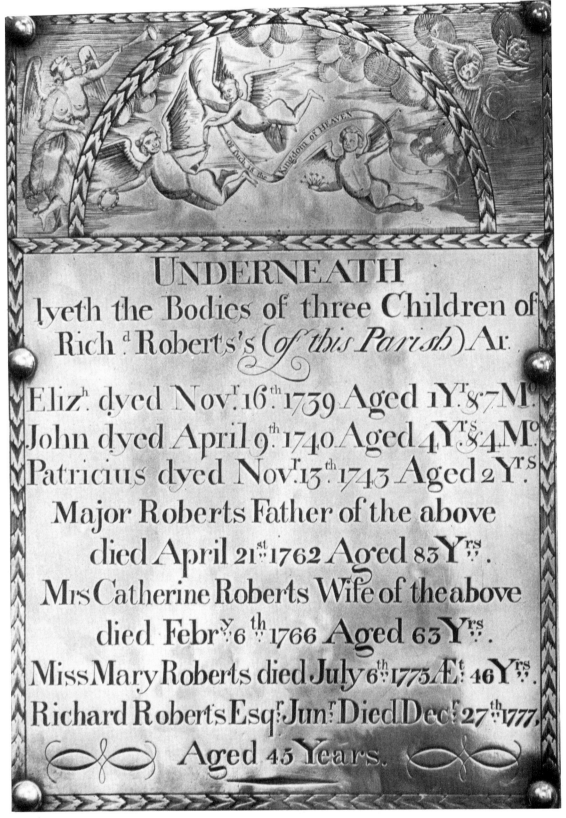

UNDERNEATH
lyeth the Bodies of three Children of
Rich.ᵈ Roberts's (*of this Parish*) A.ᵣ.

Eliz.ʰ dyed Nov.ʳ 16.ᵗʰ 1739 Aged 1 Y.ᵣ & 7 M.ᵒ
John dyed April 9.ᵗʰ 1740 Aged 4 Y.ʳˢ & 4 M.ᵒ
Patricius dyed Nov.ʳ 13.ᵗʰ 1743 Aged 2 Y.ʳˢ

Major Roberts Father of the above
died April 21.ˢᵗ 1762 Aged 83 Y.ʳˢ

Mrs Catherine Roberts Wife of the above
died Febr.ʸ 6.ᵗʰ 1766 Aged 63 Y.ʳˢ

Miss Mary Roberts died July 6.ᵗʰ 1775 Æt. 46 Y.ʳˢ

Richard Roberts Esq.ʳ Jun.ʳ Died Dec.ʳ 27.ᵗʰ 1777.
Aged 45 Years.

266. Brass to the Roberts family (1743–77), Pershore Abbey, Worcs.; probably Midlands work. Length 0·41m (16in). Photo Bailey.

267. Thomas Fromond, Esq. (1542), and wife, Cheam, Surrey; London work 'G' series. Length of male effigy 0·23m (9in). Photo K. & S.

268. Miscellaneous fifteenth and sixteenth century pieces, on reverse of Thomas Fromond, Esq. and wife, Cheam, Surrey. Photo K. & S.

269. Philip Mede, Esq. and wives (1475), St. Mary Redcliffe, Bristol, Glos.; probably London work though possibly Bristol. Length 0·58m (23in). Photo K. & S.

Index of Proper Names

This index covers the Introduction, all chapters, and the notes, and also the persons depicted and places recorded on the plates. The country and appropriate local geographical areas—unless repeating the place name—are stated for most places outside the United Kingdom. Place names are given in their local form (e.g. München for Munich). Places within the United Kingdom are located by the abbreviated name of the county only. These counties are long-established geographical units, and do not refer to the administrative counties as recently restructured, though note is taken of a few pre-Second World War boundary changes.

To provide a precise reference, dates for all *existing* brasses mentioned are given, supported in the case of the United Kingdom and Eire with references to the standard Mill Stephenson List, and in the case of the Continent to the standard Cameron List. This has been done to prevent confusion caused by suggested redating or revised identification. A dash has been inserted after the initials of the appropriate list, if the brass concerned has not been previously listed. Composite brasses, created by the appropriation of earlier figures, the addition of later figures, or substantial pre-nineteenth-century restorations, are indicated by dates separated by oblique lines.

Names are given as spelt on the memorial, so that (e.g.) Smith, Smyth and Smythe may refer to members of the same family. Where christian names of persons mentioned are not known, but the family name has been identified, reference is made under a general family entry. Kings and queens are listed under their christian names, but other titled persons under their titles (e.g. Gloucester). Soubriquets (e.g. The Black Prince) are given as cross-references.

Dinant, Namur, Belgium, 49
Dinaux, V., 97
Dingley, Northants, 1577 (MS.I) *Fig. 254*
Dingley, T., 118
Disney, Richard and William, 66
Dister, Allaine, *Fig. 249*
Dorchester, Oxon., 63, 116
Douai, Jakemes de, 95
Dow, Henry, 34
Downe, Kent, 1607 (MS.IV) 52–3
Doynton, Glos., 1529 (MS.I) *Fig. 231*
Dresden, East Germany, 49
Drewry, Anne, *Fig. 34*, 58
Druitt, H., 25, 101
Drury, G. Dru, 112
Dublin or Baile Átha Cliath, Eire, St. Patrick's
    Cathedral, 1528 (MS.I) 46; 1537 (MS.II)
    Fig. 220, 46; 1579 (MS.III) 46
Duke, Anne, 58
Du Mur, Jean, 91, 94
Dundrennan Abbey, Kirkcudbright, 43, 48
Dunkeld, Perth, Cathedral, 105, 119
Dürer, Albrecht, *Fig. 81*, 23, 99, 100, 104, 106
Durham, Cathedral, 57, 71, 75, 114
Düsseldorf, Nordrhein-Westfalen, West Germany,
    Haupstaatsarchiv, 40
Dutton, B., 33
Dynham, Roger, *Fig. 206*

East Ham, Essex, 1585 (MS.I) 115
East Horndon, Essex, 90
Easton Neston, Northants, 1552 (MS.I) *Fig. 213*,
    35, 112
East Sutton, Kent, 1629 (MS.I) 82
East Wickham, Kent, 1568 (MS.II) 56
Edenham, Lincs., c. 1520 (MS.I) *Fig. 47*, 64
Edinburgh, Cathedral, 1570 (MS.I) 46, 83
Edlesborough, Bucks., 1395 (MS.I—Ashridge
    House) 100; 1540 (MS.I) 35, 112
Edvarod, Valontyne, 59
Edward III, King of England, 56, 68, 75, 82
Eichler, Dr. Hans, 106, 119
Eichstätt, Bayern, West Germany, 85
Eleanor, Queen of King Edward I, 68, 83
Elham, Kent, 43
Elizabeth I, Queen of England, 37, 56
Ellis, A. C., 115
Elmdon, Essex, c. 1530 (MS.I) *Fig. 230*
Elsing, Norfolk, 1347 (MS.I) *Figs. 103, 129, and 130*,
    39, 42–3, 69, 73, 75, 103, 105
Elstow, Beds., d. 1527 (MS.II) 65
Ely, Cambs., Cathedral, 44; *Fig. 102*, 105
Emden, Niedersachsen, West Germany, 1507 (C.1)
    50, 105
Enfield, Middx., c. 1475 (MS.I) 103; 1585 (MS.II)
    115
Ercker, L., 34, 36
Erfurt, East Germany, Cathedral, 83; 1481 (C.4)
    31, 112; 1505 (C.5) 31; 1560 (C.6) 84
Escamaing family, 82
Esdaile, A. J. K., 25, 84
Essex, Henry (Bourchier), Earl of, 54
Essex, John, 101
Estofft, John Skerne of, 86
Etchingham, Sussex, 1444 (MS.II) 100

Ethelred, King and St., *Fig. 39*, 54, 65
Eton, Bucks., College Chapel, d. 1521 (MS. VI) 88
Etwall, Derbys., 1557 (MS.II) *Fig. 214*
Evans, H. F. Owen, 112, 118
    J., 114
Eversley, Hants., 1502 (MS.I) *Fig. 238*
Evesham, Epiphany, 82
Evora, Alentejo, Portugal, Museum of Duke of
    Cadaval, c. 1490 (C.2) 50, 75, 103
Evreux, Eure, France, Cathedral, *Fig. 106*, 85
Exeter, Devon, Cathedral, 1409 (MS.I) 54
Expence, Martine, 61
Eyer, Ralph, 64

Fabyan, Robert, 52, 91
Fairford, Glos., 1500 (MS.I) *Figs. 209 and 211*;
    c. 1526/1534 (MS.II) 62, 70; 1534 (MS.III)
    62, 70
Faringdon, Berks., 1443 (MS.II) 88
Faryndon, Thomas, 88
Fastolff, John, 52
Faversham, Kent, 55; 1533 (MS.XIII) 73
Felbrigg, Norfolk, 43, 112; 1416 (MS.III) *Fig.24*,
    54–5, 58
    House, 113
Felbrygge, Sir Symon, *Fig. 24*, 55, 58
Fenton, John, *Fig. 253*
Fermer, Richard, *Fig. 213*, 35
Fermoure, William, 35
Fetyplace, Susan, 58
Field, John, *Fig. 18*
Filleigh, Devon, 1570 (MS.I) 58–9; 1570 (MS.II)
    58–9
Filmer, Sir Edward, 82
Fitz Haimon, Robert, 65
Fitz Ralph, Sir William, *Fig. 122*, 41
Flanders, William, Count of, 111
Fleming, Alan, 55
Fletching, Sussex, c. 1440 (MS.II) *Fig. 239*, 31, 57
Flexney, Ralph, 42
Foljambe, Sir Godfrey, 72
    Henry, 82
Forest, Thomas, 56
Forêt, Brabant, Belgium, 111
Formelis, Simon de, 91
Forrester, Martin, *Fig. 37*, 63
Fortescue, Richard, 58
Fortey family, 55
    Agnes, *Fig. 180*
Fossebrok, John, 66
Fotheringay, Northants., 44, 114
Foxle, Sir John de, *Fig. 174*, 91
Foxwist, Richard, *Fig. 243*
Frankeleyn, John, 61
Franklyn, J., 74, 116
Frechwell, Peter, 115
Freiberg, Karl-Marx-Stadt, East Germany, 36, 55,
    83–4, 105; Cathedral, *Fig. 67*, 36, 48; 1541
    (C.1) *Fig. 105*, 106; d. 1606 (C.11) *Fig. 247*;
    d. 1617 (C.9) *Fig. 248*
Frenze, Norfolk, 1551 (MS.VII) 58
Frevile, Thomas de, *Fig. 162*
Fromond, Thomas, *Figs. 267 and 268*
Frowsetoure, Edmund, 103
Froxmere, Thomas, *Fig. 73*, 93, 118

Index of Subjects

Reference to figures in this index is in many cases selective, indicated by the prefix 'e.g.' Figure references are not cited in support of obvious entries, such as 'Foot supports'.